THE EMERGENCE OF LEÓN-CASTILE C.1065–1500

J.F. O'Callaghan (on left) with J.F. Powers and B.F. Reilly at the American Historical Association's Annual Meeting, January 2011 (Photo courtesy of Lorraine C. Attreed)

The Emergence of León-Castile c.1065–1500

Essays Presented to J.F. O'Callaghan

Edited by

JAMES J. TODESCA
Armstrong State University, USA

ASHGATE

Published by
Ashgate Publishing Limited
Wey Court East
Union Road
Farnham
Surrey, GU9 7PT
England

Ashgate Publishing Company
110 Cherry Street
Suite 3-1
Burlington, VT 05401-3818
USA

www.ashgate.com

British Library Cataloguing in Publication Data
A catalogue record for this book is available from the British Library.

The Library of Congress has cataloged the printed edition as follows:
The emergence of León-Castile, c.1065-1500 : essays presented to J.F. O'Callaghan / edited by James J. Todesca.
pages cm
Includes bibliographical references and index.
ISBN 978-1-4094-2035-4 (hardcover) -- ISBN 978-1-4094-2036-1 (ebook) -- ISBN 978-1-4724-0044-4 (ePub) 1. Castile (Spain)--History. 2. Leon (Kingdom)--History. 3. Castile (Spain)--Politics and government. 4. Leon (Kingdom)--Politics and government. 5. Law--Spain--Castile--History--To 1500. 6. Law--Spain--Leon (Kingdom)--History--To 1500. 7. Castile (Spain)--Kings and rulers. 8. Spain--History--711-1516. 9. O'Callaghan, Joseph F. I. Todesca, James J. II. O'Callaghan, Joseph F.
DP136.E63 2015
946'.302--dc23

2014029257

ISBN 9781409420354 (hbk)
ISBN 9781409420361 (ebk – PDF)
ISBN 9781472400444 (ebk – ePUB)

MIX
Paper from responsible sources
FSC www.fsc.org FSC® C013985

Printed in the United Kingdom by Henry Ling Limited,
at the Dorset Press, Dorchester, DT1 1HD

Contents

List of Figures

List of Contributors

Nicolás Agrait is Assistant Professor of History at Long Island University Brooklyn, Brooklyn, NY, USA.

Janna Bianchini is Associate Professor of History at the University of Maryland, College Park, MD, USA.

James William Brodman is Professor Emeritus of History at the University of Central Arkansas, Conway, AR, USA.

Theresa Earenfight is Professor of History at Seattle University, Seattle, WA, USA.

Manuel González Jiménez is Professor Emeritus of Medieval History at the University of Seville, Seville, Spain.

Donald J. Kagay is Professor of History at Albany State University, Albany, GA, USA.

James F. Powers is Professor Emeritus of History at College of the Holy Cross, Worcester, MA, USA.

Bernard F. Reilly is Professor Emeritus of History at Villanova University, Villanova, PA, USA.

Teofilo F. Ruiz is Distinguished Professor of History and of Spanish and Portuguese at the University of California, Los Angeles, CA, USA.

James J. Todesca is Associate Professor of History at Armstrong State University, Savannah, GA, USA.

L.J. Andrew Villalon is Professor Emeritus of History at the University of Cincinnati, Cincinnati, OH, USA.

Preface

In the summer of 1986 I attended the American Numismatic Society's Graduate Seminar in New York City on Joe O'Callaghan's recommendation. "Who knows?" he said. "Maybe they will give you a hoard to work with." I did indeed spend that summer reconstructing a hoard of thirteenth-century Castilian coins. But in the world of numismatics, the medievalist is often the red-headed step-child. Throughout the seminar, the graduate students presented updates on our projects, bringing samples of coins to the conference room to enlighten both colleagues and curators. The classicists could display beautiful high-relief Hellenistic coins—the silver *tetradachm* showing Alexander the Great in the lion-skin headdress of Hercules always got a few "ahs." Or they showed us equally well-struck coins with images of famous Roman Caesars. (Everyone had at least heard of Nero or Hadrian.) The Islamicists countered with gold *dinars* boasting epigraphy only they could read. The other medievalist in the group had one foot in Late Antiquity as he was working with Visigothic *tremisses*. Though verging on barbarous, they were at least gold and looked classical enough. Then came my turn to display small, greenish-black coins called *denarii* by the residents of medieval Europe. One needed a jeweler's loop just to make out the embarrassingly crude images and legends on these pieces. The types, next to the Roman and Hellenistic portraits, resembled children's renditions of kings.

But the worst indignities came when I spoke about the coins. As I elaborated on the monetary value of the *coronados* of Sancho IV of Castile-León (1284–95), one of the Roman historians usually stifled a giggle. For him, the name Sancho conjured up images of Don Quixote's portly squire or perhaps one of Pancho Villa's comrades complete with gun belts across his chest or, worst of all, the Frito Bandito. My colleague that summer, however, was not the first to find the names of Castilian royalty unusual. The British travel writer H.V. Morton remarked in 1955 that Castile was "a Spain of confusing kinglets, of Sanchos and Alfonsos, and of ladies named Berengaria, Constance and Urraca."[1] Indeed we find traces of similar prejudice in the Middle Ages. Philip Augustus of France (1180–1223) probably did not consider Alfonso VIII of Castile (1158–1214) a kinglet when

1 H.V. Morton, *A Stranger in Spain* (London: Methuen & Co., 1955), p. 252.

he agreed to marry his heir to one of Alfonso's daughters.[2] Yet according to a later chronicler, the French ambassadors sent to arrange the marriage did have trouble with names. Alfonso expected they would choose Urraca, the eldest of his two eligible daughters and said to be the more beautiful. To the Castilian court's astonishment, they chose the younger daughter, Blanca, because Urraca was "an ugly name for the French."[3] Somewhat analogously, the English monk Matthew Paris surely meant to be respectful when he recorded the death of the "illustrious king of Castile" Fernando III (1217–52), but he mistakenly called him Alfonso.[4] Morton would have sympathized with Matthew's confusion.

Today these "Sanchos and Alfonsos" are becoming more familiar in the English-speaking world as they are often mentioned (without snickering) in college-level texts on medieval Europe. Only 11 years after my seminar among the classicists, Peter Linehan commented that the "concept of Iberian peripherality," though venerable, "might well be regarded as both *passé* and dated."[5] Not all agree with this optimism. Adam Kosto recently argued that the paradigm of the *reconquista*, that is viewing medieval Spain narrowly as a "society organized

---

[2] The marriage was to seal the treaty of Le Goulet signed in May of 1200 between Philip and John of England (1199–1216), Alfonso's brother-in-law. John W. Baldwin, *The Government of Philip Augustus* (Berkeley, CA: University of California Press, 1986), pp. 96–7; W.L. Warren, *King John* (Berkeley, CA: University of California Press, 1961), pp. 54–6.

[3] The story appears in a chronicle attributed to Juan Rodríguez de Cuenca writing c.1400. See Eugenio de Llaguno Amirola (ed.), *Sumario de los reyes de España* (1781; reprint Valencia: Anubar, 1971), pp. iv–v, 39. The chronicler assumes a bride is being selected for King Philip himself when in reality Blanca was betrothed to the future Louis VIII (1223–26). Modern historians often assume Alfonso's mother-in-law, Eleanor of Aquitaine, played a part in the decision. While Roger of Howden attests that she journeyed to Spain as part of the negotiations, the *Sumario*'s account makes no mention of her. Cf. Amy Kelly, *Eleanor and the Four Kings* (Cambridge, MA: Harvard University Press, 1950), p. 359, who mistakenly cites the "Crónica de don Pedro Niño, conde de Buelna." See also Miriam Shadis and Constance Hoffman Berman, "A Taste of the Feast: Reconsidering Eleanor of Aquitaine's Female Descendents," in Bonnie Wheeler and John Carmi Parsons (eds), *Eleanor of Aquitaine, Lord and Lady* (New York: Palgrave Macmillan, 2002), p. 192; Ralph V. Turner, *Eleanor of Aquitaine: Queen of France, Queen of England* (New Haven, CT: Yale University Press, 2009), pp. 288–9. On the name Urraca in general see Jaime de Salazar y Acha, "Urraca: Un nombre egregio en la onamástica altomedieval," *En la España Medieval: Anejo 1* (2006): pp. 29–47.

[4] See Manuel González Jiménez, "Alfonso X and His Brothers: A Story of Not Very Fraternal Relations," below.

[5] Peter Linehan, "The King's Touch and the Dean's Ministrations: Aspects of Sacral Monarchy," in Miri Rubin (ed.), *The Works of Jacques Le Goff and the Challenges of Medieval History* (Woodbridge: Boydell Press, 1997), p. 189.

for war," continues to hinder the integration "of Iberian history into a wider European context."[6] By failing to recognize the political, economic and cultural ties between the Christian states of Iberia and the rest of Latin Europe, we run the risk of promoting the old adage that Europe stops at the Pyrenees. Indeed, a recent world civilization text includes medieval Spain in its chapter on "Early African Societies." Ignoring the complexity of the sources surrounding the Muslim conquest of Iberia and drawing loosely on Ibn 'Abd al-Hakam's ninth-century narrative, the text book tells students:

> The Muslims arrived in Spain as invited guests. The Germanic king of Spain died in 709, and in the contest over his succession one contender for the throne appealed to the Islamic *amir* of North Africa for help. The amir responded by sending an Arab-Berber expeditionary force under General Tariq ibn Ziyad, which landed in 711, defeated the other contender, and prepared to go home. But Tariq heard rumors that the legendary treasure of ... Solomon was hidden in a cellar in Toledo. He took the city and found nothing but rats in its cellars but saw to his astonishment that many of the residents welcomed his forces and converted to Islam ... For the next five centuries, Spain was linked with North Africa as the westernmost part of Islam's growing commercial and cultural network.[7]

Experts will recognize many levels of inaccuracy here; perhaps most surprising is the claim that the residents of Toledo enthusiastically embraced Islam. "The Chronicle of 754," the most nearly contemporary account of the Muslim entrance into Spain, highlights executions in Toledo and widespread slaughter elsewhere including crucifixion and the butchering of "youths and infants."[8] Placing medieval Spain among early African societies would not, however, surprise David Levering Lewis. In his recent *God's Crucible: Islam and the Making of Europe, 570–1215*, Lewis argues that the Pyrenees marked the divide between Islamic civilization and European barbarity. According to

---

6 Adam J. Kosto, "Reconquest, Renaissance, and the Histories of Iberia, ca. 1000–1200," in Thomas F.X. Noble and John Van Engen (eds), *European Transformations: The Long Twelfth Century* (Notre Dame, IN: University of Notre Dame Press), p. 100 and *passim*.

7 Edward H. Judge and John W. Langdon, *Connections: A World History*, 2nd edn (Boston, MA: Pearson, 2011), pp. 277–8. For Ibn 'Abd al-Hakam's account see the translation in Olivia Remie Constable (ed.), *Medieval Iberia: Readings from Christian, Muslim and Jewish Sources* (Philadelphia, PA: University of Pennsylvania Press, 1997), pp. 32–6.

8 "The Chronicle of 754," in Kenneth Baxter Wolf (ed.), *Conquerors and Chroniclers of Early Medieval Spain* (Liverpool: Liverpool University Press, 1990), pp. 132–3.

Lewis, Islam's inability to push north of the Pyrenees in the eighth century was not because of Frankish strength but because of the Abbasid revolution in Damascus. Moreover, the Muslim failure to advance further into Europe was "one of the most significant losses in world history and certainly the most consequential since the fall of the Western Roman Empire." It was, in Lewis' estimation, a pivotal point "in the creation of an economically retarded, balkanized, and fratricidal Europe."[9]

While oversimplifications such as these give credence to Kosto's warning that we have yet to fully appreciate Iberia's contribution to Europe, there is no denying Linehan's point that much progress has been made in Spanish medieval history in recent decades. The death of Franco in 1975 signaled a transformation in historical, archival and archaeological studies in Spain which picked up speed as the 1980s progressed. In 1983, Roger Collins began the preface to his *Early Medieval Spain* with the caveat, "Spanish history is not easy." But by the second edition of 1995 he noted the "sweeping changes" that had occurred in the direction and methodologies "of historical studies in Spain."[10] Even before these changes, however, the dogged efforts of a group of English and American scholars, including Collins, Linehan, O'Callaghan and some of the contributors to this volume, had been chipping away at the perceived "otherness" of medieval Iberia. Indeed, the quality of their early work helped guide the new medieval scholarship emerging in Spain in the post-Franco era.

As Bernard Reilly emphasizes here in his heart-warming opening essay, the work of this group of *extranjeros* in the 1960s and '70s was marked by friendly collaboration with one another and generous encouragement to a younger generation, some of whom are also represented in this volume. Now, in the second decade of the twenty-first century, medieval Iberian studies are thriving both in and outside Spain. Indeed, the tragedy of September 11, 2001 has heightened interest in the West's early contact with Islam in Iberia even if it has led some authors to overstate the case for peaceful coexistence. María Rosa Menocal's *Ornament of the World*, for example, dedicated a chapter to the career of the Jewish polymath Samuel ibn Naghrela who served as vizier for the Muslim *taifa* king of Granada in the eleventh century. But Menocal failed to mention that Samuel's son Joseph, along with many other Granadan Jews, was

---

[9] David Levering Lewis, *God's Crucible: Islam and the Making of Europe, 570–1215* (New York: Norton, 2008), pp. xxii–xxiii, 173–4.

[10] Roger Collins, *Early Medieval Spain: Unity in Diversity, 400–1000*, 2nd edn (New York: St. Martin's Press, 1995), pp. ix–xii.

later slaughtered in a backlash of Muslim resentment.[11] Her idyllic portrayal of al-Andalus certainly influenced Lewis in *God's Crucible*. Yet we should pause to consider that Lewis is a historian best known for his work on the American civil rights activist W.E.B. Dubois. His undertaking *God's Crucible*, then, testifies to how much more accessible Iberian history has become for scholars and the general public.

In bringing Spain into the mainstream of medieval studies alongside the classic trio of England, France and the "German" Empire, English-speaking historians, at least at first, tended to give less attention to the kingdom of León-Castile than to its Christian counterweight the Crown of Aragon-Catalonia or Muslim al-Andalus. When O'Callaghan compiled his bibliography for *A History of Medieval Spain* in 1975, under "General Histories" he could list Chaytor's *A History of Aragon and Catalonia*; Watt's *A History of Islamic Spain* and a translation of Oliveira Marques' *A History of Portugal*, but nothing for León-Castile.[12] Since that time a great deal has been written on medieval Iberia both in English and Spanish, and it would be difficult to quantify where the balance of scholarship now lies. But as recently as 2007, Wendy Davies, in her work on the tenth century, noted the amount of major studies undertaken on Catalonia "during the last generation" which are now "well-known beyond the Iberian peninsula."[13]

This concentration on Aragon-Catalonia is understandable. First, the royal archives of the Crown of Aragon are well preserved whereas the diplomas of the kings of León-Castile survive scattered in ecclesiastical and municipal collections. Secondly, Aragon-Catalonia was more firmly in the orbit of the post-Carolingian world and to historians trained in French history its government and society appear more familiar. Thomas Bisson in *Conservation of Coinage*, for example, examined the exploitation of coinage in "societies which succeeded to the West Frankish realm." While he included Aragon alongside Catalonia, he

[11] María Rosa Menocal, *The Ornament of the World: How Muslims, Jews and Christians Created a Culture of Tolerance in Medieval Spain* (Boston, MA: Little, Brown & Co., 2002), pp. 101–11. Cf. "Three Views of Samuel and Joseph ibn Naghrela," in Constable, pp. 89–102. The tendency of some scholars to hold up al-Andalus as an "inter-faith utopia," however, predates September 2001. For the difficulties of arriving "at a meaningful generalization of the Jewish experience in al-Andalus," see Ross Brann, *Power in the Portrayal: Representations of Jews and Muslims in Eleventh- and Twelfth-Century Islamic Spain* (Princeton, NJ: Princeton University Press, 2002), pp. 1–21.

[12] Joseph F. O'Callaghan, *A History of Medieval Spain* (Ithaca, NY: Cornell University Press, 1975), p. 684.

[13] Wendy Davies, *Acts of Giving: Individual, Community, and Church in Tenth-Century Christian Spain* (Oxford: Oxford University Press, 2007), pp. 13–14, n. 35.

qualified it as "clearly peripheral."[14] An excellent study, the book's approach is not flawed. Bisson simply chose not to follow monetary developments westward along the *camino de Santiago* into León-Castile although that kingdom shared as much in the Carolingian monetary tradition as Aragon. (An alumnus of the American Numismatic Society Seminar, Bisson had perhaps heard the same jokes about King Sancho.)

Nonetheless, the lands that gradually emerged as the kingdom of León-Castile were indeed remote for centuries. Greco-Roman civilization in the peninsula clung largely to the eastern coast and the Guadalquivir valley until the time of Christ. Even with Augustus' push into the northwest, settlements such as Astorga and near-by León on the northern *meseta* were lonely, austere places. Facing the winds from the snow-capped Cantabrian mountains in the north, the soldiers and residents of these outposts surely longed for the comfort of Cordoba, Seville or Tarragona.[15] While in the sixth and seventh centuries the Visigoths attempted to create a more centralized government by establishing a capital at Toledo, theirs was a kingdom characterized by "an extreme dearth of population" and life could not have improved much on the *meseta* north of Toledo and the *cordillera central*.[16] The Muslim invaders of the eighth century, like the Romans, again avoided these high plains. North African Berbers, newly converted to Islam, at first attempted to graze flocks there while the Arabs mainly stuck to the Romanized south and east. But, when the Berbers revolted against this arrangement in 740, famine followed civil unrest and the northern *meseta* "slipped out of Muslim hands."[17]

According to an early chronicle, Alfonso I (739–57) of Asturias, whose main residence lay just north of the Cantabrian mountains at Oviedo, moved southward onto the plain to take "many cities" including Astorga

---

[14] Thomas Bisson, *Conservation of Coinage: Monetary Exploitation and its Restraint in France, Catalonia, and Aragon (c.A.D. 1000–c.1225)* (Oxford: Clarendon Press, 1979), p. vii. On Catalonia as part of the Frankish world see also Adam J. Kosto, *Making Agreements in Medieval Catalonia* (Cambridge: Cambridge University Press, 2001), pp. 4–9.

[15] John S. Richardson, *The Romans in Spain* (Oxford: Blackwell, 1996), pp. 144, 157, 212; C.H.V. Sutherland, *The Romans in Spain, 217 B.C.–A.D. 117* (1939; reprint New York: Barnes and Noble, 1971), pp. 136–7. Richard Fletcher, *St. James's Catapult: The Life and Times of Diego Gelmírez of Santiago de Compostella* (Oxford: Clarendon Press, 1984), pp. 20–21, argues to the contrary that northwestern Spain, specifically Galicia, was "very much a part of the Roman and Mediterranean world" in late antiquity.

[16] Karl W. Butzer et al., "Irrigation Agrosystems in Eastern Spain: Roman or Islamic in Origins?" *Annals of the Association of American Geographers*, 75 (1985): pp. 483–4.

[17] Hugh Kennedy, *Muslim Spain and Portugal* (Harlow: Longman, 1996), p. 28, cf. pp. 18–29.

and León. While the chronicler claims he led the inhabitants of these towns back to the refuge of the mountains, a mixture of free landholders, tenants, servile dependents and slaves gradually populated the Duero valley under the protection of Alfonso I's successors.[18] Alfonso III (866–910), later sometimes called "the Great," completed "the occupation and extensive repopulation of the Duero valley."[19] A contemporary of other state builders like Alfred the Great (871–99) and Henry the Fowler (919–36), Alfonso may have written to the clergy of St. Martin of Tours in 906 seeking to purchase an "imperial crown ... quite suitable for our serenity."[20] His sons transferred the royal court from secluded Oviedo to León and so we can point to a nascent kingdom of León in the tenth century just as Alfred and Henry's heirs were transforming their domains into the kingdoms of England and Germany.

The disintegration of the Umayyad caliphate at Cordoba in the early-eleventh century paralleled the rise of Sancho García III of Navarre (1000–1035) in the Christian north. In his expansion, Sancho annexed the county of Castile, traditionally claimed by León. When he died, Castile fell to his second son, Fernando. Fernando then quickly defeated and killed the king of León and became Fernando I of a re-united León-Castile (1035–65), which now encompassed "an area more than the size of the kingdom of England."[21] He also extracted large sums of tribute from the Muslim *taifa* lords who rose up in the wake of Umayyad collapse. From this booty he pledged to pay the Burgundian monastery of Cluny 1,000 dinars annually, fostering connections across the Pyrenees that his father had begun. His son Alfonso VI (1065–1109) paid Cluny only sporadically, but his friendship with the monastery probably led to

---

[18] "Chronicle of Alfonso III" in Wolf, p. 170; Davies, pp. 16–21; Jerrilynn D. Dodds, María Rosa Menocal and Abigail Krasner Balbale, *The Arts of Intimacy: Christians, Jews, and Muslims in the Making of Castilian Culture* (New Haven, CT: Yale University Press, 2008), p. 29.

[19] Collins, pp. 231–7. The twelfth-century *Historia Silense* calls Alfonso "magnus," though this section of the history may have been copied from a tenth-century source. Justo Pérez de Urbel and Atilano González Ruiz-Zorrilla (eds), *Historia Silense* (Madrid: Consejo Superior de Investigaciones Científicas, 1959), pp. 149–52; Simon Barton and Richard Fletcher (trans.), *The World of El Cid: Chronicles of the Spanish Reconquest* (Manchester: Manchester University Press, 2000), pp. 10–11. See also de Llaguno Amirola, p. 11.

[20] "Coronam imperialem ... nostrae serenitati condignam." Antonio López Ferreiro, *Historia de la Santa A.M. Iglesia de Santiago de Compostela*, vol. 2 (Santiago: Imp. y Enc. del Seminario Conciliar Central, 1899), appendixes, pp. 57–60, no. 27, available at http://archive.org/stream/historiadelasant02lpez#page/56/mode/2up (accessed October 7, 2013). Cf. Fletcher, *St James's Catapult*, pp. 317–23; Collins, p. 233.

[21] Bernard F. Reilly, *The Contest of Christian and Muslim Spain 1031–1157* (Oxford: Blackwell, 1992), pp. 25–51.

his marriage with Agnes of Aquitaine by 1074. She was the first of Alfonso's five brides "from beyond the Pyrenees."[22] Soon after, in 1085, Alfonso conquered the Muslim *taifa* of Toledo, vastly increasing the size of his domain. He appointed a Cluniac monk, Bernard of Sedirac, as the city's archbishop.[23]

The Cluniac "alliance" and growing traffic along the *camino de Santiago* in León-Castile at the close of the eleventh century are recognizable facets of the "economic dynamism and ecclesiastical renewal" seen throughout Europe at this time. By 1150, both factors were helping to foster a revival of royal power in the Latin world. Older kingdoms matured and new kingdoms such as Portugal, Sicily and even Jerusalem were born.[24] While tracing it roots back to ninth-century Asturias, León-Castile, as Richard Fletcher noted, now "entered upon the fullness of a European inheritance in which she had shared but faintly and uncertainly during the preceding three centuries." He added that "the process was long and not without pain."[25]

One painful interlude began in the mid-twelfth century. On the death Alfonso VII (1126–57), his two sons divided the realm. The eldest, Sancho III, became king of Castile (1157–58) and Fernando II king in León (1157–88). While Sancho's reign was brief he managed to retain Toledo, the prestigious *urbs regia* of the Visigoths, signaling Castile's growing preeminence over León on the European stage.[26] Indeed, Sancho's son Alfonso VIII married Eleanor,

---

[22] Ibid., p. 75. See also Joseph F. O'Callaghan, "The Integration Christian Spain into Europe: The Role of Alfonso VI of León-Castile," in Bernard F. Reilly (ed.), *Santiago, Saint Denis and Saint Peter* (New York: Fordham University Press, 1985), pp. 101–20. For Fernando I and Alfonso VI's relations with Cluny see Charles J. Bishko, "Fernando I and the Origins of the Leonese-Castilian Alliance with Cluny" in Charles J. Bishko, *Studies in Medieval Spanish Frontier History* (London: Variorum, 1980), no. 2; Charles J. Bishko, "Liturgical Intercession at Cluny for the King-Emperors of León," in Charles J. Bishko, *Spanish and Portuguese Monastic History, 600 –1300* (London: Variorum, 1984), no. 8.

[23] Reilly, *Contest*, pp. 85–6. For the election of Bernard to the see of Toledo see Bernard F. Reilly, *The Kingdom of León-Castilla under King Alfonso VI, 1065–1109* (Princeton, NJ: Princeton University Press, 1988), pp. 175, 180–82.

[24] Thomas Ertman, *Birth of the Leviathan: Building States and Regimes in Medieval and Early Modern Europe* (Cambridge: Cambridge University Press, 1997), pp. 48–59.

[25] Richard Fletcher, *The Episcopate in the Kingdom of León in the Twelfth Century* (Oxford: Oxford University Press, 1978), p. 1; cf. Kosto, "Reconquest," pp. 100–107.

[26] Bernard F. Reilly, *The Kingdom of León-Castilla under King Alfonso VII, 1126–1157* (Philadelphia, PA: University of Pennsylvania Press, 1998), p. 134, suggests the division between the brothers was "determined by power" more than Alfonso VII's design. On the other hand, Peter Linehan, "Spain in the Twelfth Century," in D. Luscombe and J. Riley-Smith (eds), *The New Cambridge Medieval History*, vol. 4, part 2 (Cambridge: Cambridge

the daughter of Henry II of England (1154–89).[27] It was their child, Blanca, who married Phillip Augustus' heir, Louis VIII, despite the reported difficulties over names. Alfonso VIII gained further renown for Castile with his victory over the Almohads at Las Navas in 1212, a campaign in which his cousin, the king of León, did not participate. When Alfonso VIII's grandson, Fernando III (1217–52), became king of Castile he followed up the triumph of Las Navas by pushing hard into Muslim al-Andalus. Thus after Fernando III succeeded to the throne of León in 1230 and re-united the two kingdoms, he naturally gave pride of place to Castile in his intitulation: "Fernandus, Dei gratia rex Castelle et Toleti, Legionis et Gallecie."[28] His son, Alfonso X (1252–84) maintained this inverted order of the kingdoms.[29] Following this shift, historians writing about the kingdom from the reunification in 1230 on tend to refer to it as Castile-León or simply Castile. While I have maintained León-Castile in this volume's title, perhaps out of a preference for the seemingly simpler times of the eleventh and twelfth centuries, the authors of the later chapters herein follow the convention of putting Castile first.

Joseph O'Callaghan's scholarly interests have tended to focus on institutional developments, both secular and ecclesiastical, and he has moved easily between León-Castile and Castile-León. Following Reilly's encomium of Joe's career, the chapters in this collection trace the long and sometimes painful emergence of that kingdom beginning with royal administration in the eleventh century and ending with the dynastic struggles of the Trastamara family that led to the marriage of Isabel and Ferdinand in the late-fifteenth. They have their origin in three sessions held in celebration of O'Callaghan's eightieth birthday at the International Conference on Medieval Studies hosted by Western Michigan University in 2009. Some of the participants in those panels (including O'Callaghan) reconvened at the American Historical Association's annual meeting in Washington in January 2011. As a reflection of the strength of O'Callaghan's friendship and influence, his colleagues have assembled from these meetings a collection of essays that focus on the development of León-Castile from the point of view of the crown and speak to the kingdom's institutional ties and differences with the rest of Latin Europe. The

University Press, 2004), p. 489, argues that Alfonso deliberately granted Castile to his eldest son as it "comprised the family's patrimonial lands."

27 W.L. Warren, *Henry II* (Berkeley, CA: University of California Press, 1973), p. 117.

28 Julio González, *Reinado y diplomas de Fernando III* (3 vols, Cordoba: Publicaciones del Monte de Piedad y Caja de Ahorras de Córdoba, 1980–86), vol. 2, pp. 329–30, no. 285, *passim*.

29 Joseph F. O'Callaghan, "Image and Reality: The King Creates His Kingdom," in Robert I. Burns (ed.), *Emperor of Culture: Alfonso X and His Thirteenth-Century Renaissance* (Philadelphia, PA: University of Philadelphia Press, 1990), p. 16.

second collection to appear in his honor, these chapters carry us one step closer to fulfilling Joe's long-held ambition of seeing Spain more integrated into medieval European studies.[30]

In the process of editing, I have tested the patience of many. I am very grateful to my friend and colleague Michael Price of Armstrong State University's History Department. He took time from his duties as department head to read early drafts of most of the chapters and offer written comments and affable conversation about each. His perspective as a non-medievalist was invaluable. I am further indebted to several anonymous readers whom I asked to comment on specific chapters as well as the anonymous scholars who read the entire manuscript for Ashgate. Thanks goes also to Laura Barrett, Dean of the College of Liberal Arts at Armstrong, whose office provided financial support in the summer of 2012. Finally, I must thank the authors present herein. They endured and responded kindly to my many queries and requests for rewrites and clarification. I hope they agree that the final product is better for it.

James J. Todesca
Savannah, Georgia
Feast of All Saints 2013

[30] Donald J. Kagay and Theresa M. Vann (eds), *On the Social Origins of Medieval Institutions: Essays in Honor of Joseph F. O'Callaghan* (Leiden: Brill, 1998).

Chapter 1

Medieval Iberian Studies in the United States

Bernard F. Reilly

In the United States of the mid-twentieth century, Iberian studies was pursued less than English, French, German or Italian history since these latter fields were perceived as having more relevance to American developments and interests.[1] There had been honorable exceptions of course, beginning with William H. Prescott. His *History of the Conquest of Mexico* (1843) and *History of the Conquest of Peru* (1847) bear comparison with other works of European history by American authors.[2] Of course Prescott's subjects—I can recall still having discovered them with delight in the years of my early teens—were also central to the development of much of the Americas. As such they found worthy and linear succession in the work of Roger B. Merriman, *The Rise of the Spanish Empire in the Old World and in the New*, whose four volumes I stumbled across in the stacks as a college freshman.[3] More usual, and later, was the outstanding work of Garrett Mattingly. His *Catherine of Aragon* and then *The Armada* dealt with Iberian phenomena of importance certainly, but whose import, for him, stemmed from their impact on early-modern English history.[4]

The development of Iberian medieval history by American historians as a field proper has occurred largely since the end of World War II and is associated above all with three scholars. The first of them, chronologically, was Charles

---

1 See Peter Novick, *That Noble Dream: The "Objectivity Question" and the American Historical Profession* (Cambridge: Cambridge University Press, 1998), pp. 309–14.

2 William H. Prescott, *A History of the Conquest of Mexico* (New York: Harper Brothers, 1843); William H. Prescott, *A History of the Conquest of Peru* (New York: Harper Brothers, 1847). Both volumes are reprinted in Wilfred Howard Munro (ed.), *The Works of William H. Prescott* (22 vols, New York: J.B. Lippincott Co., 1968).

3 Roger B. Merriman, *The Rise of the Spanish Empire in the Old World and in the New* (4 vols, New York: Macmillan, 1918–34).

4 Garrett Mattingly, *Catherine of Aragon* (Boston, MA: Houghton Mifflin, 1941); Garrett Mattingly, *The Armada* (Boston, MA: Houghton Mifflin, 1959).

Julian Bishko (1906–2002). At the University of Virginia from 1938, he taught and trained a generation of younger scholars in what was a virtuoso creation of a then effectively new field of knowledge. The second was the Jesuit scholar Robert I. Burns (1921–2008) who did much the same, first at the University of San Francisco between 1958 and 1976 and subsequently at the University of California, Los Angeles until his official retirement in 1991. Third in this list is Joseph F. O'Callaghan, to whom these collected studies are dedicated, who taught at Fordham University in New York City from 1954 until, in turn, he retired in 1994.

All three not only established a new field of medieval studies in America and trained up a subsequent generation of scholars, but they nurtured those young people as well. As individuals and as professors their kindnesses are legendary. If personal reminiscences may be excused as most readily available, this author recalls that as a struggling doctoral candidate in an outlying province, Bryn Mawr College, he was advised to write to C. Julian before undertaking thesis research in Spain. With some trepidation I did so and shortly received in response two pages, typewritten, both sides, setting forth a guide to archives and archivists in Spain without which I suspect I might have been, literally, lost. Subsequently Julian was to read and comment upon each of the typewritten chapters of my first scholarly book, that on Queen Urraca.[5]

I do not recall when I met Joe O'Callaghan for the first time, but we were hardly more than superficially acquainted personally, when he sent me what must have been close to his entire collection of typewritten transcriptions of the royal charters of Alfonso VII made, I am sure, on long, hot, dusty afternoons in the reading room of the Archivo Histórico Nacional in Madrid. Nor do I recollect when I first met Father Burns, though it well may have been among the booksellers' stalls, for he haunted them, at some meeting of the American Historical Association. Over the years he was to furnish to me, in a variety of short, sometimes cryptic, handwritten notes, information concerning work being done, the historians doing it, and the preferable avenues of approach to both. Probably most important in this respect were his advice and admonitions concerning the use of the materials of the Archivo Histórico de la Corona de Aragon in Barcelona. For a then historian of the medieval realms of León and Castile, the former were *terra incognita* indeed.

The publications of each of these scholars naturally provided formal guidance to students and associates. In addition, critical research managed to

---

[5] Bernard F. Reilly, *The Kingdom of León-Castilla under Queen Urraca, 1109–1126* (Princeton, NJ: Princeton University Press, 1982).

get communicated at odd moments of scholarly conferences, though perhaps not at exactly the conferences or the moments one would expect. In particular, Julian generally refused to attend any conference at all, and I can recall only one meeting, an annual American Historical Association conference in Washington, DC, where he attended a reunion celebration of some of his former students. As for the rather august meetings of the Medieval Academy of America, its attendees ordinarily did not know what to make of us. Things Iberian for them largely meant unpleasant associations with the like of Franco and Salazar and the victory of the wrong side in the Spanish Civil War of the 1930s. The same tended to be true of the American Historical Association with the additional disadvantage that its meetings were so huge that our interests tended to get lost in the crush.

The annual Congress on Medieval Studies at Western Michigan University in Kalamazoo was generally more congenial and more welcoming. There, between sessions, one slept in unoccupied student dorms, fed in the student dining halls, drank cocktails or beer in the basement recreation room of John Sommerfeldt's home, and dined at The Black Swan restaurant after these exertions. At Western Michigan, far from the more proper and patrician halls of Harvard, we found the freedom to organize panels of papers particularly suited to the needs of our own interests and passions.

These sessions, two or three of them usually, were sponsored by our freshly created American Academy of Research Historians of Medieval Spain. That organization sprang from the initiative of Father Burns when he invited Joe O'Callaghan, Jim Powers, and me out to dinner at the University of San Francisco during the course of the annual American Historical Association meeting in 1974. Having survived the most hair-raising of rides (Father Burns was a careful historian but behind the wheel had the instincts of an Indy 500 contestant), we four discussed the formation of such an academy over dinner. The formal organization as it developed was not quite what Burns originally had in mind. He had conceived it as a rather informal gathering of medieval Iberian scholars to exchange research notes and information concerning personal projects in development. Imperatives of wider recognition and recruitment soon forced it into a more traditional mode but we did avoid the burden of a journal. Over the ensuing years the Academy has served quite creditably to advance the development of the field.

The "Research Historians" of the title has, one suspects, often conveyed a rather starchy, perhaps even stuffy, connotation to on-lookers and outriders, but it addressed a reality peculiar then, and even now, to Iberian studies. Briefly put, one might say that in terms of scholarship the European nineteenth century never happened on that peninsula. Wars, civil discord, and general political repression had left Iberian archives in the most dreadful state and the publication of their contents at a level scarcely above that of the eighteenth-century *España sagrada* volumes.[6] Such catalogs as were extant tended to date from the same era and modern archivists were part-time, untrained clerics who had more important concerns or hapless veterans from the victorious side of the civil war of the 1930s who lacked other congenial employment. To do research there, one had to be one's own paleographer, one's own diplomatist, and one's own cataloger if one cared to be a serious historian. It was a great adventure composed, like most great adventures, of breath-taking discoveries alongside institutional frustrations, tedium, bad lighting, and insufficient heat. Mercifully, there was very good coffee and brandy to match.

Such circumstances placed a premium on individual experience and communication with fellow workers in the vineyard. In havens such as the *residencias* of the *Consejo Superior de Investigaciones Científicas* in Madrid and Barcelona one could hope to find scholarly commerce and solace during and after dinner. But, these establishments were primarily the resort and refuge of austere, elderly bachelors. One had to be introduced to their rules of access and institutional peculiarities. More pressing problems faced those of us arriving for a year, or even a summer, with a wife and family to house and feed.

Up on the Avenida General Mola (now, in more republican days, the Avenida Principe de Vergara) there was a new, comfortable apartment block constructed at the behest of Franco for his erstwhile generals and supporters. By one device or another, the American professor Donald Cutter had managed to purchase an apartment blessed with five bedrooms and two baths in that complex. To my knowledge Joe O'Callaghan was the first to rent it for a summer. He passed the very good word on to Jim Powers who leased it in 1971. The following summer, for the entirely satisfactory rent of $250 per month, I installed my wife and brood of seven there where we found not just comfort but the shopping notes of Jim Powers' wife.

Given the intrinsic difficulties posed in the mid-twentieth century by the state of knowledge and the general disinterest in, if not a polite distaste for, the medieval history of Iberia, one asks what moved the young Charles Julian Bishko to devote his career to it. In the absence of his personal papers, we can seek the answer in his published academic ones. Unlike Father Burns or Joe O'Callaghan, Julian never published a book, although many of his individual articles were later

[6] Enrique Flórez et al. (eds), *España sagrada* (52 vols, Madrid: Antonio Marín et al., 1754–1918).

reprinted in collections.[7] At Harvard his doctoral thesis already dealt with Iberian monasticism, and his first article in 1941 was entitled "Spanish Abbots and the Visigothic Councils of Toledo."[8] Here he perhaps drew upon the earlier, lonely efforts of Aloysius K. Ziegler at Catholic University whose *Church and State in Visigothic Spain* appeared in 1930.[9] In Iberian monasticism and its import for the history of the peninsula, Bishko found a subject that was to engross him for four decades down until his "The Abbey of Santa María de Batres and the Cluniac Presence at Toledo from Alfonso VI to Alfonso VII" published in 1987.[10] But another early strand of his work is represented by "The Peninsular Background of Latin American Cattle Ranching" which, appearing in 1952, had a slender American precedent in Julius Klein's *The Mesta*.[11] Forty-five years later this stubborn preoccupation still endured to find its latest echo in Julian's article on the municipal *mestas* of New Castile and Murcia in 1997.[12]

Father Robert Burns' intellectual explorations were more singular in inspiration. In 1960 he published "Journey from Islam: Incipient Cultural Transition in the Conquered Kingdom of Valencia (1240–1280)."[13] That theme, variants upon it, and subjects closely allied to it monopolized his interests down to the publication of his final study, "100,000 Crossbow Bolts for the Crusader King of Aragon," in 2004.[14] If Iberian studies were exotic in the America of the

---

7 Charles Julian Bishko, *Studies in Medieval Spanish Frontier History* (London: Variorum Reprints, 1980); Charles Julian Bishko, *Spanish and Portuguese Monastic History, 600–1300* (London: Variorum Reprints, 1984).

8 Charles Julian Bishko, "Spanish Abbots and the Visigothic Councils of Toledo," in *Humanistic Studies in Honor of John Calvin Metcalf* (New York: Columbia University Press, 1941): pp. 139–50.

9 Aloysius K. Ziegler, *Church and State in Visigothic Spain* (Washington, DC: Catholic University Press, 1930).

10 Charles Julian Bishko, "The Abbey of Santa María de Batres and the Cluniac Presence at Toledo from Alfonso VI to Alfonso VII," in *Estudios sobre Alfonso VI y la reconquista de Toledo: Actas del II congreso internacional de estudios mozárabes* (4 vols, Toledo: Instituto de Estudios Visigótico-Mozárabes, 1987): vol. 1, pp. 187–218.

11 Charles Julian Bishko, "The Peninsular Background of Latin American Cattle Ranching," *The Hispanic American Historical Review*, 32 (1952): pp. 491–515; Julius Klein, *The Mesta: A Study in Spanish Economic History, 1273–1836* (Cambridge, MA: Harvard University Press, 1920).

12 Charles J. Bishko, "The Municipal Mestas of New Castile and Murcia: Sites, Sources and Structures, XII–XV Centuries," *Cuadernos de Historia de España*, 79 (1997): pp. 7–27.

13 Robert I. Burns, "Journey from Islam: Incipient Cultural Transition in the Conquered Kingdom of Valencia (1240–1280)," *Speculum*, 35 (1960): pp. 337–56.

14 Robert I. Burns, "100,000 Crossbow Bolts for the Crusader King of Aragon," *The Journal of Medieval Military History*, 2 (2004): pp. 159–64.

1960s, the Crown of Aragon was, to paraphrase Churchill, a mystery wrapped in an enigma. If one speculates upon the influences that led Father Burns in the lonely direction that marked his career one might look at the stirrings in his beloved Catholic Church that in time exploded at the Second Vatican Council. In particular, the Council's declaration *Nostra aetate* pointed optimistically to a rapprochement between Christianity and Islam.[15] Perhaps in his scholarly pursuits, Burns saw the opportunity for the past to be tutor to the present.

Finally we come to the scholarly "hijra" of Joseph F. O'Callaghan. One need be rather more tentative here for Joe's scholarly work is not finished, nor would we care for it to be just yet. Joe came to medieval studies, indeed the scholarly life, in rather different fashion than either Bishko or Burns. His early years were influenced by the Christian Brothers at La Salle College in Philadelphia, Pennsylvania, then a tiny, sturdily middle-class, urban, and Catholic institution from which Joe graduated in 1950. From there he went to Marquette, a Jesuit institution, graduating with the M.A. in 1952. Beginning later that same year at Fordham, another urban and Jesuit university, he earned his doctorate in 1957 and continued to teach at Fordham until his retirement 42 years later in 1994.[16]

Not surprisingly, given his training within institutions run by religious orders, his earliest publication was "'Difiniciones' of the Order of Calatrava Enacted by Abbot William II of Morimond, April 2, 1468" appearing in 1958. His extended three-part essay, "The Affiliation of the Order of Calatrava with the Order of Citeaux," followed quickly in 1959 and 1960.[17] Such studies of medieval Iberian religious orders were to form one of the enduring staples of his rich historical legacy.[18] While his early interest in monastic orders parallels that

[15] "Declaration on the Relation of the Church to Non-Christian Religions: *Nostra aetate*," available at http://www.vatican.va/archive/hist_councils/ii_vatican_council/documents/vat-ii_decl_19651028_nostra-aetate_en.html (accessed January 13, 2012).

[16] The stability, love, and respect for tradition evident in O'Callaghan's commitment to Fordham have been mirrored in other aspects of his life and career. His professional endeavors have always been accompanied by a loving and conscientious dedication to family and friends. The former could be light-hearted or serious as is illustrated by his post-retirement publication Joseph F. O'Callaghan, *The O'Callaghan Family of County Cork: A History* (Dublin: Irish Family Names, 2004).

[17] Joseph F. O'Callaghan, "'*Difiniciones*' of the Order of Calatrava Enacted by Abbot William II of Morimond, April 2, 1468," *Traditio*, 14 (1958): pp. 231–68; Joseph F. O'Callaghan, "The Affiliation of the Order of Calatrava with the Order of Citeaux," *Analecta Sacri Ordinis Cisterciensis*, 15 (1959): pp. 161–93; 16 (1960): pp. 3–59, 255–92.

[18] Many of his studies of the Order of Calatrava are gathered together in Joseph F. O'Callaghan, *The Spanish Military Order of Calatrava and its Affiliates* (London: Ashgate, 1975). He also edited a collection of studies on the Cistercian Order and even translated the autobiography of Saint Ignatius Loyola. Joseph F. O'Callaghan (ed.), *Studies in Medieval*

of Bishko, O'Callaghan, like the latter, quickly pursued another independent theme: the law and legal practices of secular institutions. "The Beginnings of the Cortes of León-Castile" appeared in the *American Historical Review* of 1969 and the "The Cortes and Royal Taxation during the Reign of Alfonso X of Castile" in *Traditio* in 1971.[19]

O'Callaghan's continued interest in representative assemblies and secular government was affirmed by the volume he published some 20 years later, *The Cortes of Castile-León, 1188–1350,* as well as more specialized studies some of which are collected in *Alfonso X, the Cortes and Government in Medieval Spain*.[20] But at the same time his interests in religious and secular institutions led him to broader preoccupations. One thinks of his enduring attention to and sympathy for the brilliant, sometimes enigmatic, and ultimately tragic Alfonso X of Castile (1252–84).[21] Most recently he has addressed America's post-9/11 interest in the Crusades and Islam with two substantial contributions on the nature of holy war as played out in both the medieval Levant and Iberia.[22]

Cistercian History Presented to Professor Jeremiah F. O'Sullivan (New York: Cistercian Publications, 1971); John C. Olin (ed.), *The Autobiography of Ignatius Loyola*, trans. Joseph F. O'Callaghan (New York: Harper Torchbooks, 1974).

[19] Joseph F. O'Callaghan, "The Beginnings of the Cortes of León-Castile," *American Historical Review*, 74 (1969): pp. 1503–37; Joseph F. O'Callaghan, "The Cortes and Royal Taxation during the Reign of Alfonso X of Castile," *Traditio*, 27 (1971): pp. 379–98. On this theme there had been an American forerunner in Roger B. Merriman, "The Cortes of the Spanish Kingdoms in the Later Middle Ages," *American Historical Review*, 16 (1911): pp. 476–95. But again one may speculate whether O'Callaghan was not moved by the more recent development of legal theory in the post-Vatican II Catholic Church that distinguished more clearly between the claims of secular and religious law and the independent function of their respective institutions. Certainly his involvement, in retirement, in the effort to promote constitutional reorganization in the Catholic Church points in such a direction. See Joseph F. O'Callaghan, *Electing Our Bishops: How the Catholic Church Should Choose Its Leaders* (Lanham, MD: Rowman & Littlefield, 2007).

[20] Joseph F. O'Callaghan, *The Cortes of León-Castile, 1188–1350* (Philadelphia, PA: University of Pennsylvania Press, 1989); Joseph F. O'Callaghan, *Alfonso X, the Cortes and Government in Medieval Spain* (Aldershot: Ashgate, 1998).

[21] Joseph F. O'Callaghan, *The Learned King: The Reign of Alfonso X of Castile* (Philadelphia, PA: University of Pennsylvania Press, 1993); Joseph F. O'Callaghan, *Alfonso X and the Cantigas de Santa Maria* (Leiden: E.J. Brill, 1998).

[22] Joseph F. O'Callaghan, *Reconquest and Crusade in Medieval Spain* (Philadelphia, PA: University of Pennsylvania Press, 2003); Joseph F. O'Callaghan, *The Gibraltar Crusade: Castile and the Battle for the Strait* (Philadelphia, PA: University of Pennsylvania Press, 2011).

But in briefly reviewing such an impressive catalog, one must give separate place to O'Callaghan's *A History of Medieval Spain*.[23] For better than 30 years now it has been the standard for a narrative history of the Iberian Middle Ages in English. I would own that it is the single most dog-eared, scotch-taped volume of history in my personal library. (I suppose that my apologies to Joe are in order here since Cornell University Press has kept his magnum opus in print continuously since 1975 and in 1983 even brought out a paperback edition.) It is an inclusive volume of Iberian medieval history that scoops up the Visigoths, the various Muslim kingdoms and empires, and the gaggle of Christian kingdoms—Aragon-Catalonia, Castile, León, Navarra, and Portugal—in the long and disorderly pageant that preceded the emergence of the unified national monarchies in Spain and Portugal at the beginning of the modern period.

When it was published in 1975, Joe's *History* both summed up the already remarkable development of American scholarship from the end of World War II and presaged the almost equally impressive work that would be erected on that foundation by he and other American medievalists in the 35 years that have followed. It should be noted here that while neither Professor Bishko nor Professor Burns aspired personally to such a task they both encouraged and assisted, when possible, Professor O'Callaghan's assumption of that Herculean effort, as he himself noted in his preface of 1973.

From that same preface it is fitting here to quote him as to the background against which he undertook to write and his purposes in doing so:

> Until recently American and most northern European scholars have paid scant attention to the history of the Iberian peninsula in the Middle Ages and have often been content with superficial judgments founded upon antiquated and inaccurate works or on opinions clouded by the prejudices accumulated over the past four hundred years. If this book contributes to a clearer understanding of the formation of Medieval Spain it will have served a valuable purpose. As the field of medieval Spanish and Portuguese history is still relatively unexplored, I hope that readers will be encouraged to pursue more intensive investigation into many of the subjects dealt with.

On this occasion we may properly celebrate that both objectives have been roundly met. Bravo, Professor Joseph F. O'Callaghan!

---

[23] Joseph F. O'Callaghan, *A History of Medieval Spain* (Ithaca, NY: Cornell University Press, 1975).

Chapter 2

The Crown Renewed: The Administration of Coinage in León-Castile c. 1085–1200

James J. Todesca

Historians like to hold up Norman England as the most centralized European state of its day, often pointing to the crown's purported regulation of coinage and other financial machinery as proof of its sophistication.[1] W.L. Warren, however, cautioned that "the evidence for the actual operation of Norman administration is very meager."[2] In terms of the coinage, the written and numismatic evidence is perplexing but overall indicates that William the Conqueror (1066–87) and his sons struggled to maintain the monetary system of their Anglo-Saxon forebears. When Henry I (1100–35) took the throne he promised to abandon a levy called *monetagium commune* that his father had introduced though the "precise nature" of this tax is uncertain.[3] Eight years

1 Charles H. Haskins, *Norman Institutions* (1918; reprint, New York: Frederick Ungar Publishing, 1960), p. 3, concluded that "the Anglo-Norman kingdom finds no parallel in the western Europe of its time." Joseph Strayer, *On the Medieval Origins of the Modern State* (1970; reprint, Princeton, NJ: Princeton University Press, 2005), p. 47, stressed that England's "judicial and financial systems created in the eleventh and twelfth centuries" allowed for its "remarkable rapidity" in state building. More recently, Malcolm Barber, *The Two Cities: Medieval Europe 1050–1320*, 2nd edn (London: Routledge, 2004), p. 285, pointed to "the stability of the coinage in Henry (I)'s time" as evidence of Norman "uniformity and control." See also M.T. Clanchy, *England and Its Rulers, 1066–1307*, 3rd edn (Oxford: Blackwell Publishing, 2006), pp. 88–9; Peter Spufford, *Money and Its Use in Medieval Europe* (Cambridge: Cambridge University Press, 1988), pp. 93–4.

2 W.L. Warren, "The Myth of Norman Administrative Efficiency," *Transactions of the Royal Historical Society*, 5th ser., 34 (1984): p. 114.

3 Mark Blackburn, "Coinage and Currency under Henry I: A Review," *Anglo Norman Studies*, 13 (1990/91): p. 50; A.J. Robertson (ed. and trans.), *The Laws of the Kings of England from Edmund to Henry I* (1925; reprint, Clark, NJ: The Lawbook Exchange, 2009), pp. 278–9. See further n. 56 below.

later, Henry was so plagued by counterfeiters that he was forced to "snick" his coinage to show that the interior contained good silver. Then, during the Christmas season of 1124, he punished more than half of the perhaps 150 moneyers in England, probably cutting off their right hands and genitals. His monetary policy, as Warren notes, "was running into serious difficulties."[4]

As fascinating as Henry I is, this paper is concerned with monetary policy in eleventh- and twelfth-century León-Castile, a kingdom usually not awarded even honorable mention when discussing institutional development. Its government can appear far removed from what Haskins called the "precocity and vigor of (the Anglo-Norman) administrative system."[5] Bernard Reilly concluded that royal government in León-Castile and the other Christian Iberian kingdoms "was short of reach and spastic in application."[6] But Warren's contention that the venerable belief in Norman efficiency is based on meager evidence should give us pause. There are enough hints in the diplomatic and numismatic records of León to indicate its kings knew more about finance then we are apt to credit them. Indeed, while there were far fewer mints in León than in England, the Leonese monarchs may have overseen their operation better than Henry I. As far as we know, they never savagely mutilated the bulk of their moneyers.

Since the era of Charlemagne the common coin in medieval Europe was the *denarius*. By the beginning of the twelfth century, *denarii* normally weighed close to 1 gram and were 50 percent silver or less.[7] In León, Alfonso VI (1065–1109) initiated the kingdom's first large-scale denarial coinage probably after his conquest of Toledo in 1085. He seems to have produced two issues from then until his death: the star-annulet type (Figure 2.1) and the christogram type (figures 2.2–4). The star-annulet type reads from obverse to reverse ANFVS REX TOLETVM. The christogram coin also reads ANFVS REX on the obverse, but its reverse legend alternates between TOLETVO, LEO CIVITAS, S IACOBI.[8] Since Toledo, León and Santiago de Compostela

[4] Warren, "Myth," pp. 116–18; Blackburn, pp. 51–2.

[5] Haskins, p. 3.

[6] Bernard F. Reilly, *The Contest of Christian and Muslim Spain, 1031–1157* (Oxford: Blackwell, 1992), p. 239.

[7] The primary exceptions were the denarii of England and Cologne; these weighed almost 1.5 grams and were more than 90 percent fine. Spufford, pp. 101–4.

[8] The Santibáñez de la Peña hoard, said to contain 421 specimens of the star-annulet type alongside 626 of the christogram type, demonstrates the two coins were successive issues. See "Museo arquelógico de Palencia: Adquisiciones," *Memorias de los Museos Arqueológicos*, 15 (1954): pp. 187–9. Since these two types allude to Toledo, we can assume they were not minted before Alfonso VI. None of the coins appear in hoards from the thirteenth century onward, so we can further assume that they are not coins of Alfonso X (1252–84) or later. Between

Figure 2.1 Obv. **ANFVS REX** Cross
Rev. **+TOLETVM** Two stars, two annulets

Source: American Numismatic Society.

Figure 2.2 Obv. **ANFVS REX** Cross
Rev. **+TOLETVO** Christogram

Source: American Numismatic Society.

Figure 2.3 Obv. **+ANFVS REX** Cross
Rev. **+LEO CIVITAS** Christogram

Source: American Numismatic Society.

Figure 2.4 Obv. **A_ _V_REX** Cross, pellet in quadrant
Rev. **S IA_O_ _** Christogram

Source: Ángel Martinez Levas. Museo Arqueológico Nacional (N.I. 1994/50/95).

were arguably the three most prestigious towns in the kingdom, it makes sense that each had a mint. In addition, Palencia and Lugo appear to have had mints.[9] If so, these lesser operations did not sign their coins but minted using the name of one of the other three towns.

In the last years of his reign, Alfonso reluctantly turned over the mint at Santiago to the town's bishop, Diego Gelmírez, to support the building of the new cathedral. His detailed charter of donation to Diego and the cathedral chapter, probably done in May 1107, reveals much of what the king had learned about minting.[10] Like Henry I of England, he was foremost concerned with counterfeiters:

> And because all the counterfeiters of the coins of my land are accustomed to always blame the crime of counterfeiting on the moneyers of Compostela, if it pleases the bishop of this same place along with the council of his canons and they recognize in this that there is great benefit and profit for their church, I

1085 and 1200 Alfonso VII (1126–57) was the only other Alfonso to claim Toledo, León and Santiago, the towns represented on the christogram type. Conceivably the coins could belong to him, but their careful craftsmanship suggests they are earlier. See n. 35 below. Aloïss Heiss, *Descripción general de las monedas hispano-cristianas desde la invasión de los Árabes*, vol. 1 (1865; reprint, Madrid: J.R. Cayon, 1975), plate 1, nos 1–5, plate 2, no. 27, assigned the star-annulet and two of the christogram types to Alfonso VI; the third christogram type he gave to Alfonso VII. Juan Caballero Alcaráz, "Dineros de Alfonso VI: Una corrección de Heiss," *Numisma*, 13 (1963): pp. 9–16, argued convincingly that all four coins should be assigned to Alfonso VI. For a review of possible royal coinage in León before 1085, see James J. Todesca, "What Touches All: Coinage and Monetary Policy in León-Castile to 1230," Ph.D. diss., Fordham University, 1996, pp. 87–131. For an overview of known coin types for León-Castile one can now consult Miquel Crusafont, Anna M. Balaguer and Philip Grierson (eds), *Medieval European Coinage*, vol. 6, *The Iberian Peninsula* (Cambridge: Cambridge University Press, 2013), though I do not always agree with their conclusions.

9 Minting at Palencia under Alfonso VI is implied in Alfonso VII's charter of 1140. See n. 39 below. Likewise, Lugo's early mint is indicated in a charter of Fernando II. See n. 57 below.

10 The earliest copy of the charter is in *Tumbo A* of the cathedral archives of Santiago. This portion of *Tumbo A* was redacted between 1129 and 1131. Manuel Lucas Álvarez (ed.), *La documentación del Tumbo A de la Catedral de Santiago de Compostela: Estudio y edición* (León: Centro de Estudios e Investigacíon "San Isidoro," 1997), pp. 30–34, 198–200, no. 72; Andrés Gambra (ed.), *Alfonso VI: Cancillería, curia e imperio*, vol. 2, *Colección diplomática* (León: Centro de Estudios e Investigacíon "San Isidoro," 1998), pp. 481–5, no. 189. Cf. Richard Fletcher, *St. James's Catapult: The Life and Times of Diego Gelmírez of Santiago de Compostela* (Oxford: Clarendon Press, 1984), pp. 263–4, 303. For the dating of the charter itself, see also Bernard F. Reilly, *The Kingdom of León-Castilla under King Alfonso VI, 1065–1109* (Princeton, NJ: Princeton University Press, 1988), pp. 324–5.

> ordain that they change the letters of their dies, and so that they achieve this more (readily) they shall appoint a provost (*prepositum*) for their mint.[11]

To understand this passage, it is helpful to turn back to England. A set of laws attributed to King Aethelred (c. 978–1016) complains of those "who make dies in secret and sell them to forgers for money, engraving upon them a name which is that of another moneyer and not that of the guilty one."[12] By Aethelred's day, moneyers were required to use dies that carried their name as well as that of the town where they minted.[13] A dishonest moneyer naturally used counterfeit dies with another minter's name and town. He then wisely sought to pass his product into circulation away from his own home. Aethelred's laws order bishops, earls, ealdormen and reeves (*praepositis*) to "be on the watch for those who coin such base money and convey it through the country."[14] Henry I later forbid "any moneyer to change *denarii* except in his own shire ... and if he is seized changing denarii in another shire he shall be taken as a forger."[15]

Alfonso's coins do not carry an individual minter's name, but his christogram type does distinguish between Toledo, León and Santiago on its reverse. In his grant, then, Alfonso seems to accuse non-Compostelan moneyers of making inferior coins with the Compostela legend. They perhaps contrived to pass these coins in the busy markets of Santiago where, according to the twelfth-century *Liber Sancti Jacobi*, "one finds money changers, innkeepers and merchants of all sorts."[16]

---

[11] "Et quia omnes falsificatores monetarum mee patrie crimen falsitatis super Compostelle monetarios semper solent obicere, si episcopo eiusdem loci cum consilio canonicorum placuerit et profectum maiusque lucrum sue ecclesie in hoc esse cognoverint, volo ut mutent cuneorum suorum litteras et de illo unde magis impetraverint faciant sue monete prepositum." Álvarez, pp. 198–200, no. 72.

[12] The law appears in "IV Aethelred." "III Athelred" also addresses "moneyers who work in a wood." Robertson, pp. 47–9, 70–71, 74–5.

[13] Ian Stewart, "Coinage and Recoinage after Edgar's Reform," in Kenneth Jonsson (ed.), *Studies in Late Anglo-Saxon Coinage in Memory of Bror Emil Hildebrand* (Stockholm: Svenska Numismatiska Föreningen, 1990), p. 457.

[14] Robertson, pp. 76–7.

[15] Ibid., pp. 284–5.

[16] William Melczer (ed. and trans.), *The Pilgrim's Guide to Santiago de Compostela* (New York: Italica Press, 1993), pp. 122–3. The *Historia Compostellana* preserves decrees promulgated by the canons and *concejo* of Santiago in 1133 which stipulate that "the innkeepers, moneyers and money changers, as well as the citizens, should not have false marks, pounds or any false weights." *Historia compostellana*, ed. Emma Falque Rey (Turnhout: Brepols, 1988), bk. 3, chap. 33 (hereafter cited as *HC*). For the fast pace of the Santiago market see also Fletcher, *Catapult*, p. 183.

Henry I, though he had blustered about counterfeiting from the inception of his reign, was unable to control it. His summary castration of a large group of moneyers in 1124 seems born from this frustration. How he determined which of them were guilty remains a mystery since no one would put his own name on bad coins. Alfonso had a more rational solution. He suggests in his charter that if counterfeiting of Compostela's money becomes too widespread, the canons should change the coin by altering its legend.

Such a maneuver would only be effective, however, if the bishop was able to invalidate the old coins. Nicholas Oresme, in the mid-fourteenth century, explained:

> The struck motif or legend of a coin can be changed in two ways. One is without prohibiting the previous money from circulating ... This is not strictly an alteration ... The form may be changed in another way, by making new money while prohibiting the circulation of the old. This is an alteration in the proper sense and can justly be made for one of two reasons. One is if a foreign prince, or some counterfeiters, maliciously copy or counterfeit the forms (*modulos*) or dies of the money ... Then, if no other remedy could be applied, it would be well to change the forms and (hence) the motif of the struck coin. Another reason might be if perchance the old money was too much injured by age or reduced in weight.[17]

The intent behind a proper alteration of types was to force the old, worn coins and counterfeits out of circulation and hence renew the currency.[18] But, to make new coins required labor and so a mint could not afford to evenly exchange old for new. If the new money was of equal weight and fineness, then the old coinage

---

17 Translation based on Charles Johnson (ed. and trans.), *The De Moneta of Nicholas Oresme and English Mint Documents* (London: Thomas Nelson and Sons, 1956), pp. 13–14.

18 The Annals of Winchester (England) record for 1179: "Eodem anno fecit rex Henricus renovare monetam pro veteris monetae nimia falsitate." Domesday Book twice speaks of "quando moneta renovatur." English numismatists, therefore, often use the term *renovatio* to refer to recoinage. For example, Ian Stewart, "The English and Norman Mints, c.600–1158," in C.E. Challis (ed.), *A New History of the Royal Mint* (Cambridge: Cambridge University Press, 1992), p. 55, refers to "the *renovatio (or mutatatio) monetae*, as it was called." Though it is a useful term, I know of no explicit medieval reference to *renovatio monetae*. For the annals mentioning Henry II's recoinage c.1179, see Gilbert M. Stack, "English Mint Administration, Moneyers and Monetary Reform in the Reign of Henry II, 1154–1189," Ph.D. diss., Fordham University, 2004, p. 125. For Domesday, see George C. Brooke, "Quando Moneta Vertebatur: The Change of Coin-Types in the Eleventh Century," *British Numismatic Journal* 20 (1929–30): pp. 105–6.

had to be discounted at the mint, not only to cover costs but hopefully to allow a profit as Alfonso's grant to the chapter at Santiago suggests.[19]

The Carolingians on occasion attempted recoinages or renewals such as Oresme describes. Louis the Pious (814–40) seems to have recoined successfully c.818, but he expressed frustration over a second attempt begun c.822 and did not change types thereafter.[20] His son Charles the Bald (840–77) waited until 864 to recall the coinage of his realm.[21] For a brief period between 973 and 1035, the English kings renewed their coinage regularly, perhaps every six or seven years. Between 1035 and 1066, however, 14 types appeared. These more frequent changes met resistance and so by the time of Edward the Confessor (1042–66) people hoarded older types rather than surrender them.[22]

Frequent recoinages persisted under the Normans. William I and William II (1087–1100) struck 13 types between them. In addition, William I's insistence

---

[19] An example of discounting invalidated coins can be seen in a *responsum* attributed to Rashi of Troyes. The question put to Rashi was: "A person lent money to his friend, and subsequently the coins were invalidated. In what coin does he pay him back?" The *responsum*: "The debtor must ... repay the creditor with the same number of new coins. Should he want to repay him in invalidated coins, however, he would have to give him a number of coins that would now have the same exchange value as the sum he lent him had at the time the loan was made." Irving A. Agus, *Urban Civilization in Pre-Crusade Europe* (New York: Yeshiva University Press, 1965), pp. 378–9, 49–51. Alternatively, the new coins could be struck at a lighter weight than the old, so one new coin contained less silver than one old. For the complicated issue of weight variation in England before the conquest, see Stewart, "Coinage and Recoinage," pp. 469–71.

[20] It is not clear if Louis attempted a recoinage at the beginning of his reign in 814. Simon Coupland, "La chronologie des émissions monétaieres de Louis le Pieux (814–40)" in *Carolingian Coinage and the Vikings: Studies on Power and Trade in the Ninth Century* (Aldershot: Ashgate, 2007), no. 4, pp. 431–3; Simon Coupland, "Money and Coinage Under Louis the Pious" in *Carolingian Coinage*, no. 3, pp. 23–54.

[21] Alfredus Boretius and Victor Krause (eds), *Capitularia regum francorum*, Monumenta germaniae historica (2 vols, Hanover: Impensis bibliopolii Hahniani, 1883–97), vol. 2, pp. 315–17; cf. Coupland, "Money," p. 36.

[22] According to Dolley and Metcalf, Eadgar (959–75) called in the coinage in 973 and six years later his son Aethelred (c.978–1016) renewed it. Dolley and Metcalf believed that Aethelred then called the coinage in at six-year intervals until his death. R.H.M Dolley and D.M. Metcalf, "The Reform of the English Coinage Under Eadgar" in R.H.M. Dolley (ed.), *Anglo-Saxon Coins (Studies Presented to F.M. Stenton)* (London: Methuen and Company, 1961), pp. 152–8. H. Bertil A. Petersson, *Anglo-Saxon Currency: King Edgar's Reform to the Norman Conquest* (Lund: Berlingska Boktryckeriet, 1969), pp. 72–87, reviewed the evidence and argued for seven-year intervals from c.974/75 through Cnut (1017–35). Stewart has challenged the idea that the crown adhered to regular intervals. See Stewart, "Coinage and Recoinage," *passim*; Stewart, "English and Norman Mints," pp. 54–5.

on collecting payments by weight rather than tale and the introduction of the *monetagium* tax further aggravated popular consent to the crown's monetary policy.[23] Henry I continued to issue new types, but seems to have been unable to call in the old. According to his contemporary Eadmer, some eight years into the reign Henry adopted alternative measures:

> Corrupt and false money afflicted many people in many ways. Thus, the king ordered it to be corrected by such severe punishment that anyone who could be caught making false denarii should not be able to save himself by any redemption except the loss of his eyes and the lower parts of the body. And since it very often happened that when denarii were being selected they were bent, broken (and) rejected, he ordered that no denarius or half denarius (*obolus*) should be whole (*integer*). From this great good resulted at once for the entire kingdom.[24]

As surviving coins of Henry's attest, by no coin being "whole" Eadmer meant that public confidence in the money was so low that the mints now "snicked" or deliberately gouged their coins to show the interior was good silver.[25]

Unlike Henry, Alfonso in his donation to Santiago considered recoinage doable though he realized it was impractical for a single mint. If Santiago attempted a new coinage on its own, how was it to deal with coins coming from Alfonso's other mints? Pilgrims and merchants would resist exchanging Leonese or Toledan coins in Compostela since they could quickly spend them once they were again outside the bishop of Santiago's jurisdiction. Alfonso's charter, therefore, continues:

> If truly they do not realize as great a profit in the alteration of the letters of the dies (as there would be) in an alteration of all my coins, and since counterfeiting of the public money ought to be feared, I order that the provost of all my mints hold the mint (of Compostela) by your authority and legitimately guard it, and he

23 Stewart, "English and Norman Mints," pp. 55–7; Dolly and Metcalf, 158; Frank Barlow, *William Rufus* (Berkeley, CA: University of California Press, 1983), p. 60 and Figure 2; Stack, pp. 31–45.

24 Eadmeri, *Historia novorum in Anglia et opuscula duo, de vita Sanctii Anselmi et quibusdam miraculis ejus*, ed. Martin Rule (London: Longman and Company, 1884), p. 193; Blackburn, p. 62. Dolley and Metcalf, pp. 158, 152, suggested that the system of renewal ran into trouble under Edward the Confessor, but that the Normans' "efficient administration" righted it and it continued to function until the anarchy after Henry I's death. Blackburn, p. 72, proposed that the system was abandoned in 1125. Eadmer's testimony, however, indicates that Henry was hampered from the beginning of his reign.

25 Blackburn, pp. 62–3.

> shall give to you from your mint as great a profit as he shall give to me from one of the best mints of my land.[26]

The king here encourages the chapter to wait for a general change of the coinage and offers the services of his own mint provost, presumably to work with Compostela's provost mentioned earlier in the grant. Alfonso is even willing to guarantee the canons a minimum profit if they wait.

Alfonso's grant implies that he attempted at least one recoinage previously and did so by relying on the skills of his provost. We know nothing more of this "provost of all my mints," though the *Historia compostellana* tells us that the chapter at Santiago appointed Randulf, a moneyer "endowed with great talent," as their own provost or mint master.[27] Judging from his name, Randulf was a foreigner. Lopez suggested that medieval moneyers formed an international brotherhood, often moving about to "promote their trade." Indeed, Randulf may have come from Normandy.[28] Although we do not know the name of Alfonso's own *prepositus*, he surely was as skilled as Randulf. While these journeyman

26 "Si vero non tantum lucrum sibi in commutione [*sic*] litterature cuneorum cognoverint quantum in omnium mearum monetarum comunitate [*sic*], timendo communis monete falsitatem, mando ut prepositus omnium mearum monetarum de iure vestro teneat et legitime custodiat, et tam magnum vobis lucrum tribuat de vestra sicuti michi dederit de una ex melioribus monetis mee parie, et sic vobis de vestra sicut michi ex una de meis melioribus complaceat et in omnibus satisfaciat." I assume that "in omnium mearum monetarum comunitate," literally "in the community of all my mints," should read "in omnium mearum monetarum commutatione" or "in an alteration of all my coins." Álvarez, pp. 198–200, no. 72; cf. Gambra, pp. 481–5, no. 189.

27 *HC*, bk. 1, chap. 28. See also Emma Falque Rey (trans.), *Historia compostelana* (Madrid: Ediciones Akal, 1994) p. 123, n. 277.

28 Lopez also observed that "no man could become a moneyer, as a rule, unless he was a descendant of a moneyer." Robert S. Lopez, "An Aristocracy of Money in the Early Middle Ages," *Speculum*, 28 (1953): pp. 2–6. One of four minters known in Normandy under William the Conqueror was named Randulf. His son Osbern appears to have succeeded him in Normandy before 1066. Another son, Waleran, became an important moneyer in England. Could Randulf of Santiago have been a member of this same Norman family? David C. Douglas, *William the Conqueror* (Berkeley, CA: University of California Press, 1964), pp. 135–6, 304; cf. Haskins, p. 280, n. 23; Fletcher, *Catapult*, p. 184. In 1121, a moneyer named Randulf witnessed an act of Alfonso I of Aragon at the siege of Tardajos just west of Burgos. Had the Aragonese king recruited Randulf of Santiago or was this perhaps another member of the same family? José María Lacarra (ed.), *Documentos para el estudio de la reconquista y repoblación del valle del Ebro (números 1 a 319)* (Zaragoza: Anubar, 1982), pp. 90–91, no. 75.

moneyers supplied the know-how, it is unlikely that they alone inspired Alfonso to reform his coinage. The exigencies of war probably demanded it.[29]

In the early part of his reign Alfonso seems to have struck few if any denarii. He and his father reportedly enjoyed vast tribute from Muslim clients and the treasure he subsequently gained from conquering Toledo in 1085 was substantial.[30] But the intervention of the North African Almoravids in 1086 signaled the end of easy money for León. Almoravid forces wintered in the peninsula for the first time in 1090–91 to begin their conquest of al-Andalus. In February and March of 1091, Alfonso, citing the Almoravid threat, sought to collect a tax of 24 denarii from each household in the "land" of León.[31] Around the same time Diego Gelmírez apparently attempted a similar levy, ordering every household in the bishopric of Santiago to pay 12 denarii so as to strengthen

---

29 Bernard F. Reilly, *The Kingdom of León-Castilla under King Alfonso VII, 1126–1157* (Philadelphia, PA: University of Pennsylvania Press, 1998), p. 318, warns that it is perhaps anachronistic to speak of royal economic policy in eleventh and twelfth-century León. Nonetheless, as Stewart points out, "competent governments are normally ready to respond to circumstances and to develop their policies in the light of experience." Stewart, "Coinage and Recoinage," p. 480; cf. Christopher Dyer, *Making a Living in the Middle Ages* (New Haven, CT: Yale University Press, 2002), pp. 57–8.

30 For the *paria* payments, see James J. Todesca, "Means of Exchange: Islamic Coinage in Christian Spain, 1000–1200" in Larry J. Simon (ed.), *Iberia and the Mediterranean World of the Middle Ages: Studies in Honor of Robert I. Burns S.J.* (Leiden: E.J. Brill, 1995), pp. 250–51. For the treasure of Toledo, see the pact between Alfonso's sons-in-law in Rui Pinto de Azevedo (ed.), *Documentos medievais portugueses: Documentos régios* (Lisbon: Academia Portuguesa da História, 1958), pp. 3–4, no. 2; cf. Bernard F. Reilly, *The Kingdom of León-Castilla under Queen Urraca (1109–1126)* (Princeton, NJ: Princeton University Press, 1982), p. 27, n. 55; Todesca, "What Touches All," pp. 119–31.

31 A royal charter dated March 31, 1091 to Bishop Pedro of León, Count Martín Laíñez and the inhabitants of the "terra de Legione" grants *fueros* regulating litigation between Christians and Jews in exchange for the levy. A second version of the text addressed more generally to the "infanzones" and "villanos" of León is dated Thursday, February 7, with the year given as 1090. In 1090, however, February 7 fell on Wednesday. The correct year should be 1091, when February 7 was on Thursday. The less than two months between these charters suggests that Alfonso reached an agreement on the tax with his court early in 1091 and had charters drawn up and distributed, similar to the *cuadernos* of later royal courts. Gambra, pp. 273–5, no. 105, pp. 295–8, no. 114; cf. Claudio Sánchez-Albornoz, "Notas para el estudio del 'petitum,'" in *Estudios sobre las instituciones medievales españolas* (Mexico: Universidad Nacional Autónoma de México, 1965), pp. 485–6. Adriano Cappelli, *Cronologia, cronografia e calendario perpetuo: Dal principio dell'era cristiana ai nostri giorni* 6th edn (Milan: Ulrico Hoepli, 1988), pp. 80, 96. For the Almoravids, see Hugh Kennedy, *Muslim Spain and Portugal: A Political History of al-Andalus* (Harlow, England: Pearson Education Ltd, 1996), pp. 162–5.

the Torres del Oeste at the mouth of the Ulla river against Almoravid attack. The *Historia compostellana* reports that after the bishop collected the tax he did not have enough to cover the cost of repairs because "the money at the time was base and weak, both in weight and fineness."[32]

Henry II of England's (1154–89) collection of *danegeld* in 1156 seems to have revealed the poor state of the kingdom's currency and prompted his recoinage of 1158.[33] Likewise in León the household levies c.1091, possibly the first extraordinary tax in the kingdom, may have prompted Alfonso to take monetary policy more seriously. Perhaps soon after 1091, he issued the star-annulet coin (Figure 2.1), invalidating what remained of sundry weak and worn denarii in the realm.[34] When the star-annulet coin showed signs of age—the Anglo-Saxons

[32] The account of the levy in Santiago is in chapter 33 of the first book of the *Historia Compostellana*. Beginning "hec autem inserendo inserimus," this chapter and chapter 34 were added to the first book at a later date probably by the canon Gerald writing as late as the 1140s. Chapter 34 implies that the tax occurred after 1102, but it is unlikely the coinage was "base and weak" that late in Alfonso's reign. *HC*, bk. 1, chaps 33–4, cf. bk. 2, chaps 23–4; Bernard F. Reilly, "The *Historia Compostelana*: The Genesis and Composition of a Twelfth-Century Spanish *Gesta*," *Speculum*, 44 (1969): pp. 84–5; Falque Rey (trans.), *Historia*, p. 133, n. 323.

It makes most sense to place the levy in the early 1090s. While Diego Gelmírez did not become bishop of Santiago until 1100, a royal grant to the monks of Montesacro dated January 28, 1090 has him confirming as "majorinus et dominator Compostelle honoris." Reilly believed Alfonso VI appointed him *merino* in anticipation of the deposition of Bishop Pedro of Cardeña at the Council of León in March 1090. Fletcher, following HC, bk. 1, chap. 4, argued that a Galician assembly entrusted Diego with these administrative duties c.1093. Possisbly Diego added his confirmation to the Montesacro grant after that date. More recently, Gambra declared the Montesacro document a forgery, but he is in the minority. At any rate, as Fletcher concludes, "for the greater part ... of the last decade of the eleventh century Diego Gelmírez had had charge of the temporalities of the see." *HC*, bk. 1, chap. 4 adds that Diego "cepit destructa restaurare et restaurata consevare et conservata quasi ad statum rectitudinis multo labore perducere." This langauge seems echoed by *HC*, bk. 1, chap. 33 in describing the tax levy. Gambra, pp. 270–72, no. 104; Reilly, *Alfonso VI*, pp. 216–18; Fletcher, *Catapult*, pp. 104–8; Falque Rey (trans.), *Historia*, p. 132, n. 318. For dating the Council of León, see Simon Barton and Richard Fletcher (trans), *The World of El Cid: Chronicles of the Spanish Reconquest* (Manchester: Manchester University Press, 2000), p. 34.

[33] W.L. Warren, *Henry II* (Berkeley, CA: University of California Press, 1973), pp. 263–5; Stack, pp. 55–65, does not consider this possibility.

[34] In 2001 researchers opened an eighteenth-century silver urn at the monastery of Silos containing the remains of Santo Domingo. Along with the human remains and a "gran cantidad de tierra y pequeños cascotes" the reliquary yielded a star-annulet coin. Miguel C. Vivancos, "Hallazgo de un dinero de Alfonso VI en el monasterio de Santo Domingo de Silos," *Numisma*, 51 (2001): 169–74, argued that in 1088 monks opened an older tomb

considered six to seven years a reasonable life for a coinage—Alfonso replaced it with the christogram, struck with three reverse legends—TOLETVO, LEO CIVITAS and S IACOBI (figures 2.2–4).[35] The christogram denarius must have been in circulation for a few years when, in his grant of May 1107, Alfonso accused counterfeiters of targeting the coins of Compostela, i.e., those reading S IACOBI. As far as we can tell, he did not undertake a third issue in the last chaotic years of his life.

The following May Alfonso's son, Sancho, fell fighting the Almoravids. Alfonso then designated his daughter Urraca (1109–26) as successor and arranged her marriage to Alfonso I of Aragon (1104–34). The two married shortly after the old king's death in the summer of 1109. A party in Galicia, however, promoted young Alfonso Raimúndez' claim to the throne. The boy was Urraca's child by her first husband, Raymond of Burgundy. The tension between this Galician faction and Urraca, combined with her inability to get along with Alfonso of Aragon, plunged León into an anarchical period similar to the years in England after the death of Henry I.

---

of the saint's to extract relics for the three newly built apses of the monastic church and inserted the coin to mark the event. Additionally, eighteenth-century written records of the monastery report that four coins reading "Adefonsus Toletum" were found in (or near) an altar in the church's lower apse, presumably retired in 1088. The whereabouts of these four coins, however, are not known today. The evidence here is intriguing but multilayered. Though the new apses do seem to have been consecrated c.1088, I am not convinced the coins were deliberately placed there at that time. Cf. Elizabeth Valdez del Álamo, *Palace of the Mind: The Cloister of Silos and the Spanish Sculpture of the Twelfth Century* (Turnhout: Brepols, 2012), pp. 32–8.

35 In a study of 180 of the TOLETVO christogram coins, Metcalf found that the dies were "extremely uniform" which indicates central control of their engraving. He noted attention to details such as the consistent alignment of the beginning of the legend with the top of the christogram. He added that "the weights of individual flans were controlled with a quite impressive accuracy," estimating their intended weight at "between 1.07 and 1.09" grams. D.M. Metcalf, "A Parcel of Coins of Alfonso VI of León (1073–1109)," in Mário Gomes Marques and D.M. Metcalf (eds), *Problems of Medieval Coinage in the Iberian Area III* (Santarém: Sociedade Numismática Scalabitana, 1988), pp. 293–9. The uniformity of the christogram coins is reminiscent of the careful design of Charlemagne's reform coinage. Spufford, p. 43.

Less can be said about the star-annulet coin because of the few specimens available. In the 1990s, the combined trays of the American Numismatic Society and the Museo Arqueológico Nacional contained 32 specimens; 17 weighed between 0.90 and 1.19 grams. See Todesca, "What Touches All," pp. 492–4. Of the 421 star-annulet coins said to have been in the Santibáñez de la Peña hoard, 23 now remain in the Museo Provincial de Palencia. 19 of these are of one variety (with a point in each annulet); 13 weigh below 0.80 grams.

During the turmoil, Urraca, Alfonso Raimúndez and Alfonso of Aragon all struck coins in León-Castile as they vied for power. Though Urraca herself issued at least five types there is no evidence that she was able to recall older coins. A few charters between 1113 and 1120 mention *moneda de medietate* or coins of half silver and *moneda de tercia*, that is coins of only one-third silver.[36] Most likely Alfonso VI's reformed denarii had been half silver, a respectable fineness for a denarius of southern Europe, but at some point during Urraca's reign the standard dropped to one-third. While this drop may have been prompted by the expenses of civil war, it was also in keeping with larger monetary trends. By 1130 the popular coinage of Melgueil and probably the *jaccensis* of Aragon were also one-third fine.[37]

Urraca's death in 1126 brought a gradual restoration of peace as Alfonso Raimúndez, now Alfonso VII (1126–57), consolidated his power. After the death of Alfonso of Aragon in 1134, Alfonso VII emphasized his hegemony in the peninsula by using the title of emperor as his grandfather occasionally had. Heiss, in his pioneering catalogue of Spanish coinage, therefore assigned Alfonso VII a large array of coin types some of which carry no ruler's name but invoke the Leonese *imperium*.[38] While there is no certainty that all these coins belong to Alfonso VII, a good many of them probably do. Beside this puzzling array of coins, we have only a few scattered documentary references that help shed light on Alfonso VII's administration of the coinage.

In 1140, Alfonso confirmed the privileges of the bishop of Palencia, agreeing that:

> For that fur (coat) and also that mantle of gray fur which my predecessors established be given to the bishop of Palencia when the money was changed (*quando mutatio monete fierit*), I, the Emperor Alfonso, concede and order that

[36] Cristina Monterde Albiac (ed.), *Diplomatario de la reina Urraca de Castilla y León* (Zaragoza: Anubar Ediciones, 1996), pp. 104–6, no. 58, pp. 221–3, no. 140; José María Fernández Catón (ed.), *Colección documental del archivo de la catedral de León (775–1230)*, vol. 5 *(1109–1187)* (León: Centro de Estudios e Investigacíon "San Isidoro," 1990), pp. 47–9, no. 1349, pp. 69–70, no. 1359; Todesca, "What Touches All," pp. 197–200, 226–31, 236–40.

[37] J. Rouquette and A. Villemagne (eds), *Cartulaire de Maguelone, tome premier* (Montpellier: Librairie Louis Valat, 1912), pp. 108–12, no. 55; Todesca, "What Touches All," pp. 245–53.

[38] Heiss, plates 1–4. Estaban Collantes Vidal, "Intento de ordenación de las acuñaciones de Alfonso VII," *Acta Numismática*, 2 (1972): pp. 167–214, indentified 53 types or variations of types. Despite his resolve to "distinguir tipos" from "las piezas que realmente son variantes," a more rigorous study remains to be done.

the present bishop of Palencia, Lord Pedro, and his successors are to be given fifty *morabetinos* when there is a change to new money in Palencia ...[39]

"Quando mutatio monete fierit" here is reminiscent of Domesday's "quando moneta renovatur" or "quando moneta vertebatur" and implies that changes to the coinage occurred regularly. When Innocent II affirmed the bishop of Palencia's right three years later he spoke of "fifty morabetinos at each change of the money."[40] Also, it is clear that these changes generated profit. Rather than fur garments, Alfonso now promised the bishop 50 *morabetinos*, gold dinars procured from the Almoravids whose hold over al-Andalus was rapidly diminishing.[41] Alfonso VII's charter, then, underscores his grandfather's grant to Compostela in 1107. Both kings did not change coins haphazardly but attempted what Nichols Oresme called proper changes where the old money was invalidated and called in at a discount.

Alfonso's stipend in gold may also have compensated the new bishop of Palencia, Pedro II (1139–48), for accepting a reduced share in regular mint profits. Urraca had allowed the bishop's predecessor a half of overall mint revenue, but Alfonso's charter of 1140 is silent about that half. A subsequent royal charter of 1146, however, states that the bishop held only a tenth of the mint.[42] A similar tactic can be seen in Alfonso's dealings with Segovia. In late March 1135, he granted the bishop there "a third part of the money which

39 "Pro quadam, quoque, pellicia et quodam pallio grisis, que mei antecesssores palentinis episcopis, quando mutatio monete fieret, stabilierunt donari, ego, imperator Adefonsus, presenti palentino episcopi, domno Petro, suisque successoribus quinquaginta morabitinos, quando in Palencia monete nove fiet mutatio ... donari concedo et iubeo." Teresa Abajo Martín (ed.), *Documentación de la catedral de Palencia (1035–1247)* (Burgos: Ediciones J.M. Garrido Garrido, 1986), pp. 80–82, no. 35.

40 "In singulis monete mutacionibus quinquaginta morabetionos, quos rex Aldefonsus tibi et ecclesie tue reddi constituit." Abajo Martín, pp. 90–93, no. 41, cf. pp. 129–32, no. 62, pp. 191–4, no. 93. For Domesday, see Brooke, pp. 105–6.

41 The old payment in fur is worth noting. Pamela Nightingale, "The London Pepperers' Guild and Some Twelfth-Century English Trading Links with Spain," *Bulletin of the Institute of Historical Research*, 58 (1985): pp. 123–32, suggests that English merchants were visiting Palencia in the early twelfth century. Deorman, an English trader of "silks and rich fabrics," may have owned a church in London dedicated to St. Antonin, patron of the see of Palencia. He also seems to have come from a family of moneyers, further support of Lopez's point that moneyers at this stage were an international group.

42 Abajo Martín, pp. 62–3, no. 25, pp. 93–7, no. 42. For Pedro II, see Emiliano González Diéz, "Formación y desarrollo del dominio señorial de la iglesia palentina (1035–1351)" in *Actas del I congreso de historia de Palencia*, vol. 2, *Fuentes documentales y Edad Media* (Valladolid: Diputación Provincial de Palencia, 1987), p. 285.

shall be made in Segovia."[43] But in early April 1136, almost exactly a year after the previous grant, Alfonso drew up another charter. While the syntax here is cryptic, the king seems to grant "a fourth part of the money which shall be made in Segovia and (a fourth part) of the whole *cambiacio* however much that shall come to be."[44] As with Palencia, Alfonso reduced the bishop's general profit but compensated him with a share of the more occasional revenue from a *cambiacio* or exchange of the coinage.

Other sources attest that Alfonso paid close attention to his mint revenues. As early as 1119, while still co-ruling with his mother, he increased the crown's portion of minting at Sahagún from one-third to one-half.[45] After his mother's death, he boldly challenged Diego Gelmírez by attempting to reclaim mint revenues in Compostela. According to the *Historia compostellana*, the aging Diego, now archbishop, shamed him into confirming his grandfather's privilege. After Diego's death in 1140, however, Alfonso won back half the mint profits of Santiago apparently by promising that it would be the sole mint in Galicia. It may have been at this time that the king closed down minting at nearby Lugo.[46]

At Alfonso VII's death in 1157 at least seven episcopal towns—Toledo, León, Compostela, Segovia, Salamanca, Burgos and Zamora—had the right to mint. Segovia had begun minting during the anarchy of Urraca. The mints at Salamanca and Burgos either emerged in her time or in the first years of Alfonso VII's sole rule.[47] Alfonso also allowed a mint at Zamora sometime before the death of Bishop Bernard in 1149 but does not appear to have licensed any

---

43 Luis-Miguel Villar García (ed.), *Documentacíon medieval de la catedral de Segovia (1115–1300)* (Salamanca: Ediciones Universidad de Salamanca, 1990), pp. 60–61, no. 18. Minting began in Segovia during the chaotic years of Urraca's reign. Todesca, "What Touches All," pp. 226–30.

44 "Quartam partem monete que in Secobia facta fuerit et totius cambiacionis a quecumque parte venerit." A confirmation of 1139 repeats the clause. Villar García, pp. 62–3, no. 19, pp. 75–7, no. 29.

45 Urraca established a mint at Sahagún in 1116, giving a third of the revenue to the monks of Sahagún and a third to the nuns of San Pedro de las Dueñas. In 1119, Alfonso spilt the mint revenues between himself and the monks, ignoring the nuns. Monterde, pp. 158–60, no. 100; José Antonio Fernández Flórez (ed.), *Colección diplomática del monasterio de Sahagún (857–1300)*, vol. 4 *(1110–1199)* (León: Centro de Estudios e Investigacíon "San Isidoro," 1991), pp. 58–9, no. 1201.

46 *HC*, bk. 3, chaps 12–13. Alfonso VII's successful reclaiming of half the Compostella mint is made clear in a charter of Fernando II done in 1171. Álvarez, pp. 289–91, no. 121; see further Todesca, "What Touches All," pp. 311–13. For minting at Lugo dating back to Alfonso VI's reign, see n. 57 below.

47 For Salamanca and Burgos, see Todesca, "What Touches All," pp. 290–94, 298–303.

others.[48] Rather, he closed Lugo and apparently the monastic mint at Sahagún for we hear no more of the latter after 1119. Likewise, Palencia ceased minting late in the reign which presumably allowed Alfonso to renege on his pledge of 50 *morabetinos* to the bishop every time the coinage was changed.[49] Considering the variety of coins that survive today, however, it is evident the king changed coin types frequently. That process would have been difficult with only seven mints. William I of England, for example, had 68 at his disposal.[50] The shorter the interval between new issues, the harder it was for the mints to successfully remove the older coins. Confusion and resentment among Alfonso's subjects was inevitable.

An extreme example of the ills of coinage renewal can be seen in the reign of Alfonso's contemporary, Duke Vladislav I of Bohemia (1109–25). Vladislav may have issued 29 coin types in 16 years prompting Cosmas of Prague, who lived during the reign, to speak of "not dukes, but thieves ... who change the money three and four times in a year."[51] In Cosmas's opinion, "frequent changes and fraudulent debasements of the coinage" did more harm than if "an enemy

---

48 A mint at Zamora under Bishop Bernardo is attested by a later grant of Alfonso IX. Julio González, *Alfonso IX* (2 vols, Madrid: Consejo Superior de Investigaciones Científicas, 1944), vol. 2, pp. 135–7, no. 91. See also Richard Fletcher, *The Episcopate in the Kingdom of León in the Twelfth Century* (Oxford: Oxford University Press, 1978), 42–4. Urraca's grant of 1124 to Bernard of Zamora does not appear to mention *moneta* as Reilly believed. See Monterde, pp. 280–81, no. 187. Reilly, *Alfonso VII*, pp. 221–2, also concluded there was a mint at Oviedo. The evidence comes from a cartulary copy of a charter of Pedro Ansúrez dated c.1088–91 which reads "metkales de auro obetensis monete." Most likely "obetensis" was originally some form of "obtimus" as in "vas aureum obtimun" later in the text. José Manuel Ruiz Asencio (ed.), *Colección documental del archivo de la catedral de León (775–1230)*, vol. 4 *(1032–1109)* (León: Centro de Estudios e Investigacíon "San Isidoro," 1989), pp. 557–9, no. 1262. Finally, mints in Sigüenza and Soria probably opened after Alfonso VII's death in 1157. Todesca, "What Touches All," pp. 329–32.

49 The mint at Palencia was reopened by Fernando II. See n. 58 below.

50 Philip Grierson, "The Monetary System under William I," in *Domesday Book: Studies* (London: Alecto Historical Editions, 1987), p. 78.

51 Bertold Brethloz (ed.), "Die Chronik der Böhmen des Cosmas von Prag," in *Scriptores rerum germanicarum*, n.s., vol. 2, Monumenta germaniae historica (Berlin: Weidmannsche Buchhandlung, 1923), bk. 1, chap. 33; cf. Cosmas of Prague, *The Chronicle of the Czechs*, trans. Lisa Wolverton (Washington, DC: The Catholic University of America Press, 2009), pp. 85–7. On the coinage see Ruth Mazo Karras, "Early Twelfth-Century Bohemian Coinage in Light of a Hoard of Vladislav I," *American Numismatic Society Museum Notes*, 30 (1985), pp. 205–10. Despite Cosmas' remarks, Lisa Wolverton, *Hastening toward Prague: Power and Society in the Medieval Czech Lands* (Philadelphia, PA: University of Philadelphia Press, 2001), pp. 25, 165–73, argues that the ducal coinage was "quite stable" and that the changes in type represented an "iconographic program."

ravaged the whole land with fire and pillage."[52] The situation in León, however, was not as dire. While Alfonso may have changed types often, none of the sources accuse him of debasing at the same time.[53] Still, if his monetary policy did not quite ravage the land, his frequent change of types did cause distress. In February of 1155, the papal legate Hyacinth held a council in the town of Valladolid attended by Alfonso, his two sons, the leading prelates of Spain and an assembly of noblemen.[54] One of the canons of the council addresses Alfonso's changing coin types:

> The emperor for the sake of God and the salvation of his soul should establish whatever money at a good weight and at four *denarii* of silver without any price, (and) never in his day change it, but rather confirm it so that it remains thus.[55]

Medieval mints designated fineness by a special use of the term *denarius*. Pure silver was said to be 12-*denarii* fine; a coin of half silver therefore was 6-*denarii* fine. The Council of Valladolid, then, exhorted Emperor Alfonso to settle on one coin at 4-*denarii* fine, i.e., one-third silver, and of good weight. At the same time it asked him to maintain this coin without asking "any price." Hyacinth and the council were surely alluding to redemption of coinage where a ruler demanded payment for forgoing a recoinage. Louis VII of France (1137–80) allowed the knights and burghers of Orleans to "redeem" their local coinage by paying him 100 pounds every three years. The unpopular *monetagium commune* collected

---

[52] Brethloz, bk. 1, chap. 33.

[53] In relation to the gold morabetino, the *denarius* of León appears to maintain the same purchasing power as the *jaccensis* of Aragon. With one brief exception, the *jaccensis* remained one-third fine silver until late in the century. Todesca, "What Touches All," pp. 266–80.

[54] Julio A. Pérez Celada (ed.), *Documentación del monasterio de San Zoilo de Carrión (1047–1300)* (Burgos: Ediciones J.M. Garrido Garrido, 1986), pp. 60–61, no. 36.

[55] "Monetam quidquam bene pensatam et quatuor denariorum argenti mittet imperator sine omni precio propter Deum et anime sue salutum nunquam in diebus suis mutandum, sed eam ita mansuram firmat." This canon survives as the last decree attributed to a council held by Hyacinth later that spring in Lérida. Addressed to the "emperor," the canon was clearly aimed at Alfonso VII and must have originated at the Valladolid meeting. The decrees for Valladolid survive in the Cathedral of Tuy, copied "in a crabbed little hand" onto the back of a charter. They closely parallel those of Lérida but this final canon is missing. Ferran Valls Taberner, "Ein Konzil zu Lérida im Jahre 1155," in Albert Brackman (ed.), *Papsttum und Kaisertum* (Munich: Verlag der Münchner Drucke, 1926), p. 368; Carl Erdmann, *Das Papsttum und Portugal im ersten Jahrhundert der portugiesischen Geschichte* (Berlin: Verlag Akademie der Wissenschaften, 1928), pp. 55–8; Thomas Bisson, *Conservation of Coinage: Monetary Exploitation and its Restraint in France, Catalonia and Aragon (c.A.D. 1000–1225)* (Oxford: Oxford University Press, 1979), pp 81–2; Fletcher, *The Episcopate*, p. 208.

from "cities and counties" which Henry I promised to abolish in England was likely a similar monetary tax imported from Normandy.[56]

Alfonso died two years after the Valladolid meeting and so did not have time to commit to a single coin. On his death the realm split between his two sons; Fernando II (1157–88) held León while Sancho III (1157–58) ruled briefly in Castile followed by his son, Alfonso VIII (1158–1214). Fernando moved to undo some of his father's hard stance against the bishops. In 1158, citing a charter of his great-grandfather, Alfonso VI, he reestablished the mint of Lugo and the local bishop's right to a third of the profit.[57] In 1163, acting as regent for his nephew Alfonso VIII and seeking allies in Castile, he reopened the mint in Palencia and affirmed its bishop's right to half the mint revenue.[58] And, in 1171, Fernando restored to the cathedral chapter of Santiago full rights to their mint as Alfonso VI had intended.[59]

Eleven years later, in 1182, Fernando made a pilgrimage to Compostela and confirmed that the archbishop and chapter held the mint in full. His charter on that occasion further reveals that despite the recommendation of the Council of Valladolid in 1155 he was not willing to abandon the practice of changing the coinage. In the document, he explains that the archbishop holds the mint freely:

> So that however much I lord king F(ernando) or my son lord king A(lfonso) or any of our successors may wish to remove the money from the kingdom or permit its value to be diminished, you and your successors shall be able to let this money of yours continue at full and firm value, valid and steadfast, in your town of Santiago and throughout your entire archdiocese as long as you wish. And this

---

56 Bisson, *Conservation*, pp. 14–15, 31–2; Robertson, pp. 278–9. Grierson and others have argued that William I introduced two distinct taxes to England: the geld *de moneta*, levied on those boroughs with a mint, and the more general *monetagium commune*. I am not convinced these terms refer to separate taxes. Philip Grierson, "Domesday Book, the Geld *De Moneta* and *Monetagium*: A Forgotten Minting Reform," *British Numismatic Journal*, 55 (1985), pp. 84–94; Grierson, "The Monetary System," pp. 75–9; D.M. Metcalf, "The Taxation of Moneyers under Edward the Confessor and in 1086," in J.C. Holt (ed.), *Domesday Studies* (Woodbridge: Boydell Press, 1987), p. 282.

57 César Vaamonde Lores, "De monetaria gallega," *Boletín de la Academia Gallega*, 30 (1935), pp. 114–15.

58 "Volo, igitur, et precipio quod deinceps fiat moneta in palentina civitate et ibidem fabricetur, sicuti quondam fieri solebat, de lucro cuius palentinus episcopus habeat medietatem in omnibus et per omnia et rex alteram medietatem." Abajo Martín, pp. 132–4, no. 63.

59 Álvarez, pp. 289–91, no. 121.

> money of yours, granted and conceded to you, will suffer minimum damage due to any commutation (*commutationem*) and diminishment of value.[60]

Sánchez Albornoz saw the reference here to diminishment in value as evidence that the monarchy was prone to the "vulgar recourse" of debasement. But Fernando is not talking about debasement; he is talking about the mechanics of a commutation or recoinage.[61] His charter clarifies that a commutation in León involved diminishing the legal value of the older coinage so that it could be removed. At the same time, the charter underscores our reading of Alfonso VI's original grant. Fernando reaffirms Compostela's freedom not to participate in general renewals. Alfonso VI had allowed that freedom but had hoped the cathedral chapter would elect to participate under the guidance of his provost. Fernando adds that if Compostela did not participate in a general recoinage, its unaltered coins could continue to circulate in Santiago at full value. Outside the archdiocese, however, they would not be current and so would be subject to discount.

Fernando issued four basic types, and his son, Alfonso IX (1188–1230), struck at least another two.[62] In time, the resentment toward coinage renewal evident at Valladolid reared up again. In March of 1202, Alfonso IX presided over an assembly at Benavente attended not only by his bishops and lay vassals but also by "many men from each town," only the second clear reference to townsmen at a royal *cortes* or court in León. The charter recording the acts of this meeting clearly attests to an ongoing practice of coinage renewal:

---

[60] "Ita quod, quamuis ego rex domnus F(ernandus), vel filius meus rex donnus Adefonsus aut aliquis de mea progenie monetam voluerit tollere de regno, aut permiserit eius valorem diminuere, vos et successores vestri per villam vestram Sancti Iacobi et per totum archiepiscopatum vestrum hanc monetam vestram in rigoris pleno valore, quamdiu volueritis, ratam et firmissmam permanere facere possitis, et propter ulam commutationem et valoris diminutionem hec vestra moneta vobis data et concessa lesionem minime suscipiat." I follow here Álvarez, pp. 328–30, no. 140, though his text reads "hanc monetam nostram." Both Sánchez-Albornoz and Grassotti, following López Ferreiro, agree that it reads "hanc monetam vestram." Claudio Sánchez-Albornoz, "La primitiva organización monetaria de León y Castilla," *Anuario de Historia del Derecho Español*, 5 (1928), p. 337, n. 80; Hilda Grassotti, "Dos problemas de historia castellano-leonesa," *Cuadernos de Historia de España*, 49–50 (1969), pp. 186–7, n. 89.

[61] Sánchez-Albornoz, "La primitiva," pp. 338–9. Grassotti, p. 187, understood that the document speaks of replacing one coin for another but still saw it as evidence that "era habitual, o por los menos previsible, la quiebra del valor de la moneda."

[62] The two types of Alfonso IX survive in several variants which might represent separate issues. Todesca, "What Touches All," pp. 518–21. See further Antonio Orol Pernas, *Acuñaciones de Alfonso IX* (Madrid: Editorial Vico, 1982).

> Also, in this curia it was judged, just as it always was, that if the king should again wish to change his coinage for another, everyone from his kingdom must accept it equally.[63]

Merchants and artisans whose capital was apt to be largely in cash were more hurt by frequent renewals than landed lords.[64] The Benavente assembly, perhaps prompted by the burghers present, took the step that the Council of Valladolid had tried to avoid. They agreed to pay the king if he would forgo renewal. The charter concludes:

> These things were done and firmly established at Benavente in a full curia of the lord king ... when the lord king sold his money to the people of the land from the Duero to the sea for seven years, receiving from each for this sale a single *morabetino*.[65]

Besides being a tax on one's capital in cash, a renewal carried the danger that the crown might use the opportunity to issue a debased coin, the shameful practice that Cosmas of Prague lamented. While the crown appears not to have debased since the days of Urraca, the men gathered at Benavente had reason to fear such a maneuver. Alfonso VIII of Castile had issued the debased *pepión* by 1192 and Pedro II of Aragon-Catalonia (1196–1213) would lower the finenes of the *barcelonés* c.1209. Both monarchs later succumed to pressure and re-valued the coins.[66] As the thirteenth century progressed, representative assemblies in

---

[63] "In ipsa curia etiam iudicatum fuit sicut etiam semper fuerat quod si rex de novo voluerit suam monetam mutare in aliam, universi de suo regno equaliter recibere debent." González, *Alfonso IX*, vol. 2, pp. 236–7, no. 167. Joseph F. O'Callaghan, *The Cortes of Castile-León 1188–1350* (Philadelphia, PA: University of Pennsylvania Press, 1989), p. 16.

[64] Spufford, pp. 93–5.

[65] The charter continues: "Similiter eodem anno, et tempore simili eorum empta fuit moneta in tota Extremadura." There is no indication in the text that Santiago was exempted from the tax, implying its mint was no longer independent of the crown. An undated mandate of Alfonso IX also indicates he expected Santiago to accept his coin. González, *Alfonso IX*, vol. 2, pp. 236–7 no. 167, p. 733, no. 653.

[66] The *pepión* is cited in the *Liber censum* compiled in 1192. Paul Fabre (ed.), *Le Liber censum de l'eglise romaine*, fascicule 2 (Paris: Bibliothèque des Écoles Française d'Athènes et de Rome, 1889), pp. 17, 218, available at https://archive.org/details/lelibercensuumde02fabruoft (accessed September 10, 2014); cf. I.S. Robinson, *The Papacy, 1073–1198* (Cambridge: Cambridge University Press, 1990), p. 260. For Pedro II, see Thomas N. Bisson, "Coinages of Barcelona (1209 to 1222): The Documentary Evidence," in C.N.L. Brooke et al. (eds), *Studies in Numismatic Method Presented to Philip Grierson* (Cambridge: Cambridge University Press, 1983), pp. 193–204.

both León and Castile preferred to redeem the coinage by consenting to the levy that became known as *moneda* or *moneda forera* rather than submit to renewals. As at Benavente, the *moneda* tax was normally allowed every seven years.[67] Paid not to alter the coinage, Fernando III (1217–52), who reunited León and Castile in 1230, simply continued to issue the coin types of his predecessors, Alfonso VIII's in Castile and Alfonso IX's in León. He never put his own name on a coin. In England, the successors of Henry II did the same.[68] One of the chief grievances against Alfonso X (1252–84) when he was effectively deposed in 1282 was his dishonest manipulation of this arrangement. He collected *moneda* while introducing several new and debased coins.[69]

Overall, royal administration of coinage as it developed in twelfth-century León-Castile does not look dramatically different from the more famous English model. In this regard, the seven-year period governing the Leonese *moneda* tax as it emerged at Benavente should not escape our notice. The Anglo-Saxon kings may have considered seven years the appropriate interval for renewals. In the twelfth and thirteenth century, the monarchs of Aragon and Portugal also shared this assumption.[70] As with the *denarius* itself, this seven-year time frame probably came to Iberia and England via the Carolingians though there is no evidence of it in Carolingian documents.[71] In their study of medieval

---

[67] The *carta de hermandad* of 1282 drawn up by supporters of *infante* Sancho's rebellion against Alfonso X (1252–84) recognized Sancho's right to "moneda, a cabo de siete annos do la solíen dar et como la solíen dar, non mandando los reyes labrar moneda." Alfonso García Gallo, *Manual de historia del derecho español*, 3rd edn (2 vols, Madrid, 1967), vol. 2, p. 936; O'Callaghan, p. 24.

[68] Henry II introduced the short-cross type in the recoinage of c.1180. The type was maintained until 1247. Nicholas Mayhew, "From Regional to Central Minting, 1158–1464" in C.E. Challis (ed.), *A New History of the Royal Mint* (Cambridge: Cambridge University Press, 1992), p. 100.

[69] James J. Todesca, "The Monetary History of Castile-León (c.1100–1300) in Light of the Bourgey Hoard," *American Numismatic Society Museum Notes*, 33 (1988), pp. 160–78.

[70] Todesca, "What Touches All," p. 362; Todesca, "Monetary History," pp. 147–9; Bisson, *Conservation*, p. 75.

[71] While, to my knowledge, there is no evidence for the seven-year interval in Carolingian sources, both Louis the Pious and Charles the Bald attempted to call in old money by Martinmas (November 11). English chronicles agree that Henry II introduced his short-cross coinage on November 11, probably in 1180. Stack, p. 125. Bisson pointed out that November resurfaces with "curious frequency" as a time for changing the coinage. Ramiro II of Aragon (1134–37) and Alfonso II of Aragon-Catalonia (1162–96) both changed the money in this month. And the *Chronicle of Saint-Maixent* from Poitou reports that in 1120 "the coins were changed in the month of November." Boretius and Krause, vol. 1, p. 306, vol. 2, p. 316; Bisson, *Conservation*, p. 5 n. 2, pp. 7–8.

finance, Lyon and Verhulst complained that "nationalism, chauvinism, and particularism" has too often prevented historians from recognizing parallel financial developments in Western Europe: "This common bond between institutions, not as visible perhaps as that which united the church of western Christendom or that which gave thought and art a like vocabulary and expression, nevertheless existed."[72]

The kings of León never developed an office to rival the English exchequer nor did their mint output approach the volume of England's. Nonetheless, the monetary policies of the two governments were analogous. Both kingdoms lay outside the Carolingian empire and were largely spared the aristocratic grab for power of the ninth and tenth centuries. In western and eastern Francia (Germany), "feudal" coinages emerged as "the monopoly of minting was taken over by vassals."[73] By the twelfth century, Louis VII of France controlled nine mints in the limited Île-de-France, but each struck different coins.[74] In England, by contrast, the Normans inherited a centrally controlled currency that reached back to the tenth century. While the kings of León did not have a tradition of minting reaching back that far, they did not allow their sovereign right to be usurped. Alfonso VI and his heirs established a small but effective network of mints and, by periodically recalling coin types, provided a stable royal currency up to the mid-thirteenth century.

72 Bryce Lyon and A.E. Verhulst, *Medieval Finance: A Comparison of Financial Institutions in Northwestern Europe* (Providence, RI: Brown University Press, 1967), pp. 8, 97.

73 Lopez, p. 12; Marc Bloch, *Feudal Society*, trans. L.A. Manyon (2 vols, Chicago, IL: University of Chicago Press, 1961), vol. 1, pp. 181–7.

74 Spufford, p. 197.

Chapter 3

Towns on the Edge: Twelfth-Century Municipal War Policy in León-Castile and France

James F. Powers

Since Charles Julian Bishko's seminal address at the American Historical Association meeting in 1955, the field of medieval frontier history has developed widely.[1] My own research has examined the manner in which the monarchs of León-Castile, along with those of Navarre, Aragon and Portugal, exploited towns as a resource for frontier expansion. Their strategies included granting liberal freedoms for settlers, aiding those settlers in site fortification, and urging the maintenance of well-organized militia forces for both territorial defense and offensive raiding. A similar pattern can be observed in the competition of the Angevin and Capetian monarchs for the control of Western France. This paper explores the possibility that these rulers north of the Pyrenees indeed may have been influenced by the Iberian frontier model.

In Iberia, frontier expansion and the evolution of institutions needed to sustain it occurred over a substantial period of time. The struggle for the central *meseta* was well over 100 years old by the turn of the millennium. By the early eleventh century, towns had been organized for their own defense, an obligation made clear by their charters or *fueros*.[2] But the collapse of the Umayyad caliphate and the disintegration of al-Andalus into competing *taifa* states gave these towns much needed respite. By the mid-twelfth century, the municipalities

---

1 Charles Julian Bishko, "The Frontier in Medieval History" (paper presented at the annual meeting of the American Historical Association, Washington, DC, December, 1955), available at http://libro.uca.edu/aarhms/essays/bishko.html (accessed July 11, 2012). See further James Muldoon and Felipe Fernández-Armesto (eds), *The Medieval Frontiers of Latin Christendom: Expansion, Contraction, Continuity* (Farnham: Ashgate, 2008).

2 James F. Powers, *A Society Organized for War: The Iberian Municipal Militias in the Central Middle Ages, 1000–1284* (Berkeley, CA: University of California Press, 1988), pp. 18–39, 136–46.

were capable of waging offensive warfare, both independently and as a part of a royal expeditionary army.[3] The disorganized *taifa* states in the Muslim south could produce no effective response to this development and faced individual conquest one after another.[4] Despite the temporary reunifications of al-Andalus achieved under the North African Almoravids and Almohads during the later eleventh and twelfth centuries, the Christian frontier thrust steadily southward. The towns played their role by the vigilance of their defense within their regional boundaries and the extra surge they could add to the occasional royal offensives. However, the Muslim threat counted for only one of the influences that impacted the kings and their towns.

The freedom of the Christian states to expand against Muslim territory, supported by a sympathetic international papacy, has enjoyed ample attention from historians of the medieval frontier.[5] Less concern, however, has been directed to the competition between the Iberian Christian states themselves. With León and Castile separated from 1157 to 1230, intra-Christian rivalry became particularly intense. Not only did these kings vie against each other, but León struggled with Portugal to the west, while Castile competed with Aragon to the east. The evidence strongly suggests that the Christian kingdoms feared each other and took that threat into consideration in formulating their municipal strategies. Yet they also drew upon each other for institutional expertise, demonstrated by the municipal law codes in which that tradition is expressed.[6] This legal tradition developed rapidly in the twelfth century, signifying the elaboration of the institutional structures to which the laws gave force. Muslim expansiveness seems to have had a part in intensifying the rhythm of legal development, as the Almohad pressure of the later twelfth century indicates.

The emerging territorial states shaped the role of the towns in the absorption of frontier areas in a number of ways. Towns occasionally undertook expansion on their own volition, but were no match by themselves for the incursions from Morocco by the Almoravids and the Almohads. It was as a segment of a larger state and as an element of a collective force that they constituted a real

3 Powers, *Society*, pp. 29–50, 147–61.

4 See, for example, David Wasserstein, *The Rise and Fall of the Party-Kings: Politics and Society in Islamic Spain, 1002–1086* (Princeton, NJ: Princeton University Press, 1985).

5 See most recently Joseph F. O'Callaghan, *Reconquest and Crusade in Medieval Spain* (Philadelphia, PA: University of Pennsylvania Press, 2003).

6 James F. Powers, "Frontier Competition and Legal Creativity: A Castilian-Aragonese Case Study Based on Twelfth-Century Municipal Military Law," *Speculum*, 52 (1977): pp. 465–87. James F. Powers, "The Creative Interaction of Portuguese and Leónese Municipal Military Law, 1055–1279," *Speculum*, 62 (1987): pp. 53–80; Powers, *Society*, pp. 41–5, 219–29.

threat. The Christian monarchs, therefore, established general norms by which municipalities could function both as defensive and offensive elements of war. Thus appeared the large formularies of law in the *fuero* families, whereby a code written for one town could be modified for use by others. Most noteworthy here is the early twelfth-century charter of Salamanca borrowed by the Portuguese king for the Numão-Trancoso family of *forais* (the Portuguese equivalent of Spanish *fueros*); the nearly contemporary Ávila charter borrowed from the Évora family in Portugal; and the impact of the late eleventh-century *Fuero de Sepúlveda* for Castile and the contemporary *Fuero de Jaca* for Aragon. All of these families established the limits by which military service would be rendered and their respective bases on the frontier secured.[7] The ability to bring entire regions under a set policy gave the Christian royal military establishments a consistency mostly lacking in the Muslim south.

By the middle of the twelfth century, charters impressive in their length and in their detail began to appear. Toledo's *fuero* provided an emerging model for Castile, although it was less extensively formulated than others soon to come. By 1179, a new prototype *foral* or law code *foral* more extensive in its military law than the earlier Trancoso or Évora families was awarded to Lisbon, Santarém and Coimbra in Portugal.[8] But the most impressive development occurred in the competitive frontier growing between Castile and Aragon along the rugged Cordillera Ibérica. *Fueros* laden with ever-increasing specifications of military obligations appeared on both sides of the frontier during the reigns of Alfonso VIII (1158–1214) of Castile and Alfonso II of Aragon (1162–96).[9] By the end of the twelfth century, both kingdoms had produced prototypes that marked a quantum leap in the evolution of medieval Iberian municipal law, the *fueros* of Cuenca (Castile) and of Teruel (Aragon). Each of these was a full-scale municipal code, approximately 200 pages in modern printed editions, with military requirements specified in hitherto unprecedented detail. Moreover, they were remarkably similar in content, clearly a product of interacting royal policies in the two kingdoms. It is not insignificant that these two towns were less than 100 miles apart on opposite sides of the same range. Shortly thereafter,

---

7 Powers, *Society*, pp. 219–37.

8 For a complete listing of the Portuguese families of municipal charters (*forais*), see Powers, *Society*, 215–18.

9 Rafael de Ureña y Smenjaud (ed.), *Fuero de Cuenca* (Madrid: Typografía de Archivos, 1935); James F. Powers (ed. and trans.), *The Code of Cuenca: Municipal Law on the Twelfth-Century Castilian Frontier* (Philadelphia, PA: University of Pennsylvania Press, 2000); Jaime Caruana Gómez de Barreda (ed.), *El fuero latino de Teruel* (Teruel: Artes Gráficas y Ediciones S.A., 1974).

a new charter, longer than any prior Léonese prototype, was given to the frontier town of Ciudad Rodrigo hard by the Portuguese frontier. It was a seminal document that provided the nucleus of the Coria-Cima-Coa family of the thirteenth century, ultimately possessed by towns on both sides of the Léonese-Portuguese frontier.[10] These lengthy codes taken together with contemporary chronicles suggest a royal policy of territorial expansion in which the towns and their militias played an integral part.

While Muslim weakness tended to direct the town's expansive force southward, such force by no means had to be exclusively vented there. Town charters specified defensive measures aimed at any exterior force threatening the towns, and Christian towns could and did attack their co-religionist neighbors. Iberia constituted a zone of territorial conflict among ambitious states. Initial Muslim attacks may have provoked a counter-assault, but once the machinery of expansion was in place all targets were viable. This reality may explain why we need not search exclusively along the exterior frontiers of Europe to find a comparative contemporary model of the use of towns. Internal frontiers could provoke similar results as long as the circumstances remained comparable: developing state systems, municipal growth, and territorial competition. The process at work between Portugal-León on one hand and Castile-Aragon on the other can also be observed in France in the struggle between the Capetian monarchy and the Angevin Empire.

In northwestern Europe, military service for townsmen first appeared in charters dating from the late-eleventh century. Some historians have taken particular note of the Norman role in this expansion of urban franchise and obligations. Around 1060, William fitz Osbern, a close ally of Duke William of Normandy, granted a charter to the town of Breteuil southeast of Rouen (and possibly also to the nearby town of Verneuil). After the Norman conquest of England, fitz Osbern was granted the town of Hereford on the Welsh frontier, giving it a new charter containing the laws of Breteuil.[11] Mary Bateson first sorted out the family of charters issued subsequently which were influenced by Breteuil's laws and recreated a model of the Breteuil charter (the original

---

[10] Powers, *Society*, pp. 225–7. The original copy of the Ciudad Rodrigo charter did not survive, but the *fueros* and *forais* of Alfaiates, Castelo Rodrigo, Castel Melhor, Coria, Castello-Bom, Cáceres and Usagre were all derived from it.

[11] Robert Bartlett, *The Making of Europe: Conquest, Colonization and Cultural Change, 950–1350* (Princeton, NJ: Princeton University Press, 1993), pp. 172–3. Keith D. Lilley, *Urban Life in the Middle Ages, 1000–1450* (New York: Palgrave, 2002), pp. 78–83. Norman preeminence on the European frontier has been a major theme since the days of Charles H. Haskins, *The Normans in European History* (Boston, MA: Houghton Mifflin, 1915).

no longer exists), working especially from the charter of Preston.[12] Some of the charters in the Breteuil family contained a reference to a military obligation for expeditionary and escort service, strictly limited to returning the same day they left.[13] In no case was the one-day limit extended, in effect limiting service to a 10-mile radius of the town. Subsequently Adolphus Ballard compared the military obligations in the Breteuil family of charters with similar ones in other charters including Haverfordwest, Swansea and Pembroke in England, and Lorris, Sées and Beaumont-en-Argonne in France.[14] From the Breteuil group and these other charters, we might conclude that a severely limited urban military obligation was standard in Western Europe north of the Pyrenees up to the middle of the twelfth century.[15] This tradition continues, for example in Lübeck's charter of 1188, which includes a specific exemption from expeditionary service enabling municipal citizens to remain focused on urban defense and the garrisoning of town walls.[16]

The late-twelfth century in northwestern France witnessed a remarkable expansion of these responsibilities, namely the emergence of towns able, and indeed required, to field a militia clearly able to operate for longer than one day as a part of holding royal territory. These were usually, although not invariably, municipalities possessing the status of communes. Charles Petit-Dutaillis argued that there appears to have been no precedent for this in Capetian history.[17]

---

12 Mary Bateson, "The Laws of Breteuil," *English Historical Review*, 15 (1900): pp. 73–8, 302–18, 496–523, 754–7; 16 (1901): pp. 92–110, 332–45.

13 Some excuses from this service were allowed but were voided if the king led the expedition. Mary Bateson, "The Laws of Preston," *English Historical Review*, 15 (1900): pp. 449, 511–12; Bateson, "Breteuil," 15: p. 755.

14 Adolphus Ballard, "The Laws of Breteuil," *English Historical Review*, 30 (1915): p. 650.

15 For a possible but unspecified defensive obligation on the occasion of a general mobilization in 1066 established by the Bishop of Liège for Huy in Belgium see André Joris, *Huy, ville médievale* (Brussels: Le Renaissance du Livre, 1965), pp. 38–50. See also David Nicholas, *The Growth of the Medieval City: From Late Antiquity to the Fourteenth Century* (London: Longman, 1997), pp. 212–13.

16 "Cives vero iam dicte civitatis nullam expeditionem ibunt, sed civitatem suam defensabunt." Friedrich Keutgen, *Urkunden zur Städtischen Verfassungsgeschichte* (Berlin: Verlag von Emil Felber, 1901), p. 185.

17 Charles Petit-Dutaillis, *Les communes françaises: Caractères et évolution des origines au XVIIe siècle* (Paris: A. Michel, 1947), pp. 116–17. For an English translation without notes and sources, see Charles Petit-Dutaillis, *The French Communes in the Middle Ages*, trans. Joan Vickers (Amsterdam: North-Holland Publishing Co., 1978), pp. 70–71. Petit-Dutaillis's argument is part of an extended critique of the work of Alphonse Giry and Achille Luchaire. Giry does mention an eleventh-century requirement for the town of Saint-Jean

Rather, the precedent for French municipal militias seems to lie in a document on the Angevin side, granted by Henry II (1154–89) of England at La Rochelle, undated but placed between 1172 and 1178 by Petit-Dutaillis on the basis of internal evidence. In the charter, Henry grants this port city of the Poitou region a commune by which it can defend itself against the local rebellious barony.[18] No specific military services for Henry are mandated, but the charter implicitly requires the formation of some kind of militia for self-defense. Potential length of service was not specified. Far more specific are two laws contained in the charter known as the *Établissements de Rouen* granted by Henry II, which specify that the mayor of that town is authorized to form a militia capable of making an expedition, indicating severe punishments for those who fail to serve. The grant is undated, but Petit-Dutaillis surmised that it had probably been given between 1160 and 1170.[19] Since we cannot be certain, it is also possible that it was granted a few years after 1170, closer to that of La Rochelle.

Were there events in the 1160s or 1170s that could have provided an inspiration and context for Henry II's remarkable and unprecedented military service laws at Rouen and La Rochelle? In the wake of Becket's death, revolt sprang up against Henry both in England and on the continent. The ensuing siege laid by King Louis VII (1137–80) against Rouen in 1174, climaxed by Henry II's relief of the town, could have provoked the English king's sense of need.[20] But, could inspiration for the creation of municipal militias possibly have

d'Angély which negates the exemption normally enjoyed from military service if there is to be a *bellum campestre*, a kind of public warfare, similar to the *lid canpal* in the Iberian fueros. Giry offers no source for this reference, however. See Alphonse Giry, *Les Établissements de Rouen: Études sur l'histoire de institutiones municipales de Rouen, Falaise, Pont-Audemer, Verneuil, La Rochelle, Saintes, Oleron, Bayonne, Tours, Niort, Cognac, Saint-Jean-d'Angély, Angoulême, Poitiers, etc.* (2 vols, Paris: F. Vieweg, 1885), vol. 1, p. 495. Albert Vermeesch, *Essai sur les origines et la signification de la commune dans le Nord de la France, (XIe et XIIe siècles)* (Heule: UGA, 1966), pp. 135–48, distinguishes municipal groups designed to keep the "Peace and Truce of God" from conventional militias.

[18] Petit-Dutaillis, *Les communes*, pp. 117–18. King John later specified more clearly the raising of a military force in his charter for La Rochelle in 1208. See Giry, *Les Établissements*, vol. 2, pp. 67–8.

[19] Giry, *Les Établissements*, vol. 2: 36–7; Petit-Dutaillis, *Les communes*, pp. 118–19. Petit-Dutaillis argued that the reference to Henry and his sons does not mention Prince Henry's coronation in 1170, after which young Henry should have been referred to as *rex*. On the other hand, John H. Round, arguing from internal evidence, believed that the likely date of the Rouen charter should be placed between 1170 and 1189. See John H. Round, *Commune of London and Other Studies* (Westminster: A. Constable, 1899), pp. 248–52.

[20] W.L. Warren, *Henry II* (Berkeley, CA: University of California Press, 1973), pp. 134–40.

come from Iberia? We know that Alfonso VIII of Castile had been in contact with Henry at some point during the 1160s. Shortly after reaching his majority in 1169, Alfonso was betrothed to Henry's daughter Eleanor (Leónor), then aged 9. Royal marriages were rarely achieved without months and even years of prior negotiations and contact. The creation of this close diplomatic relationship between the kingdom of Castile and the Angevin monarchy could easily have initiated the exchange of information regarding Alfonso's expanding southern frontier and the techniques of its achievement.[21] Moreover, about the time of the marriage's consummation c.1176–77, Henry II acted as arbitrator in a territorial dispute between his son-in-law Alfonso and King Sancho VI *el Sabio* of Navarre (1150–94).[22] Alfonso VIII sought the return of territories seized by Navarre during his minority and sent three representatives to the court of Henry II to represent Castile's position during the arbitration in London.[23] Alfonso did not expect to respect the arbitration's findings; rather he sought a truce with Navarre to free his forces for an extended siege of the Muslim town of Cuenca in 1177. His growing alliance with Alfonso II of Aragon had enabled this possibility, and the arbitration purchased sufficient time to execute this plan.[24] While no surviving sources indicate any collaboration on Henry's part with this overall plan, it certainly served to his son-in-law's advantage.

Such an argument is circumstantial but potentially viable. That is, the more developed municipal militias of the Iberian Peninsula possibly impacted upon the Plantagenet-Capetian struggle. Consider that the Iberian municipalities were approximately a half-century ahead of their French counterparts in establishing an offensive or expeditionary capability, as evidenced by contemporary chronicles and *fueros*. These militias could range hundreds of kilometers from their home base. They enhanced the king's territorial control and assisted in the

---

21 Julio González, *El reino de Castilla en la época de Alfonso VIII* (3 vols, Madrid: Consejo Superior de Investigaciones Científicas, 1960), vol. 1, pp. 144–5, 179–95. Warren, *Henry II*, pp. 117, 222. The marriage produced its first offspring, Berenguela, in 1180.

22 Thomas Rymer and Robert Sanderson (eds), *Foedera, conventiones, literae, et cujuscunque generis acta publica, inter reges Angliae* et al.*ios quosvis imperatores, reges, pontifices, principes, vel communitates: ab ingressu Gulielmi I en Angliam, A.D. 1066 ad nostra usque tempora habita aut tractata*, vol. 1, part 1, *Ab anno MLXVI ad annum MCCLXXII* (London: George Eyre and Andrew Strahan, 1816–69), pp. 32–4. See further, Fernando Luís Corral, "Alfonso VIII of Castile's Judicial Process at the Court of Henry II of England: An Effective and Valid Arbitration?" *Nottingham Medieval Studies*, 50 (2006): pp. 22–41; Esther Pascua Echegaray, *Guerra y pacto en el siglo XII: La consolidación de un sistema de reinos de en Europa* (Madrid: Consejo Superior de Investigaciones Científicas, 1996), p. 32.

23 Luís Corral, pp. 31–2.

24 Ibid., pp. 35–9.

defense of Castile's frontier. Of course, their use involved a certain amount of risk: they were capable of attacking Muslim towns during periods of royal truce, they could attack each other, and they could provide unwonted resistance to royal authority.[25] There exists a striking similarity of spirit that links one of the laws in the *Établissements de Rouen* to the *Forum Conche* granted by Alfonso VIII c.1190–91. Both charters speak of the concern experienced by the town when its militia has departed on campaign, leaving the municipality comparatively defenseless to strangers or malingerers. First at Rouen:

> If the commune has to go outside the country by command of the king or his justiciar, the mayor and aldermen shall decide who are responsible for guarding the city. Whoever is found in the city after the hour of departure shall be arrested by those who have remained to guard the city and shall be at the mercy of the mayor and his alderman for the destruction of his house or condemnation to a fine of a hundred *solidi* if he has no house.[26]

Then in the laws of Cuenca:

> When the council wants to make a military expedition [of the town's militia] against the enemy, before it departs, watchmen should be placed in each parish who should guard and keep watch over the city day and night. There should remain also two sworn parish representatives [*alcaldes*] together with an acting mayor [*judex*] whom the annual Mayor leaves in his place. And these *alcaldi* together with this *judex* should concern themselves with protecting the city, as has been said. It also remains established by the code that once the council has departed [on expedition], all strangers should be expelled from the city. After sunset, if the guards find anyone walking in the streets without carrying a light, they should seize all his belongings and put him in confinement until the following morning. In the morning, he should be brought before the [acting] council, and if he was a

---

25 Powers, *Society*, pp. 24–50.

26 "Si communia precepto domini regis vel justicie sue debeat iter facere, major et eschevini providebunt quos statuant remansuros ad urbem Rothomagi custodiendam, et qui, post horam nominatam exeundi, inventus fuerit in civitate dicta, ille convictus erit per illos qui custodes urbis remanserunt, et erit in misericordia domini regis et in misericordia communie de domo sua prosternanda vel de centum solidis, si domum non habuerit." Giry, *Les Établissements*, vol. 2, pp. 36–7; Petit-Dutaillis, *Les communes*, p. 119.

citizen or the son of a citizen, he should be absolved; but if he was a stranger, let him be hurled from the city cliffs.[27]

While both Rouen and Cuenca address the question of the town preparing to go on a military expedition, Rouen concerns itself with the problem of obligated citizens who stayed behind thus refusing to render the required service, threatening them with a severe sanction. On the other hand, Cuenca assumes that its system of fines and legal excuses will obviate that consideration, but is deeply concerned by the threat to security caused by strangers skulking about the streets after the town has dispatched most of its military effectives on campaign. The contrast suggests that Castile has the greater experience with frontier warfare and its nuances.

Regrettably, we possess only later copies of a charter that appears to have evolved over time. Like Cuenca, Rouen received a charter intended as a precedent for other towns in the region, and its rapid spread suggests that the modern form emerged early in its evolution, certainly before Henry II's death. Rouen's *Établissements* were formed in a period of worsening relationships between Henry II and Louis VII after 1167. Henry's concern for his continental towns and their ability to defend themselves proved well founded, as the 1174 siege of Rouen clearly indicated. As in León, Castile and Aragon, the *Établissements* mandate that the mayor of Rouen lead the municipal contingent on expedition. The king punished those refusing to serve without a royal excuse by having their houses torn down or, if they owned no house, by levying upon them a heavy fine of 100 *solidi*.[28]

The precedent set by the Plantagenets at Rouen, in Petit-Dutaillis's mind, was the initiation of an offensive capability for the municipal militia. The militia could be summoned to join the royal army for an expedition. This went

[27] "Cum concilium in hostem exercitum facere voluerit, antequam proficiscatur, de unaquaque collatione ponat vigiles, qui die ac nocte vigilent et excubent civitatem. Et etiam remaneant duo alcaldes adjurati cum judice facticio, quem judex annalis vice sua reliquerit. Et isti alcaldes cum hoc judice faciant custodire civitatem sicut dictum est. Sit itaque in foro, quod postquam concilium exierit, omnes ignoti expellantur ab urbe. Post solis occasum quemcumque excubie de nocte per calles ambulantem invenerint ignem non portantem, omnes exuvias illius accipiant custodes, et mittant eum in cipo usque mane. Mane facto tradant eum in concilio, et si vicinus vel filius vicini fuerit exutus, sit solutus; set si ignotus fuerit, precipitetur." de Ureña y Smenjaud, pp. xxx, 1; Powers, *Code*, p. 165. A nearly identical law appears in the Aragonese charter for Teruel at about the same time as the Cuencan version, an indication of the closeness of the Castilian and Aragonese regional legal traditions in the later twelfth century. See Caruana Gómez de Barreda, ccccxxvi.

[28] Giry, *Les Établissements*, vol. 2, pp. 36–7.

significantly beyond simply securing one's own environs with an emergency defensive force. This development saw no parallel in Henry II's England, not even on the Scottish, Welsh or Irish frontiers. The charters of La Rochelle and Rouen suggest that Henry viewed with concern both the rebellious continental baronage and the growing capability of the Capetian monarchy. In the face of such challenges, Henry seized the opportunity these charters presented to implement the changes necessary to hold the French frontier territories. Once established in Angevin lands, the concept of a municipal offensive capability was exploited, particularly by John, in the face of the looming Capetian offensive of the early thirteenth century.[29]

On the other side of the frontier, the new king, Philip II Augustus (1180–1223), moved to adopt the Plantagenet innovation for some of his own towns. This tended to take the form of granting commune status to a number of municipalities, primarily those on threatened frontiers near Flanders, Normandy, Anjou and Poitou. Some of this was doubtless assisted when communes gave a good military account of themselves, as in the case of Mantes's resistance to Henry II in 1188.[30] If origination of the concept belonged to Henry II on the Angevin side of frontier, Philip's acute administrative perceptiveness, combined with the former solid Capetian alliance with the towns, certainly enabled him to grasp the possibilities. He clearly intended to renew his father's pressure on the Angevin Empire. As in Iberia, frontier situations tend to replicate the workable policies of one side on the other, a kind of historical mimesis. It is also notable that for both Plantagenet and Capetian this frontier expedient constituted an exception to the urban policy in the heart of their respective states. Such awards of liberties and encouragement of bellicose capabilities did not occur in England or at the heart of the Capetian royal domain, certainly not in London or Paris.

By 1199, a crisis was brewing that led to an intensification of municipal military development on both sides of the Capetian-Plantagenet frontier. Despite Richard's victories against Philip, the French king brought the question

---

29 W.L. Warren, *King John* (Berkeley, CA: University of California Press, 1961), pp. 90–99.

30 John W. Baldwin, *The Government of Philip Augustus: Foundations of French Royal Power in the Middle Ages* (Berkeley, CA: University of California Press, 1986), pp. 59–64. Elizabeth Hallam, *Capetian France, 987–1328* (London: Longman, 1980), pp. 161–3. Petit-Dutaillis, *Les communes*, pp. 116, 120–21. Michael Wolfe, *Walled Towns and the Shaping of France: From the Medieval to the Early Modern Era* (New York: Palgrave Macmillan, 2009), pp. 19–31, provides a useful recent survey of the role of towns during this English-French conflict.

of the dual loyalties of the barony in the Angevin Empire to a head.[31] Philip further granted communal status to an increasing number of towns both before and after 1204.[32] Giry and Petit-Dutaillis note that on the Plantagenet side a number of Norman towns received the status of commune, particularly Bayeux (1195–98), Alençon (September 6, 1199), Evreux (July 7, 1202), Harfleur and Montivillier (July 8, 1202), Fécamp (July 30, 1202), Falaise (January 31, 1203), and Domfront (February 25, 1203).[33] Giry and Petit-Dutaillis see the purpose of the communal awards as efforts by Richard I and John to secure militias from these towns, but I find that among these only Fécamp, Harfleur and Montvillier had a clearly stated military obligation.[34] To these one can add on the Plantagenet side the military obligations assigned to the island of Oléron (treated as a kind of collective commune which received an added military obligation in February 28, 1205),[35] La Rochelle (December 31, 1208),[36] and Montierneuf (May 4, 1199).[37] The town of Niort, south of Parthenay in Poitou, received a military service obligation from Philip in September, 1204, but John counter-claimed it on December 28, 1205.[38]

Both John and Philip thus sought to advantage themselves of this new municipal potential, although for John it would prove too little too late as the northern possessions of the Angevin Empire fell before Philip's onslaught.[39] Our sources fail to clarify exactly what role the municipal resource played in Philip's achievement. As in Iberia, chroniclers tended to have their eyes fixed on the king, churchmen and the nobility. But in the battle of Bouvines of 1214 we have a climactic conflict in which the municipal militias participated. In this great struggle between Philip and John's imperial ally Otto IV, the French

---

31 J. Holt, "The End of the Anglo-Norman Realm," *Proceedings of the British Academy*, 61 (1973): pp. 259–65.

32 Baldwin, pp. 62–4, 472.

33 Charles Petit-Dutaillis, *La monarchie féodale en France et en Angleterre, Xe–XIIIe siècle* (Paris: La Renaissance du Livre, 1933), p. 194. For the English translation, see Charles Petit-Dutaillis, *The Feudal Monarchy in France and England from the Tenth to the Thirteenth Century*, trans. E.D. Hunt (1936; reprint, New York: Harper & Row, 1964), p. 176. Giry, *Les Établissements*, vol. 1, pp. 47–8.

34 *Rotuli Litterarum Patentium en Turri Londinensi Asservati*, vol. 1, part 1, *ab anno MCCI ad annum MCCXVI*, ed. Thomas D. Hardy (London: G. Eyre and A. Spottiswoode, 1835), pp. 13–14.

35 *Foedera*, vol. 1, part 1, p. 92.

36 Giry, *Les Établissements*, vol. 2, pp. 67–8.

37 Ibid., vol. 1, p. 354.

38 Ibid., vol. 2, pp. 125–6. *Rotuli Chartarum in Turri Londinensi*, vol. 1, part 1, *1199–1216*, ed. Thomas D. Hardy (London: G. Eyre and A. Spottiswoode, 1837), p. 161.

39 Warren, *King John*, pp. 90–99. Baldwin, *Philip Augustus*, pp. 191–219.

king positioned the detachments of five of his communes from the Flemish frontier in the central wing of battle, mixed with some of his knights. The five militias from Corbie, Amiens, Arras, Beauvais, and Compiègne, apparently all infantrymen, collapsed before the charge of the imperial cavalry, threatening the life of King Philip, who was unhorsed as a result. Two years earlier, at Las Navas de Tolosa, the municipal militias of the Castilian king caused Alfonso VIII a certain amount of concern as well. Yet the important matter remains that municipal armies could serve at all, coordinate with aristocratic cavalry, absorb any shock, and compel the royal enemies to expend considerable resources to deal with them.[40] Kings in frontier conflict had found institutional devices through employing their municipalities to seize and hold territory, laying a basis for permanent expansion.

The preceding examples provide the foundation for the basic point that should be made. Namely, twelfth-century monarchies in the west were already sufficiently precocious to devise institutions that would enable them to expand and hold territory. Moreover, they achieved their most rapid and inventive progress when they were in direct competition with each other. In that context, another relatively new entity, the emerging municipalities, could bargain with these monarchs for freedoms in exchange for their military and settlement contributions. Frontier zones therefore constituted a crucible of enormous legal and institutional creativity in the twelfth century. Yet it is also clear that these frontiers produced similar institutional activity simply by operating within comparable sets of circumstances in the world of developing territorial state systems.

The issue here is not the borrowing of texts but of ideas and concepts. The background of municipal militias in Iberia more than accounts for the evolution of these laws in the Spanish and Portuguese kingdoms.[41] But while lessons learned from Castile could have influenced the creation of expeditionary town militias elsewhere, it was also possible that King Henry had his own ideas regarding the full expression of legal concepts in documentary form. These in turn may have informed King Alfonso's framing of the extensive municipal codes that would mark the latter part of the Castilian's reign. In the twelfth century, the fledgling European monarchies were grappling with the great questions of institutional power and territorial management. Frontier expansion provided a catalyst for creativity. This indicates that the European states, long before Columbus and the

---

[40] Baldwin, pp. 215–18. Petit-Dutaillis, *Les communes françaises*, pp. 122–3. Powers, *Society*, pp. 52–5, 207–8.

[41] For background regarding Castilian and Aragonese law, see Powers, *Society*, pp. 48–50 and Powers, *Code of Cuenca*, pp. 16–18.

so-called world systems of the Later Middle Ages, could assemble the machinery of territorial expansion. If the argument for Plantagenet borrowing of Castilian concepts appears uncertain, one can at least conclude that the connection between municipal freedom and military service arose simultaneously in the different realms of an expanding Europe.

Chapter 4

Foreigners and Foes in the Leonese Succession Crisis of 1230[1]

Janna Bianchini

Rodrigo Jiménez de Rada, the archbishop of Toledo, observed that the prospective unification of León and Castile in 1230 "displeased almost everyone."[2] Certainly it had displeased the late king of León, Alfonso IX (1188–1230), who spent over a decade laboring to ensure that the union would not take place. But it did take place. And because the reestablishment of a single monarchy was, institutionally at least, the basis for León-Castile's existence as a concept from 1230 on, historians have given considerable attention to how it happened.

Their debate engages a pressing concern about the history of power: how much influence did the various elites of León (monarch, magnates, prelates, town councils) have in determining the outcome of a royal succession dispute in the early thirteenth century?[3] Claudio Sánchez-Albornoz and Carlos Estepa Díez have argued that town councils played a significant role in this crisis.[4] That

1 I am grateful for the comments and suggestions that this chapter received from Thomas Bisson, Michael McCormick, Simon Barton, Arthur Eckstein, Philip Soergel, Ken Holum, Joseph O'Callaghan, James Powers, Bernard Reilly, and James Todesca, among others. Any errors or omissions, however, are entirely my own.

2 Rodrigo Jiménez de Rada, *Historia de rebus Hispanie*, ed. J. Fernández Valverde (Turnhout: Brepols, 1987), bk. 9, chap. 15, p. 297.

3 Cf. Ana Rodríguez López, "Sucesión regia y legitimidad política en Castilla en los siglos XII y XIII: Algunas consideraciones sobre el relato de las crónicas latinas castellano-leonesas," in Isabel Alfonso, Julio Escalona, and Georges Martin (eds), *Lucha política: condena y legitimación en las sociedades medievales* (Paris: Ens Éditions, 2004), p. 33.

4 Claudio Sánchez-Albornoz, "La sucesión al trono en los reinos de León y Castilla," in *Viejos y nuevos estudios sobre las instituciones medievales españoles*, 2nd edn (2 vols, Madrid: Espasa-Calpe, 1976), vol. 2, pp. 1148–9; Carlos Estepa Díez, "Curia y cortes en el reino de León," in *Las cortes de Castilla y León en la Edad Media* (2 vols, Valladolid: Simancas Ediciones, 1988), vol. 1, p. 100; Julio González, *Reinado y diplomas de Fernando III* (3 vols, Córdoba: Monte de Piedad y Caja de Ahorros de Córdoba, 1980–86), vol. 1, p. 257.

argument corresponds to wider evidence that councils were increasingly involved in governance after 1200.[5] At the same time, the Leonese succession contest's outcome has often been attributed to gender because it pitted a male claimant to the throne, Fernando III of Castile (1217–52), against two female ones, his half-sisters, Sancha and Dulce. In this reading, Fernando III's masculinity made his triumph practically inevitable.[6]

Both arguments have merit. However, historiography about the succession crisis suffers from the fact that all the contemporary narrative accounts we have were written for the Castilian court. Rodrigo Jiménez de Rada, Lucas of Túy, and Juan of Osma all worked under the direction of Fernando III and his mother, Berenguela (r. 1217–46).[7] The chroniclers' proximity to the events they describe makes them invaluable. But it also leaves modern scholars without access to any discourse about the Leonese succession except the one created by (and for) Castile. Not surprisingly, the Castilian chroniclers portray Fernando III's accession in León as a triumph, in which the new king met a warm welcome from everyone but a few malcontents. Without saying a word about women's suitability as monarchs, the chroniclers have thereby contributed to the belief that Fernando III's sex made him widely preferred as León's next ruler. And without saying much at all about the Leonese nobility, they have also fed the conviction that support from bishops and town councils brought Fernando to the throne.

My aim is to complicate these narratives. We do, after all, have sources for the Leonese succession crisis besides the Castilian chroniclers. Leonese royal diplomas list the prelates and nobles who confirmed each act. In addition, both royal and non-royal charters frequently identify the occupants of royal tenancies.[8] The distribution of royal tenancies in this period serves as a barometer of a

---

5 Thomas N. Bisson, *The Crisis of the Twelfth Century: Power, Lordship, and the Origins of European Government* (Princeton, NJ: Princeton University Press, 2009), pp. 429, 491–2.

6 Peter Linehan, *History and the Historians of Medieval Spain* (Oxford: Clarendon, 1993), p. 394; Miriam Shadis, *Berenguela of Castile (1180–1246) and Political Women in the High Middle Ages* (New York: Palgrave Macmillan, 2009), p. 115.

7 Lucas of Túy, *Chronicon mundi*, ed. E. Falque Rey (Turnhout: Brepols, 2003); *Chronica latina regum Castellae*, ed. L. Charlo Brea (Turnhout: Brepols, 1997). Juan of Osma is now generally accepted as the author of the so-called *Chronica latina*. See Derek W. Lomax, "The Authorship of the *Chronique latine des rois de Castille*," *Bulletin of Hispanic Studies*, 40 (1963), pp. 205–11.

8 Holding a tenancy gave one administrative, financial, and judicial rights in a town or region of the king's desmesne; the tenant (or, increasingly, his proxies) acted basically as the king's agent. See Simon R. Doubleday, *The Lara Family: Crown and Nobility in Medieval Spain* (Cambridge, MA: Harvard University Press, 2001), pp. 13–14, 45, 51.

monarch's relationship with his or her nobles.[9] Particularly in León, the crown could still grant or revoke tenancies at will in the early thirteenth century, and it exercised this power frequently. Possession of tenancies therefore indicates a noble's favor with his monarch; conversely, a loss of tenancies reflects a loss of favor. Confirmation lists are an even more direct index of royal goodwill. Whether or not the people who confirmed royal diplomas were physically present for the act, their inclusion shows that they were members of the royal curia, the assembly that (however figuratively) sanctioned royal acts by their witness and consent.[10] The record of tenancy distribution and diplomatic confirmations in León between 1217 and 1230 reveals information about the succession crisis that cannot be found in the chronicles.

A Binary Queenship

Alfonso IX of León had married twice. Between 1191 and 1193, he was married to Teresa of Portugal, daughter of King Sancho I (1185–1211); between 1197 and 1204, his wife was Berenguela of Castile, daughter of King Alfonso VIII (1158–1214). Both marriages had produced children before Rome annulled them for consanguinity. By 1217, however, Alfonso IX had only two surviving sons, Fernando and Alfonso. Both were offspring of his marriage to Berenguela.

Alfonso IX had duly recognized his elder son, Fernando, as heir to León. But in 1217, an unexpected turn of events threw Fernando's status into doubt. Thirteen-year-old King Enrique I of Castile (1214–17) died that spring. Because he left no children, the throne of Castile went to his oldest sister, Berenguela of Castile, Alfonso IX's erstwhile wife. Berenguela then established her son Fernando as her co-sovereign. The presumptive heir to León was now also the king of Castile. If Fernando succeeded Alfonso IX as planned, the two crowns would be united. So Alfonso IX promptly disinherited his son.

---

9 See Cristina Jular Pérez-Alfaro, "*Alfoz* y *tierra* a través de documentación castellana y leonesa de 1157 a 1230: Contribución al estudio del dominio señorial," *Studia Histórica: Historia Medieval* 9 (1991), p. 41; Carlos Estepa Díez, "Frontera, nobleza y señoríos en Castilla: El señorío de Molina (siglos XII–XIII)," *Studia Histórica: Historia Medieval* 24 (2006), pp. 17–20; Janna Bianchini, "The Distribution of Tenancies in León, c.1200–1250: Charter Evidence for a History of Power," *Journal of Medieval Iberian Studies*, 5 (2013), pp. 33–46.

10 Bisson, *Crisis*, pp. 98–9; Estepa Díez, "Curia y cortes," pp. 56–9, 77; José Manuel Cerda, "The Assemblies of Alfonso VIII of Castile: Burgos (1169) to Carrión (1188)," *Journal of Medieval Iberian Studies*, 3 (2011), pp. 67–8

Fernando's replacements as heirs to León were his older half-siblings, the *infantas* Sancha and Dulce, who were the children of Alfonso IX's marriage to Teresa of Portugal. Until this point, Sancha and Dulce had never challenged Fernando's claims. Leonese custom allowed women to inherit the throne—de facto as well as *de iure*, as Queen Urraca had proved in 1109—but only in the absence of a direct male heir. Still, once Alfonso IX chose to exclude his sons from the line of succession, Sancha and Dulce offered a viable alternative.

The *infantas* were already persons of consequence in León. In January 1217, Alfonso IX had awarded them queen's rents—13 castles and 8 towns, along with lesser properties. Significantly, their new domain lay almost entirely within the old kingdom of Galicia.[11] Galicia had close cultural ties to its southern neighbor, Portugal. And not only were Sancha and Dulce the daughters of a Portuguese queen, but Dulce at least had been part of the Portuguese court during her childhood.[12] Their property in Galicia made the *infantas* important lords in a region especially hospitable to them and their interests. Finally, because Alfonso IX gave them a few major royal towns, such as Limia and Traba, Sancha and Dulce also gained authority over the royal tenants who held those towns.

By early 1217, then, Sancha and Dulce's status within León was already rising. But once Berenguela and Fernando III came to power in Castile that June, the Leonese *infantas* became indisputably their father's heirs. Beginning in late May of 1217—the very time when King Enrique of Castile suffered his fatal injury—Sancha and Dulce appear regularly in Alfonso IX's diplomas, first as confirmers and then as co-issuers.[13] They even began issuing diplomas in their own names.[14] And from 1217 on, Alfonso IX identified them as his successors in

[11] Julio González, *Alfonso IX* (2 vols, Madrid: Consejo Superior de Investigaciones Científicas, 1944), vol. 2, pp. 448–51, no. 342 (1/6/1217).

[12] *Documentos de d. Sancho I (1174–1211)*, ed. R. de Azevedo, P. Avelino de Jesus da Costa, and M. Rodrigues Pereira (2 vols, Coimbra: Centro de História da Universidade de Coimbra, 1979), vol. 1, p. 298, no. 194 (10/1210).

[13] González, *Alfonso IX*, vol. 2, pp. 453–6, nos 346–7 (5/28 and 5/29/1217); Archivo Histórico Nacional, Madrid (hereafter AHN), Cód. 323, fols 60v–61r (3/14/1218; confirmed by Alfonso IX 6/26/1228); González, *Alfonso IX*, vol. 2, pp. 486–7, no. 372 (4/28/1219); González, *Fernando III*, vol. 3, p. 29, no. 518 (2/16/1221); González, *Alfonso IX*, vol. 2, p. 526, no. 411 (10/4/1221), pp. 530–32, nos 415–16 (11/14/1221 and 2/8/1222); AHN, Cód. 1045, pp. 13–14 (9/23/1223); González, *Alfonso IX*, vol. 2, pp. 550–51, no. 436 (12/15/1223), pp. 554–5, no. 441 (4/24/1224). June 6 is the date usually given for Enrique I's death; however, a major reshuffling of Alfonso IX's court from May 28 onward indicates that, at minimum, he knew the Castilian king was *in extremis*. See Janna Bianchini, *The Queen's Hand: Power and Authority in the Reign of Berenguela of Castile* (Philadelphia, PA: University of Pennsylvania Press, 2012), p. 125.

[14] González, *Alfonso IX*, vol. 2, pp. 493–4, no. 378 (10/6/1219).

agreements both with foreign powers and with his own subjects.[15] At the same time, Fernando III disappears from his father's documents; no extant diplomas from that spring and summer include him.

By confirming, issuing, and co-issuing royal diplomas, Sancha and Dulce took on the same roles played by Alfonso IX's male heirs in the past.[16] Clearly, the king intended his daughters to inherit León.[17] But beginning in April 1224, after seven years' worth of iterations of their status as heirs, Sancha and Dulce disappear from Alfonso IX's diplomas, and remain missing for several years. Their absence has led some historians to speculate that Alfonso IX was not fully committed to setting two women on the Leonese throne.[18] I believe, instead, that it was due to unexpected consequences of the king's strategies to ensure Sancha and Dulce's inheritance.

Diplomatic evidence reveals that between 1223 and 1226 Alfonso IX became increasingly unable to control the fractious nobles of León. Their discontent was probably partly due to the prospect of rule by two women. While women could inherit the Leonese throne, they were far more acceptable to their subjects if they ruled with a male partner, such as a husband or son.[19] But Sancha and Dulce had never married, and by 1223 they were both at least 30—well past the age when most royal women first married and past the peak of their fertility too. They had no masculine figure to associate with themselves in power.

Alfonso IX tried to find one for them, of course. He may have negotiated a marriage with Jaime I of Aragon (1213–76); he certainly did so with Jean of Brienne, the king of Jerusalem (c. 1210–25), during that worthy's tour of western Europe in 1224. However, Queen Berenguela succeeded in marrying Jean to her own (much younger) daughter instead.[20] Alfonso IX's plans to provide a husband for at least one of his daughters, and a male monarch for León, had failed. And it

15 González, *Alfonso IX*, vol. 2, p. 521, no. 406 (3/10/1221). See also ibid., vol. 2, pp. 458–9, no. 350 (11/26/1217); ibid., vol. 2, p. 488, no. 373 (6/13/1219).

16 See, e.g., González, *Alfonso IX*, vol. 2, pp. 241–7, nos 170–74 (9/8/1202–3/12/1203), and pp. 389–91, nos 290–91 (4/17 and 4/22/1213).

17 Even Rodrigo Jiménez de Rada, bk. 9, chap. 14, p. 295, acknowledges this.

18 González, *Alfonso IX*, vol. 1, p. 170. The king never seems to have promoted one daughter over the other; he acknowledged them jointly as heirs. He may have meant to divide the kingdom between them, but there is no contemporary evidence for this.

19 See Bernard F. Reilly, *The Kingdom of León-Castilla under Queen Urraca, 1109–1126* (Princeton, NJ: Princeton University Press, 1982); María del Carmen Pallares and Ermelindo Portela, *La reina Urraca* (San Sebastián: Editorial Nerea, 2006).

20 *Chronica latina*, chap. 42, pp. 84–5. See also Guy Perry, *John of Brienne: King of Jerusalem, Emperor of Constantinople, c.1175–1237* (Cambridge: Cambridge University Press, 2013), pp. 129–31.

is probably not by chance that this failure coincides with our clearest evidence of a breach between Alfonso IX and his magnates: the mass departure of the Leonese nobility from their king's court.

To say that the Leonese nobles left only out of frustration that the *infantas* were still unmarried, however, is to rely too heavily on the old narrative of gender bias. There were other reasons for the magnates' growing unrest, and they arose much more from xenophobia than from misogyny.

Foreign Allies

From the moment of Fernando III's and Berenguela's accession in Castile, Alfonso IX had looked outside León for men who could support his daughters' claim to his throne. He turned first to the Lara brothers, three powerful Castilian magnates whose active opposition to their new king and queen made them unwelcome in Castile and gave them a vested interest in keeping Fernando III off the Leonese throne. The three brothers received important offices in the Leonese court, along with a slew of royal tenancies close to the Castilian border; this put them in the front line of defense, and of offense, in any clash between the kingdoms. One of the Lara brothers soon died, however, and the others—for reasons that the documents do not reveal—went one by one into exile. Alfonso IX initially replaced them with another Castilian, Álvaro Pérez de Castro, who received many of the same tenancies previously held by the Lara.[21] Yet this alliance, too, faltered a few years later, and after that Alfonso IX abandoned his efforts to cultivate Castilian nobles. He turned instead to the royal house of Portugal.[22]

Sancha and Dulce's mother, Teresa, was a daughter of Sancho I of Portugal, who had endowed her and her sisters with extensive properties in his kingdom.[23] Her brother Afonso II (1211–23) fought throughout his reign to recover those bequests. Teresa had resisted him with the help of Alfonso IX, her former

---

[21] See Simon Barton, "From Mercenary to Crusader: The Career of Álvar Pérez de Castro (d. 1239) Re-examined," in Therese Martin and Julie A. Harris (eds), *Church, State, Vellum, and Stone: Essays on Medieval Spain in Honor of John Williams* (Leiden: Brill, 2005), pp. 111–30.

[22] The Castilians were in favor between 1217 and 1223. Álvaro Pérez's ascendancy in León overlapped that of the youngest Lara brother, Gonzalo Núñez, as well as that of Martim Sanches of Portugal. See Bianchini, *The Queen's Hand*, pp. 153–6, 189–90.

[23] See *Documentos de d. Sancho I*, vol. 1, pp. 297–300, no. 194 (10/1210).

husband.[24] In 1218, Teresa and Alfonso IX both found a new source of support in Teresa's illegitimate half-brother, Martim Sanches.[25]

From his first appearance at the Leonese court in March 1218, Martim Sanches held the tenancy of Limia, in Galicia.[26] Within a year, he had acquired a host of other important Galician tenancies—including Baronceli, Ledesma, Montenegro, Ribadavia, and Sarria—as well as Buyeza and the Bierzo, valuable tenancies close to Portugal.[27] By 1222, he also held Toroño and perhaps the cathedral city of Lugo as well.[28] The Portuguese *infante* was becoming a major power in western León, particularly in Galicia.

This was no accident. For one thing, the border between León and Portugal was perhaps most hotly disputed in Galicia; by placing Martim there, Alfonso IX followed the same strategy that had led him to position the Lara brothers and Álvaro Pérez de Castro along the Castilian border. For another, the properties that Alfonso IX had bestowed on Sancha and Dulce in 1217 were overwhelmingly Galician. Martim was now tenant of one of those properties, Limia, which put him under the *infantas*' lordship and created a personal tie of loyalty between them.[29] Alfonso IX expected his new ally not only to support Teresa, but also to put his weight behind Teresa's daughters and their claim to the Leonese throne.

---

24 *La documentación pontificia de Gregorio IX (1227–1241)*, ed. E. Sáinz Ripa (2 vols, Rome: Instituto Español de Historia Eclesiástica, 2001), vol. 1, pp. 323–8, no. 245 (12/15/1231); see also Humberto Baquero Moreno, "Portugal no tempo de Fernando III de Castela (1201–1252)," in *Fernando III y su tiempo: VIII actas del congreso de estudios medievales* (León: Fundación Sánchez-Albornoz, 2003), pp. 316–17.

25 Baquero Moreno, p. 314.

26 AHN, Cód. 323, fols 60v–61r (3/14/1218). González lists a diploma dated 1217, whose confirmation list includes Martim Sanches (*Alfonso IX*, vol. 2, pp. 460–61, no. 352). The diploma names Álvaro Núñez de Lara as the king's majordomo, which dates it to May 1217 or later. But its confirmation list bears little resemblance to the (admittedly few) other diplomas known from this year. Without more satisfactory dating, I prefer not to use this diploma to determine when Martim Sanches arrived in León.

27 González, *Alfonso IX*, vol. 2, pp. 473–4, nos 360–61 (4/1218); González, *Fernando III*, vol. 1, p. 92; Rogelio Pérez-Bustamante, *El gobierno y la administración de los reinos de la corona de Castilla (1230–1474)* (2 vols, Madrid: Universidad Autónoma, 1976), vol. 1, p. 198.

28 For Martim Sanches's Galician tenancies: AHN, Clero, 1513/14 (8/29/1218); AHN, Clero, 1482/7 (1219); AHN, Clero, 538/8 (2/13/1219); González, *Alfonso IX*, vol. 2, p. 492, no. 376 (7/16/1219); AHN, Clero, 1513/20 (11/1219); AHN, Clero, 1215/5 (3/23/1220); AHN, Clero, 1797/12 (1/1222).

29 González, *Alfonso IX*, vol. 2, pp. 448–51, no. 342 (1/6/1217).

The link between royal favor in León and support for the *infantas* is made explicit by a 1223 pact between the newly crowned Sancho II of Portugal (1223–48), on the one hand, and Teresa and her sisters, on the other. The nobles who swore to uphold the agreement on Teresa's behalf were men prominent at Alfonso IX's court: Martim Sanches, Rodrigo Gómez de Traba, Rodrigo Fernández de Valduerna, Pedro Fernández de Tiedra, Fernando Pérez Tinoso, and Álvaro Rodríguez. Not only does the treaty explicitly identify these men as "barons from the kingdom of the king of León," but it reveals that they owed obedience to Teresa. They swore to uphold the treaty "at the command of the queens" (that is, Teresa and her sisters), and, as loyal vassals, they agreed to ensure that "the queens" would abide by its terms too.[30] Except for Fernando Pérez, all these men confirmed Alfonso IX's extant diplomas in 1223; indeed, they are the magnates most frequently visible at court that year. Furthermore, they all held Leonese tenancies or offices, or both, in 1223.[31] The correlation between their prominence in Alfonso IX's court and their service to Teresa of Portugal shows that Alfonso IX expected his nobles' loyalty to extend to Teresa—and, through her, to her daughters, Sancha and Dulce. Later in 1223, all the Leonese nobles named in the treaty (again, except Fernando Pérez) confirmed a diploma that Sancha and Dulce had co-issued with the king. Their confirmations were a formal acknowledgment of the *infantas*' status as heirs to León.[32]

Alfonso IX had thus enlisted several of his own nobles in support of his daughters and of Teresa, and had made Martim Sanches the dominant magnate in Galicia with the same purpose in view. But he was still keen to recruit new allies and in 1223 he found an ideal candidate. The *infante* Pedro Sanches was another of Queen Teresa's brothers, a son of Sancho I of Portugal—but, unlike Martim, a legitimate one. His emigration to León seems to have been prompted not by antagonism with his brother Afonso II but by the accession of Afonso's son, Sancho II, in March 1223; Pedro appears in León that June, as tenant of Salamanca and the city of León.[33] If he came in hopes of profit, he was not

---

30 *Documentación de Gregorio IX*, pp. 323–8, no. 245.

31 AHN, Clero, 1431/3 (5/3/1223); AHN, Cód. 1045, pp. 13–14 (9/23/1223); González, *Alfonso IX*, vol. 2, pp. 550–51, no. 436 (12/15/1223); *Colección diplomática del monasterio de Carrizo*, ed. M.C. Casado Lobato (2 vols, León: Centro de Estudios e Investigación "San Isidoro," 1983), vol. 1, p. 143, no. 124 (6/1222); AHN, Órdenes Militares (hereafter OO.MM.), 387/133 (11/1222); *Colección diplomática de Carrizo*, vol. 1, p. 148, no. 129 (2/1224).

32 González, *Alfonso IX*, vol. 2, pp. 550–51, no. 436 (12/15/1223).

33 *Documentos de los Archivos Catedralicio y Diocesano de Salamanca (siglos XII–XIII)*, ed. J.L. Martín Martín et al. (Salamanca: Universidad de Salamanca, 1977), p. 239, no. 151; *Patrimonio cultural de San Isidoro de León*, ed. M.E. Martín López (León: Universidad de

disappointed. Pedro had become Alfonso IX's majordomo by late September.[34] In the course of the following year, he also acquired a long list of tenancies that gave him authority over the southern Leonese frontiers (Extremadura and the Transierra), as well as the southern Portuguese border (Toro and Zamora).[35] At the same time, his half-brother Martim Sanches held most of the premier tenancies in Galicia. No Leonese nobles enjoyed such sweeping power in the mid-1220s, and few even came close. The Portuguese *infantes*' nearest rivals were Rodrigo Fernández de Valduerna, whose tenancies of Astorga, Benavente, Castrotierra, and Mayorga gave him a strong power base in the Leonese Tierra de Campos; Fernando Gutiérrez de Castro, who held Lemos (Galicia); and Rodrigo Gómez de Traba, who held Montenegro and Trastámara (also in Galicia). These three men were also the most frequent confirmers of Alfonso IX's diplomas, superseded only by Pedro and Martim Sanches themselves.[36]

The ascent of Pedro and Martim Sanches marks a turning point in Alfonso IX's strategies. The king had been courting the support of foreign nobles since 1217, yet there are no signs of serious discontent among the Leonese nobility through the early 1220s. But from 1223, Alfonso IX turned specifically to Sancha and Dulce's Portuguese relatives to back the *infantas*' claims. By 1224, most of the major Leonese tenancies were not in Leonese hands, and the size of Alfonso IX's court had been dramatically reduced. Although a trend toward a shrinking court is visible earlier, it is unmistakable in this period; it becomes increasingly rare to see any nobles confirming the king's diplomas except the Portuguese *infantes*, Rodrigo Fernández de Valduerna, Fernando Gutiérrez de Castro, and Rodrigo Gómez de Traba.[37] Even these few followers are not always mentioned.

Resentment at Alfonso IX's decision to favor Portuguese magnates over Leonese ones certainly contributed to this problem, which becomes most visible after Pedro Sanches's arrival. The extraordinary generosity with which Alfonso IX sought to retain the foreigners' loyalty bred hostility among his own nobles. Several major Leonese families—the Froilaz, the Cabrera, the Villalobos, the

---

León, Secretariado de Publicaciones, y Cátedra de San Isidoro de la Real Colegiata de León, 1995), p. 249, no. 219. One charter, which exists only as a copy, names Pedro as the tenant of Salamanca on April 1, 1222 (*Documentos de Salamanca*, p. 237, no. 149), but no other evidence places him in the kingdom before 1223.

[34] AHN, Cód. 1045, p. 14 (9/23/1223); Simon Barton, *The Aristocracy in Twelfth-Century León and Castile* (Cambridge: Cambridge University Press, 1997), p. 142.

[35] González, *Alfonso IX*, vol. 2, p. 551, no. 436 (12/15/1223), p. 556, no. 443 (8/31/1224).

[36] Bianchini, *The Queen's Hand*, p. 190.

[37] Ibid.

Limia—rarely or never confirmed diplomas between 1224 and 1230. Their long absence, and their long exclusion from royal favor in the form of tenancies and honors, point to a serious rift between them and their king.

But envy was not the only factor. After all, the primary reason for Pedro and Martim's good fortune in León was Alfonso IX's desire to make Sancha and Dulce his heirs. And 1224, when the absence of many Leonese nobles from court signals that the crisis had truly arrived, was also the moment when Alfonso IX failed to marry Sancha or Dulce to Jean of Brienne, the king of Jerusalem. After that, the *infantas* disappear from their father's diplomas for four years.[38] If their absence was due to the nobles' displeasure over the succession, then Alfonso IX's decision to seek the support of foreigners only exacerbated the issue.

The Problem of Consensus

From the beginning of the twelfth century, it had been customary for Leonese and Castilian royal heirs to be acclaimed by an assembly of nobles and prelates. By circa 1200, such acclamations were often accompanied by the more explicit act of homage, and the gathered notables might include town representatives. These practices reflected the growing importance of consensus in the rule of thirteenth-century monarchs. An heir to the throne was legitimized by public recognition in an assembly of elites, whose individual demonstrations of loyalty could be attested, and enforced, by their peers.[39] The performative role that nobles, prelates, and occasionally even towns had in legitimating an heir meant that those same groups had to be induced to support Sancha and Dulce in the inevitable contest for the throne.

Alfonso IX had addressed the question of noble support by concentrating power in the hands of a few faithful magnates. Once the other Leonese nobles withdrew from court, he began to woo the Church as well. In March 1226, the king issued 17 confirmations of previous monarchs' privileges to monasteries on the Galician-Portuguese border, chiefly Celanova and Sobrado.[40] He made four

---

38 They are not mentioned in surviving royal diplomas until June 1228. See González, *Alfonso IX*, vol. 2, pp. 650–51, no. 550 (6/21/1228). See also González, *Fernando III*, vol. 1, pp. 250–51.

39 Hilda Grassotti, *Las instituciones feudo-vasalláticas en León y Castilla* (2 vols, Spoleto: Centro italiano di studi sull'alto medioevo, 1969), vol. 1, pp. 202–9; Cerda, "Assemblies," pp. 70–72.

40 Between March 2 and March 23, Alfonso IX issued nine confirmations for Sobrado

more confirmations for the monastery of Meira a year later.[41] In the summer of 1228 he went on a confirmation spree in Galicia: 3 to the monastery of Montederramo,[42] 10 to the monastery of Melón, 8 to the monastery of Tojos Outos,[43] 5 to the cathedral of Túy,[44] and a whopping 17 to the cathedral of Orense.[45] In short, he confirmed nearly all his previous privileges to these recipients, and he made new grants at the same time. For a monarch to bestow such a concentrated series of royal privileges on individual institutions within such a short time is extremely unusual.[46] Alfonso IX's courtship of these powerful monasteries and cathedrals implies that he wanted to ensure their support. But the shower of privileges fell only on the churches of Galicia, where the *infantas*' support was already strongest. Still, the grants were linked to his efforts to secure the succession for his daughters; during his fit of generosity in 1228, Alfonso IX again asserted Sancha and Dulce's status as heirs. That June, he co-issued three royal diplomas with his daughters—their first appearance in his documents in four years.[47]

The loyalty of the Leonese nobles was becoming a pressing issue again, too. At the end of 1227, Martim Sanches disappears from view. Although he was the king's standard-bearer as late as October 1227, he is gone from that post and from

---

and seven for Celanova, as well as one for the monastery of Osera. González, *Alfonso IX*, vol. 2, pp 585–93, nos 474–90.

41 AHN, Clero, 1131/3–4 (3/11/1227) and 5–6 (3/12/1227).

42 AHN, Clero, 1482/13–14 (5/12/1228); González, *Alfonso IX*, vol. 2, p. 630, no. 526 (5/14/1228).

43 AHN, Sellos, 3/15; AHN, Clero, 513/8; ibid., 1440/11; AHN, Cód. 1002, fol. 32v (all 6/24/1228); AHN, Clero, 1440/13; AHN, Cód. 323, fol. 48r–v; AHN, Cód. 1002, fols 28v–30v and 34v (all 6/25/1228); AHN, Clero, 1440/14–16; AHN, Cód. 323, fols 60v–61v (all 6/26/1228); AHN, Cód. 1002, fols 32v–33v (6/27/1228); AHN, Cód. 323, fols 88v–89r and AHN, Cód. 1002, fols 31v–32r (both 6/28/1228); AHN, Clero, 556/9 (6/29/1228); AHN, Sellos, 3/14 (6/30/1228); AHN, Cód. 1002, fol. 32r–v (7/1/1228); AHN, Cód. 1002, fols 30v–31r (7/2/1228).

44 González, *Alfonso IX*, vol. 2, pp. 671–2, nos 577–8 (8/9 and 8/11/1228); ibid., vol. 2, pp. 674–7, nos 580–82 (8/13 and 8/17/1228).

45 González, *Alfonso IX*, vol. 2, pp. 631–5, nos 527–31 (5/18/1228); ibid., vol. 2, pp. 636–44, nos 533–44 (5/19–20 and 5/22–5/1228).

46 González, *Alfonso IX*, vol. 1, p. 498. Cf. James D'Emilio, "The Royal Convent of Las Huelgas: Dynastic Politics, Religious Reform and Artistic Change in Medieval Castile," in Meredith Parsons Lillich (ed.), *Studies in Cistercian Art and Architecture* (Kalamazoo, MI: Cistercian Publications, 2005), pp. 201–2.

47 González, *Alfonso IX*, vol. 2, pp. 647–8, no. 547 (6/10/1228); AHN, Clero, 1798/13 (6/12/1228; the date is from González, *Alfonso IX*, vol. 2, p. 648, no. 548); González, *Alfonso IX*, vol. 2, pp. 650–51, no. 550 (6/21/1228).

his tenancies by mid-December.[48] Two of his wealthy Galician properties, Sarria and Toroño, appear to have been retained by the crown. This decision shows Alfonso IX's estrangement from his nobles; those tenancies were useful lures or rewards for magnates who were at the court, or who should have been. Limia went to enhance Pedro Sanches's already bloated holdings, and the position of standard-bearer was given to Rodrigo Fernández de Valduerna, who had been one of Alfonso IX's few loyal Leonese followers throughout the 1220s. In short, the absence of a man who held several of León's most desirable tenancies caused hardly any change in the kingdom's constellation of power. No new figure rose to take Martim Sanches's place, but neither were his tenancies parceled out among other magnates. The rift between those magnates and the king had evidently gone too deep to be papered over with gifts.

By the spring of 1229 though, Alfonso IX made some efforts at reconciliation. His diplomas from April and May are confirmed not only by his usual retinue of loyalists, but also by representatives of some long-absent families. Diego and Ramiro Froilaz, sons of the powerful Asturian Count Fruela Ramírez, appeared at court; for them, Alfonso IX turned over Martim Sanches's former tenancy of Sarria. Fernando Yáñez de Limia also returned and received Toroño, another former Martim Sanches property; he seems to have gotten Pedro Sanches's tenancy of Zamora as well.[49] Pedro Ponce de Cabrera and Ordoño Álvarez de Asturias came to court too, though without receiving significant tenancies.[50] But Alfonso IX's efforts to woo his recalcitrant nobles were short-lived. By May 31, the court had shrunk to its usual feeble size, and the tenancies granted to the Froilaz brothers

---

[48] AHN, Clero, 3565/14 (10/1227); González, *Alfonso IX*, vol. 2, p. 617, no. 516 (12/14/1227). One non-royal charter lists him as tenant of Limia on January 3, 1228 (AHN, Clero, 1516/11), but the royal diplomas of December 14, 1227 and January 8, 1228 name Pedro Sanches as tenant there (González, *Alfonso IX*, vol. 2, p. 617, no. 516, and p. 619, no. 518). Another non-royal charter names him as tenant of Sarria on February 3, 1228 (AHN, Clero, 1215/7); in that case I have no other evidence of any tenant there between August 1227 and August 1228 (González, *Alfonso IX*, vol. 2, pp. 613–14, no. 513 [8/6/1228]; ibid., vol. 2, pp. 675–6, no. 581 [8/18/1228]). Still, the preponderance of evidence suggests that the January 3 and February 3 charters are in error. Martim Sanches's disappearance may mean that he died, of course, but I have not been able to confirm this.

[49] AHN, OO.MM., 568/12 (4/5/1229). For the Limia family, see Margarita Torres Sevilla-Quiñones de León, *Linajes nobiliarios en León y Castilla (siglos IX–XIII)* (Salamanca: Junta de Castilla y León, Consejería de Educación y Cultura, 1999), p. 333.

[50] See AHN, OO.MM., 568/12 (4/5/1229); AHN, OO.MM., 88/18 (5/1229); AHN, Cód. 1045, pp. 7–9 (5/16/1229).

and to Fernando Yáñez de Limia were revoked. Sarria and Toroño reverted to the crown, and Zamora went back to Pedro Sanches.[51]

Even then, Alfonso IX's hopes of broader support among the Leonese magnates were not extinguished. In March 1230, he reached out to his nobles again—in particular to Diego and Ramiro Froilaz. Indeed, the diploma of March 30 in which the Froilaz brothers and Pedro Ponce de Cabrera first reappear at court was co-issued with Sancha and Dulce.[52] This time, Alfonso IX had more success. The Froilaz brothers were still at court when the king issued his last confirmed diplomas that July—although Pedro Ponce de Cabrera was not.[53] And, once again, Alfonso IX used his position of strength to co-issue a diploma with his daughters, on August 1, 1230.[54] It is his last surviving diploma.

Alfonso IX died in the Galician town of Villanueva on September 24, 1230.[55] The news sped to Sancha and Dulce, who were nearby, and to Fernando III, as he abandoned a failed siege at Jaén.[56] The contest for the Leonese succession had begun in earnest.

The Contest for the Crown

Alfonso IX had tried to overcome his subjects' reluctance to accept Sancha and Dulce as their queens, first by building and enriching a nucleus of noble support, then by rewarding loyal religious institutions with an unprecedented bounty of privileges. In the first case, however, his reliance on Portuguese magnates had bred resentment among León's own nobility; in the second, his generosity was focused on Galician churches and monasteries, rather than shared among the ecclesiastics of his whole kingdom. Nevertheless, his actions were an effort to build consensus on his daughters' behalf, at least among some of his nobles and prelates.

Had he done the same among the Leonese towns? Alfonso IX was well aware of town councils' value as a legitimizing force and as a potential counter

---

51 González, *Alfonso IX*, vol. 2, pp. 698–700, no. 600 (5/31/1229).

52 González, *Alfonso IX*, vol. 2, pp. 710–11, no. 613 (3/30/1230).

53 AHN, OO.MM., 568/13 (7/1/1230); González, *Alfonso IX*, vol. 2, pp. 716–17, no. 619 (7/20/1230); AHN, Clero, 3551/17 (7/22/1230).

54 González, *Alfonso IX*, vol. 2, pp. 717–18, no. 620.

55 Lucas of Túy, bk. 4, chap. 98, pp. 337–8.

56 *Chronica latina*, chap. 60, p. 103; Rodrigo Jiménez de Rada, bk. 9, chap. 14, p. 295; Bianchini, *The Queen's Hand*, p. 191.

to noble power.[57] Yet it is impossible to say with certainty whether he wooed any Leonese towns to support the *infantas*. There are few extant royal privileges to towns from the 1220s, but such privileges are simply less likely to have survived than grants made to churches; ecclesiastical archives were better maintained than municipal ones. The Castilian chroniclers have a few things to say about the towns' roles, but they, as we will see, cannot always be trusted. And all the non-narrative sources can tell us is that, as far as the crown was concerned, a town's loyalty was closely involved with the loyalty of its noble tenant.

This is why Alfonso IX had put dangerous border regions into the care of his most trusted magnates. Sancha and Dulce's itinerary immediately after Alfonso IX's death reflects the same expectation. Although they were in Galicia when the king died, they promptly left the region and headed east with their mother, Teresa. Their first stop was the city of Astorga, then León itself; when their retinue was refused entrance there, they fell back to Benavente.[58] The *infantas* had, in other words, set out to stake their claim to the city of León and to meet any border forays by Fernando III. The towns they approached were all royal tenancies, and all were held by Alfonso IX's longtime loyalists. Pedro Sanches had held León at least since September 1223, and Astorga and Benavente were both in the hands of Rodrigo Fernández de Valduerna.[59] The *infantas* sought to demonstrate their lordship over the crown's possessions, and they expected the town councils to fall in with the will of their royally appointed tenants.

The Castilians had similar expectations—though for them it was the episcopate, not the nobility, whose influence was decisive. Rodrigo Jiménez de Rada explains:

> However, the prelates of the kingdom ... received King Fernando as their king as soon as they learned of his arrival. These were Juan of Oviedo, Nuño of Astorga, Rodrigo of León, Miguel of Lugo, Martín of Salamanca, Martín of Mondoñedo, Miguel of Ciudad Rodrigo, and Sancho of Coria. When the father had died, they all submitted themselves to the son along with their cities, and the planned revolt [by Sancha and Dulce] could not prevail.[60]

---

[57] Bisson, *Crisis*, pp. 537–40.

[58] *Chronica latina*, chap. 60, p. 103.

[59] *Colección documental del archivo de la catedral de León*, ed. J.M. Fernández Catón et al. (18 vols, León: Centro de Estudios e Investigación "San Isidoro," 1990–2003), vol. 6, p. 411, no. 1916 (9/29/1223); González, *Alfonso IX*, vol. 2, p. 533, no. 417 (2/16/1222); ibid., vol. 2, p. 718, no. 620 (8/1/1230).

[60] Rodrigo Jiménez de Rada, bk. 9, chap. 14, p. 296.

To Archbishop Rodrigo, the submission of these bishops meant the submission of their cities. For early thirteenth-century elites, the assumption that nobles or prelates could enforce their will upon the lands that they controlled was well-grounded in experience.[61] But the Leonese succession crisis did not bear out that assumption.

No evidence exists to show whether the prelates listed by Archbishop Rodrigo really did bring their cities along with them. Still, Rodrigo's omissions are telling. Although he implies that *all* "the prelates of the kingdom" immediately endorsed Fernando III, his actual list of bishops is mostly limited to those of southern and eastern León—of Asturias, the Tierra de Campos, and Leonese Extremadura. It includes only two of the five bishops of Galicia, those of Lugo and Mondoñedo.[62] The bishops of Orense and Túy, whose sees lay closest to the Portuguese border, and León's foremost prelate, the archbishop of Santiago de Compostela, are not mentioned. Sancha and Dulce were not completely lacking ecclesiastical support, especially within their Galician domains. Alfonso IX's efforts at building consensus there had borne some fruit.

His faith in the power of his noble tenants was less well repaid. Juan of Osma's *Chronica latina* reports that upon their approach to Astorga, León, and Benavente—all tenancies of the late king's loyalists—Sancha and Dulce "were not received as they wished." At Astorga and León, "the response of the people and of the bishops was that they would receive and willingly serve the *infantas* themselves, but they would not receive their knights or armed men." At Benavente, which had no bishop, "they received a similar response."[63]

A refusal to admit Sancha and Dulce's military forces was, in essence, a refusal to back their claims. The *Chronica latina*'s allusion to "the people and ... the bishops" has encouraged historians to see the opposition to the *infantas* as a popular movement, led by town councils and supported by the Church. In this view, the towns' prominence in deciding the succession contest demonstrates their increasing influence. And the *Chronica latina* and *De rebus Hispanie* both go on to claim that, conversely, town support made Fernando III's arrival in León

---

61 Lordship in this period could be understood simultaneously as command over persons and possession of lands. Bisson, *Crisis*, p. 3; John Van Engen, "Sacred Sanctions for Lordship," in Thomas N. Bisson (ed.), *Cultures of Power: Lordship, Status, and Process in Twelfth-Century Europe* (Philadelphia, PA: University of Pennsylvania Press, 1995), pp. 216–18.

62 Ana Rodríguez López, "Dotes y arras en la política territorial de la monarquía feudal castellana: Siglos XII–XIII," *Arenal*, 2/2 (1995), p. 285; Bianchini, *The Queen's Hand*, p. 195.

63 *Chronica latina*, chap. 60, p. 103.

a success. Once Sancha and Dulce had retreated from Benavente to Zamora, whose bishop was their partisan and where they were welcomed, the Castilians advanced across the border.[64] The towns of Mayorga and Mansilla, two more erstwhile tenancies of Rodrigo Fernández de Valduerna, received Fernando III gladly. So did Toro, a town close both to the Portuguese border and to Zamora, where Sancha and Dulce had taken refuge from Fernando III's forces. Like the city of León, Toro had been Pedro Sanches's tenancy before Alfonso IX died. But as in León, Pedro's tenancy there did not ensure the town's loyalty. Toro declared for Fernando III, and the king marched on the city of León.[65]

So far, then, events seem to bear out the conclusion that town councils were decisive in the succession contest. Mayorga's and Mansilla's welcome gave Fernando III a valuable foothold in the kingdom; conversely, the *infantas*' cold reception at Astorga, León, and Benavente kept them from pressing their early advantage. Perhaps, then, Alfonso IX's and Archbishop Rodrigo's belief that towns obeyed their lords was born of an antiquated faith in the power of arbitrary lordship, and did not reflect thirteenth-century realities.

However, although the Castilian chronicles imply that Astorga, León, and Benavente rejected the *infantas* in order to support Fernando III, this is not necessarily so; nor were these towns altogether free of seigneurial pressure. León and Benavente—and Mayorga and Mansilla, for that matter—lay in the Tierra de Campos, a region on the Castilian border where Fernando III's mother, Berenguela, had long-established interests and allies. Berenguela had also had connections to Astorga during her marriage to Alfonso IX.[66] The loyalties of these towns may not have been swayed by their royal tenants, but the councils could still be influenced by other lords with other claims.

Moreover, even Archbishop Rodrigo acknowledges that the Leonese towns were not all committed to Fernando III's cause. He writes:

> we received knights and envoys who came from other cities, who seemed somewhat irresolute about receiving the king. For the lord king's sisters, Sancha and Dulce ... were preparing to revolt with their supporters.[67]

---

64 *Chronica latina*, chap. 60, p. 103. The bishop of Zamora is not among the prelates whom Archbishop Rodrigo lists as Fernando III's partisans (see n. 60 above).

65 Rodrigo Jiménez de Rada, bk. 9, chap. 14, pp. 295–6; Bianchini, *The Queen's Hand*, p. 197.

66 Julio González, *El reino de Castilla en la época de Alfonso VIII* (3 vols, Madrid: Consejo Superior de Investigaciones Científicas, 1960), vol. 3, pp. 204–8, no. 681 (12/8/1199); ibid., vol. 3, pp. 365–74, no. 782 (3/26/1206); Lucas of Túy, bk. 4, chap. 85, p. 325.

67 Rodrigo Jiménez de Rada, bk. 9, chap. 14, p. 296.

The ambivalence of these "other cities" echoes the hesitation of the towns that the *infantas* first approached. Indeed, a town's refusal to admit the *infantas*' forces was more a declaration of neutrality than an endorsement of the king. And in some areas, hostility to the Castilians was downright emphatic: "In that time great unrest was made in the kingdom of León. For many Galician and Asturian knights ... strove to resist King Fernando if they could."[68] Galicia, of course, was the *infantas*' stronghold, and the principal magnates of Asturias were Diego and Ramiro Froilaz, their partisans. Alfonso IX's efforts to secure support for his daughters had at least partly succeeded, both with the Church and among the lesser nobility ("knights") who dominated town councils.[69]

What about the great magnates? The loyalty of tenants may not have determined the loyalty of their cities, but Alfonso IX had spent vast effort and wealth to secure the personal fidelity of his noble partisans. Were they effective?

To some extent, they were. Sancha and Dulce had at least enough resources—whether their own or their allies'—to assemble the retinue of "knights and armed men" who were turned away at Astorga and León. Juan of Osma further observes that "Rodrigo Fernández, known as *el Feo*; the sons of Count Fruela; and many others from the land of León supported those noble ladies."[70] Rodrigo Fernández de Valduerna had been a mainstay of Alfonso IX's court throughout the 1220s, and "the sons of Count Fruela," Diego and Ramiro Froilaz, had reconciled with the king in the months before his death. Indeed, Diego Froilaz was responsible for the best-recorded early resistance to Fernando III. Before the city of León could welcome the king—joyfully, according to his chroniclers—the city's council and bishop had to overcome Diego Froilaz, whose men had occupied the canonry of San Isidoro and the royal palace.[71] They achieved this not by force of arms, but (says Lucas of Túy) through the intervention of San Isidoro himself. And although Lucas implies that Diego Froilaz's change of heart was enough to deliver the city to Fernando III, Juan of Osma reports that the king had to stay in León a long time, trying to wrest its fortifications from the control of García Rodríguez Carnota, one of Alfonso IX's officials.[72] Clearly, Sancha and Dulce had a substantial power base, including some of the magnates their father had so assiduously cultivated.

---

[68] Lucas of Túy, bk. 4, chap. 99, p. 338.

[69] Estepa Díez, "Curia y cortes," pp. 81–3.

[70] *Chronica latina*, chap. 60, p. 103.

[71] Lucas of Túy, bk. 4, chap. 99, pp. 338–9; Rodrigo Jiménez de Rada, bk. 9, chap. 15, pp. 296–7.

[72] Lucas of Túy, bk. 4, chap. 99, pp. 338–9; *Chronica latina*, chap. 60, p. 104.

But nowhere do the narrative sources mention the man who should have done the most to support the *infantas*: their uncle, Pedro Sanches. Although he appears in the last confirmed diploma Alfonso IX is known to have issued, Pedro was already exploring more attractive options in Aragon-Cataluña by 1230.[73] His failure to assist his nieces left their success entirely in the hands of the Leonese nobility—the very group that Alfonso IX had tried to circumvent by inviting Pedro and Martim Sanches to León.[74] And the *infantas*' support among the great Leonese magnates proved predictably sparse.

Yet these nobles' reluctance to back Sancha and Dulce did not make them ardent supporters of Fernando III. Although Alfonso IX had died at the end of September, it was not until mid-December that the succession crisis was resolved. Having occupied the city of León, Fernando III began to issue diplomas as king of Castile and León in early November. But not one Leonese noble confirmed these diplomas—neither Alfonso IX's die-hard loyalists, nor the many magnates whose estrangement from the king had removed them from court for nearly a decade. The great noble families may have had doubts about Sancha and Dulce's succession, but they did not rush to Fernando III's side simply because he was male. Notably, although the Castilian chroniclers name a handful of the *infantas*' noble supporters, they never identify Leonese magnates who supported Fernando III. Apart from the "knights" (*milites*) of Toro and the ambivalent knightly envoys who visited the king from "other cities," the pro-Castilian partisans mentioned in the chronicles are exclusively townspeople (*ciues*) and ecclesiastics.

This is rhetorical sleight-of-hand, meant to persuade the reader that although Fernando III faced some modest resistance, most Leonese were eager to accept him as their king. Consequently, the Castilian chroniclers' discourse emphasizes the role of bishops and councils (some, though not all, of whom did support Fernando) and passes over the role of the Leonese magnates. The magnates, for their part, were not all active partisans of Sancha and Dulce. Most of them held aloof, watching the struggle play out before deciding where to commit themselves. Sancha and Dulce offered their half-brother terms by early December. But only after they formally renounced their claims in the Treaty of Benavente (December 11, 1230) did Leonese nobles acknowledge Fernando III's authority by confirming his diplomas.[75] Even then, Fernando's victory was incomplete. Galicia and

[73] AHN, Clero, 3551/17 (7/22/1230). See González, *Fernando III*, vol. 1, pp. 92, 254; *Documentación de Gregorio IX*, vol. 1, pp. 220–21, no. 146 (6/4/1229).

[74] Bianchini, *The Queen's Hand*, p. 192.

[75] González, *Fernando III*, vol. 2, pp. 311–14, no. 270 (12/11/1230); ibid., vol. 2, pp. 314–17, no. 272 (12/19/1230).

Asturias, where Alfonso IX had worked so hard to build support for his daughters, remained restive for more than a year before the new king could travel there to "reduce [them] from disorder to peace."[76]

Modern interpretations of the succession contest that rely too heavily on the rising power of towns are therefore throwbacks to a narrative created by the Castilian court. Interpretations that rely only on gender, meanwhile, fail to account for the *infantas*' robust support in some parts of the kingdom and for the rather tepid reception of Fernando III as a male alternative.[77] By considering documentary evidence alongside the narrative sources, however, we can reach a more nuanced understanding of how elite powers competed with each other in the early thirteenth century.

First, royal succession relied increasingly on elite consensus—and the broader that consensus was, the better. But much of it was based on old mechanisms of lordship, which produced the procedural approval of vassals and subjects. In Galicia, where Alfonso IX built a strong power base for his daughters, he did it by winning the loyalty of Galicia's great magnates—such as Rodrigo Gómez de Traba, who remained conspicuously absent from Fernando III's diplomas for more than a month after Sancha and Dulce conceded defeat[78]—and putting substantial tenancies into the hands of those he trusted, like Martim Sanches. He encouraged the Galician Church's support by awarding it unprecedented numbers of privileges and confirmations. And he forged bonds of fealty by establishing Sancha and Dulce themselves as the lords of numerous Galician towns and castles. The *infantas*' confidence in their Galician partisans is illustrated by their willingness to leave the region when the moment of crisis came; Galicia's long-drawn-out resistance to Fernando III's authority shows that their trust was not misplaced.

Second, although towns were undeniably important in consensus-building, the Castilian narrative overstates their centrality. Fernando III's support among Leonese towns was not as immediate or as widespread as his chroniclers imply. Support among prelates, while stronger, was still not universal. What ultimately tipped the scales in Fernando's favor were the Leonese magnates—not because they endorsed him, but because they refused to endorse anyone. Without their express backing, Sancha and Dulce's civic and ecclesiastical partisans in western León and Galicia could not overcome Fernando III's adherents along

[76] *Chronica latina*, chap. 62, p. 105; González, *Fernando III*, vol. 2, pp. 475–7, no. 415 (2/26/1232); ibid., vol. 2, pp. 524–5, no. 455 (5/29/1232).

[77] For the complex role of gender in this dispute, see Bianchini, *The Queen's Hand*, pp. 180–207.

[78] See González, *Fernando III*, vol. 2, pp. 342–3, no. 297 (1/20/1231).

the Castilian border, at least not when those adherents had an entire kingdom's wealth and military might behind them. Still, it was only after the *infantas* admitted defeat that the Leonese magnates accepted their new king.

Third, it was more than misogyny that held the Leonese nobles back. There were drawbacks to enthroning Sancha and Dulce, certainly. But enthroning Fernando III meant the unification of Castile and León—evidently an unpalatable prospect for the Leonese. Under such circumstances, the Leonese nobles could perhaps have been brought to the *infantas*' side. But here Alfonso IX miscalculated badly. Faced with his nobles' hesitation, the king elevated a few loyalists over the rest, and enriched them spectacularly with tenancies that they could then secure for the *infantas*. This was bound to foster bad blood. But Alfonso IX compounded the problem by singling out foreigners for special favor. His strategy relied on twelfth-century habits of lordship: personal, affective fidelity that shaded over into familial bonds.[79] Apart from whatever oaths they had made to the crown, Pedro and Martim Sanches were connected to Sancha and Dulce by blood; therefore they were more likely than other magnates to promote the *infantas*' interests.

As it turned out, though, the Portuguese *infantes*' blood tie to Sancha and Dulce did little to reinforce their loyalty. Leonese magnates like Diego Froilaz proved far more valuable to the *infantas*, even though their lordly bonds were of a simpler kind. Alfonso IX's mistake lay partly in failing to establish such bonds between his daughters and a majority of his nobles. Partly, too, it lay in assuming that hostility toward the Portuguese was any less potent than hostility toward the Castilians. The Leonese magnates had no incentive to endorse a monarchy dominated by their Portuguese counterparts. And they might certainly have thought that the ascendancy of two half-Portuguese *infantas*, and their mother, would leave them as unwelcome at court after Alfonso IX's death as they had been before it. In this scenario, there was not much to choose between Sancha and Dulce's court and that of Fernando III, which would be similarly dominated by Castilians.

A monarch's success, and succession, depended on consensus—or, more precisely, on the *display* of consensus, on the professed subjection of as many elite groups as possible.[80] Its importance is reflected in the discourse of the Castilian chronicles, which strive to create an impression of broad-based support for Fernando while eliding details about his opposition. Still, for all the attention paid to towns by medieval chroniclers and modern historians, Fernando III's

---

[79] Thomas N. Bisson, "Medieval Lordship," *Speculum*, 70 (October 1995), p. 746.

[80] Bisson, *Crisis*, pp. 562–3.

accession to the Leonese throne—and hence the union of León-Castile—was less the result of conciliar action than of noble inaction. And what held the Leonese magnates in check was their anxiety, not about rule by women, but about domination by foreigners, be they Castilian or Portuguese. Ultimately, the unification of Castile and León did not happen because Fernando III had won popular support. It happened because Alfonso IX failed to rally enough nobles to his daughters' cause—a characteristically twelfth-century problem that the Castilians concealed behind thirteenth-century rhetoric. The process of royal legitimation was indeed changing. But the discourse of royal legitimation was changing even faster.

Chapter 5
Alfonso X and His Brothers: A Story of Not Very Fraternal Relations[1]

Manuel González Jiménez

In 1252 Matthew Paris from the English monastery of St Albans near London recorded the death of Fernando III (1214–52), King of Castile and León, in the following terms:

> The illustrious King of Castile, Alfonso [*sic*], who is called King of all Spain because of his eminence after his famous deeds and great conquests of the Muslims in Spain, which to be told would need long and special treatises, undertook the road of all mortals ... He left, however, behind him very noble offspring and illustrious and genteel knights who offer effective resistance to the perverse Saracens.[2]

Matthew believed that Fernando's achievements against Islam were secure, in part, because he left "behind him very noble offspring." From his marriage to the German princess Beatrice of Swabia six sons survived him: Alfonso, Fadrique, Enrique, Felipe, Sancho and Manuel. While the eldest was designated to succeed to the throne as Alfonso X (1252–84), Fernando made provisions to assure his younger sons a princely future. The second son, Fadrique, was to have the Duchy of Swabia from his mother's inheritance. Fernando granted the next eldest, Enrique, the town of Morón. He intended to make him holder of an extensive lordship along the frontier from Morón to Alcalá de los Gazules

[1] Translated from the Spanish by Mary O'Sullivan, University of Seville. An earlier, partial version of this chapter appeared as Manuel González Jiménez, "Alfonso X y sus hermanos (I)," *Minervae Baeticae: Boletín de la Real Academia Sevillana de Buenas Letras*, 32 (2004): pp. 203–14.

[2] Matthew Paris, *Chronica majora*, ed. H.R. Luard (7 vols, London: Longman, 1872–1883) vol. 4, p. 311. Derek W. Lomax, "La conquista de Andalucía a través de la historiografía europea de la época," in Emilio Cabrera (ed.), *Andalucía entre Oriente y Occidente (1236–1492)* (Córdoba: Excma. Diputación Provincial de Córdoba, 1988), pp. 35–49.

that included Arcos, Jerez, Lebrija and Medina Sidonia once they had been conquered.[3] Sancho and Felipe were, in their father's plans, destined to occupy the archiepiscopal sees of Toledo and Seville respectively.

Over the following 30 years, Alfonso X overcame two uprisings by the nobility, in 1255 and 1272–73, only to be effectively deposed by his son Sancho in 1282. He died in 1284, king in name only. Four of his five brothers took part to some extent in these political conflicts. The only brother with whom Alfonso had no dispute was Sancho, but he died young. What were the reasons behind Alfonso's bad relationship with his brothers? We shall try to enter into the private life of the royal household and its internal rivalries to help explain what, in the end, constituted a serious problem for the royal family of Castile-León.

Infante Enrique

Let us begin with the first of the conflicts. In the autumn of 1255, while Alfonso X was in Burgos, Enrique rose in revolt in Andalusia. Almost at the same time, another rising took place in Vizcaya, instigated by Diego López de Haro, Lord of Vizcaya. Diego had been exiled to Navarre some months previously because of his differences with the king.[4] Jaime I of Aragon (1213–76), father-in-law but at the time enemy of Alfonso X, encouraged and promised aid to both rebellions.

The events in Vizcaya were rapidly dealt with by the king, but our sources for the revolt headed by Enrique in Andalusia are scarce and not explicit. According to Juan Manuel, a member of the royal family writing in the fourteenth century, Enrique wished to marry Constanza, daughter of Jaime I, and accepted her demand that he first acquire a kingdom. So Enrique decided to conquer the kingdom of Niebla, west of Seville, ruled by Ibn Mahfuz, a vassal of Alfonso X. When his attempt failed, he was forced to flee Castile.[5] While Juan Manuel's explanation of Enrique's motives sounds utterly false, it

[3] The charters given by Fernando III to Enrique have not reached us. Consequently, we do not know the reasons behind such an exceptionally generous donation, nor do we know the legal terms it included. Manuel González Jiménez (ed.), *Diplomatario Andaluz de Alfonso X* (Sevilla: El Monte, Caja de Huelva y Sevilla, 1991), p. 14, no. 15; cf. Manuel González Jiménez, *Alfonso X el Sabio* (Barcelona: Ariel, 2004), pp. 81–5.

[4] Diego López de Haro died in Bañares (La Rioja) on October 4, 1254. Joseph F. O'Callaghan, *The Learned King: The Reign of Alfonso X of Castile* (Philadelphia, PA: University of Pennsylvania Press, 1993), pp. 74–5.

[5] Andrés Giménez Soler, *Don Juan Manuel: Biografía y estudio crítico* (Madrid: Real Academia Española, 1932), pp. 683–4.

is possible that he did attempt to occupy Niebla. We know from other sources that he tried to take over Écija to the east of Seville.

His attempt to conquer Écija, however, was repelled by the *tenente* of the town, Nuño González de Lara, who pursued Enrique as far as Lebrija where they engaged in battle. González de Lara had been joined by the king's uncle, Rodrigo Alfonso, and together they defeated Enrique and his followers. Yet Enrique did not fall prisoner. He managed to escape and reach El Puerto de Santa María. From there he went to Cádiz and boarded an Aragonese ship bound for Valencia. So began an adventure that would lead him through France, England and Tunisia.[6]

The origin of the enmity between *infante* Enrique and Alfonso X was without doubt their incompatibility of character. Enrique was impulsive, more given to action than reflection, inclined more to take up arms than appreciate the literature and learning of the court Alfonso had already established as *infante*. The first public confrontation between the two took place shortly after their father's conquest of Seville in December of 1248. They clashed at a meeting of the *curia regia* over the question of how the fertile lands of Seville were to be distributed among the nobles who had taken part in the campaign. Alfonso was of the opinion that the concessions (*donadíos*) should be feudal, with submission (*homenaje*) and loyalty due to the king and his successors. Enrique argued that the *donadíos* should be free of feudal obligations as he considered them payment for service to the crown. When they could not come to an agreement, Enrique stormed out.[7] This difference of opinion might explain why Fernando III, incapable of finding a solution, deferred the question of distributing land in Seville. Eventually Alfonso undertook the task in May 1253, at the end of his first year as king. And he did not forget what had happened between himself and Enrique.

In the spring of 1253, the new king conquered Lebrija and Arcos in the vicinity of the River Guadalete. Instead of handing over the towns to Enrique, as Fernando III had promised, Alfonso demanded his brother show him the charters on which he based his claim and then tore them up in his face. Thus Enrique lost all hope of becoming lord of an extensive and prosperous territory. With the destruction of the charters, he also lost the right to Morón and its villages, which were subsequently incorporated into the territory and jurisdiction of Seville. A concession in the territory of Alcalá de Guadaíra of 800 *aranzadas*

6 Manuel González Jiménez et al. (eds), *Crónica de Alfonso X según el ms. II/2777 de la Biblioteca del Palacio Real, Madrid* (Murcia: Real Academia Alfonso X el Sabio, 1998), pp. 22–5.

7 O'Callaghan, *Learned King*, p. 73; cf. González Jiménez, *Diplomatario*, p. 5, no. 3.

of olive and fig trees was small compensation for this great loss. We do not know if Enrique owned other lordships and rents in Castile or León. It is possible that he did, but the loss of Morón left him at his brother's mercy. Like the other great noblemen of the kingdom, he received a royal stipend and, thanks to these annuities, managed to keep his princely status and circle of vassals.

It was in retaliation for his loss and humiliation that Enrique chose to confront his brother in 1255. Unfortunately his only followers were his own vassals, in addition to Ramiro Rodríguez and other noblemen of lesser rank.[8] No magnates supported him in his revolt, and Jaime I of Aragon, despite his promises, did not lift a finger to help. For some time after his subsequent exile, Enrique wandered the courts of France and England. Eventually he moved to Tunisia, where he gained fame and fortune as a mercenary of the emir. In 1260 he left Tunisia for Italy and entered the service of the pope, who named him "governor" or "senator" of Rome, hence his sobriquet, the "senator." Resentful of not receiving the title of king of Sardinia from the pope, Enrique defected to Conradin, grandson of the emperor Frederick II. Defending Conradin's right to the throne of Sicily in 1268, he fell prisoner to Charles I (1266–85), the Angevin king of Sicily, at the battle of Tagliacozzo. In fairness it must be said that Alfonso did all in his power to persuade Charles to free Enrique but without success.[9] The brothers did not see each other again.

Enrique's dreams of power and glory came to an end in Canosa and in the many other castles where he was held prisoner. In both Castile and in Italy he had been incapable of measuring his strength against that of his enemies and was, at the end of the day, a victim of his own impulsive and ambitious character. "After 26 years in Italian prisons," Enrique finally returned to Castile in 1293 where his nephew, Sancho IV (1284–95), now sat on the throne.[10] When Sancho died in 1295, Enrique became tutor to his son, Fernando IV (1295–1312), until the boy came of age in 1302. A year later, Enrique died in Roa (Burgos).

Infante Fadrique

The personal trajectory of *infante* Fadrique, the second eldest of the brothers, appears quite different from that of Enrique though we know little about

---

8 González Jiménez, *Alfonso X*, p. 84.

9 O'Callaghan, *Learned King*, p. 210, concludes that after demanding "an explanation from Charles ... Alfonso X did not press the issue." Cf. Peter Linehan, *Spain, 1157–1300: A Partible Inheritance* (Oxford: Blackwell, 2008), p. 167.

10 Linehan, p. 229; O'Callaghan, *Learned King*, p. 210.

his life. It has been recorded that during Fernando III's reign Fadrique spent time in Palermo at the court of his uncle, Emperor Frederick II Hohenstaufen (1212–50). His time in Sicily was probably intended to help him procure the duchy of Swabia as part of his mother's inheritance. If this is true, Fadrique must have soon waived his rights, yielding to pressure exerted by his elder brother, Alfonso X.[11] Alfonso was generous in compensating him for renouncing Swabia. In 1253, the year after their father's death, he granted Fadrique the largest and best of the concessions registered in the distribution of land (*repartimiento*) in Seville. He was also allotted the Moorish palace in the city of Seville itself where he constructed a magnificent Gothic tower, which still stands today. These chambers must have witnessed readings from the book of *Sendebar*, which was translated from Arabic at Fadrique's behest and whose tales revolve around a king's false accusation against a prince.[12]

Fadrique did not support the revolt led by Enrique, even though it appears he felt more empathy for him than for his brother the king. And so between the years 1255 and 1260 he led a normal, obscure life at court. If we are to believe the chronicles, he was disappointed in 1258 when the Norwegian princess Kristin chose to marry his brother Felipe, who had recently abandoned his ecclesiastical career, instead of himself. We do not know what role Alfonso X played in the matter or to what extent the event influenced Fadrique's decision to leave the kingdom. Perhaps there was an argument between the two brothers or perhaps he was tired of his irrelevant role at court. In 1260, he followed Enrique to Tunisia. Since he had abandoned the kingdom without the king's permission his properties were confiscated and handed over to the archbishop of Seville.[13]

Always in his brother's shadow, Fadrique next followed Enrique to Italy to join the Hohenstaufen cause. He may have been present at the battle of Tagliacozzo where Enrique was taken captive. He eventually arrived in northern Italy and tried unsuccessfully to win the support of the Ghibelline cities. In 1271, he returned to Castile in the company of William VII, Marquis of Monferrat, representative of Alfonso X's imperial interests in Italy.[14]

---

11 Cf. Linehan, p. 104. Linehan also notes that Fadrique had been given "the Spanish form of a German name."

12 María Jesús Lacarra (ed.), *Sendebar* (Madrid: Ediciones Cátedra, 1989); Jerrilynn D. Dodds, María Rosa Menocal and Abigail Krasner Balbale, *The Arts of Intimacy: Christians, Jews and Muslims in the Making of Castilian Culture* (New Haven, CT: Yale University Press, 2008), pp. 235, 238.

13 González Jiménez, *Alfonso X*, pp. 140–41.

14 Ibid., pp. 232–4.

Reconciliation between Fadrique and Alfonso took place in Murcia. The king received his brother with the honors due an *infante* of Castile, though without much affection. There never had been much love between them and it took time before Fadrique was fully accepted at court. Some of the lands that had been confiscated in 1260 were, however, returned to him—Brenes, Sanlúcar de Albaida, and Rianzuela, all of them close to the city of Seville. He was also appointed *tenente* or royal representative in Villa Real (known today as Ciudad Real). Not until the eve of Alfonso X's departure for Lombardy in 1274 (to resolve his claim to the Roman Empire) do we see *infante* Fadrique witnessing the king's charters. Around this time Fadrique became tied to one of the most prestigious lineages in Castile when one of his daughters married Simón or Ximén Ruiz, Lord of the Cameros in Rioja.[15]

In 1275, on the death of Alfonso's eldest son and heir, Fernando de la Cerda, several nobles in the realm supported the claim of Fernando's young sons to their grandfather's throne. The rights of these boys, the *infantes* de la Cerda, were also defended by their uncle Philip III (1270–85) of France. At a *cortes* held in Burgos in 1276, Fadrique and his son-in-law, Simón de los Cameros, along with many others, advocated the candidacy of *infante* Sancho, Alfonso's second son. Alfonso appears to have designated Sancho heir at this meeting.[16] In the spring of 1277, however, with Alfonso increasingly ill, Fadrique made the great mistake of being drawn into a mysterious conspiracy along with Simón de los Cameros. Since contemporary texts barely touch on the episode, we do not know what made the king dictate the severest of sentences: the execution of Fadrique and Simón. The account in the *Crónica de Alfonso X* could not be more disappointing. It simply states that "because the king discovered certain matters about his brother and about don Simón Ruiz ... (he) ordered don Fadrique to be strangled."[17] Alfonso sent Sancho to capture Simón, who was subsequently

15 Ibid., p. 233.

16 O'Callaghan, *Learned King*, pp. 238–48, argues convincingly that Alfonso acknowledged Sancho in 1276 and gave him greater responsibility in 1278. Linehan, p. 174, echoes the older view of Ballesteros that Sancho was not actually confirmed as heir until 1278; cf. Antonio Ballesteros Beretta, *Alfonso X, el Sabio* (1963; reprint, Barcelona, 1984), pp. 789–91, 824–41.

17 Shelby Thacker and José Escobar (trans), *Chronicle of Alfonso X* (Lexington, KY: The University Press of Kentucky, 2002), chap. 68, pp. 219–20; González Jiménez, *Crónica*, p. 194. The conspiracy must have been discovered before July 7, 1277, the day the king donated *infante* Fadrique's lordships to the loyal archbishop of Seville, Raimundo de Losana. González Jiménez, *Diplomatario*, pp. 40–43, no. 43.

burned.[18] What crime had Fadrique and the lord of the Cameros committed that warranted such severe justice?

The meager information in contemporary texts has led to much speculation. Whatever happened, it was of the utmost gravity. Not even during the darkest times of the revolt of the nobles from 1272–73 did Alfonso X act with such vehemence and lack of mercy. Fadrique had never been his favorite brother and it is possible that Alfonso's own health problems, which had afflicted him for many years, influenced such an unwonted decision. On the other hand, we cannot ignore the hypothesis that, tired of so much defiance, Alfonso decided to use the executions as a warning against insubordination. Still the episode does not tally with Alfonso's normal behavior; he was more given to clemency than anger, to negotiating than imposing his own will.

Jerónimo Zurita, writing in the sixteenth century, proposed Fadrique was put to death because the king feared a prophecy which stated "he was to die, disinherited from the kingdom of Castile and León, at the hand of a man of his lineage."[19] But this suggestion is pure fantasy. Antonio Ballesteros Beretta, in his well-known biography of Alfonso X, came to the conclusion that Fadrique and Simón were indeed involved in a conspiracy in favor of *infante* Sancho.[20] Yet if Ballesteros is correct, either Sancho was totally unaware of what his followers were doing behind his back, or he was a callous scoundrel who had no problem in obeying his father's order to execute Simón Ruiz, knowing that he was conspiring in his favor.

Richard Kinkade, basing his analysis on one of the poems from the *Cantigas de Santa Maria*, defended an older theory that Fadrique and Simón were guilty of homosexuality.[21] *Cantiga* 235, in three different passages, talks about two rich men (*ricos hombres*) who, together with the majority of the nobles, took part in a conspiracy to expel the king from his kingdom and divide it up among themselves. The end of the *cantiga* tells us that these *ricos hombres* were sentenced to be burnt at the stake because "just as a long candle burns, so did the flesh

---

18 Thacker and Escobar, chap. 68, pp. 219–20; González Jiménez, *Crónica*, p. 194.

19 Jerónimo Zurita y Castro, *Anales de la Corona de Aragón*, ed. Ángel Canellas López (9 vols, Zaragoza: Institución Fernando el Católico, Consejo Superior de Investigaciones Científicas 1967–1985), vol. 2, p. 16.

20 Ballesteros, p. 824.

21 Richard P. Kinkade, "Alfonso X, *Cantiga* 235, and the Events of 1269–1278," *Speculum*, 67 (1992), pp. 313–18. Gaspar Ibáñez de Segovia, *Memorias históricas del rey d. Alfonso el Sabio* (Madrid: Casa de Joachin Ibarra, 1777), p. 345, expressed the opinion that during their stay in Tunisia both Enrique and Fadrique adopted Muslim customs and differed "little from them in their behavior and scandalous way of life."

burn of those who did not love women."[22] Fadrique, however, was not burnt at the stake. The royal chronicle states that he was "strangled," perhaps meaning hanged.[23] Furthermore, Jesús Montoya has argued that the conspiracy of the nobles referred to in the *cantiga* took place in 1272–73, not 1277, and that the two magnates involved were condemned because they sympathized with the Catharist or Albigensian heresy.[24]

Considering the growing unpopularity of the king, who had given sufficient signs of political incompetence and mental instability, I am inclined to believe that Fadrique, as the eldest of the king's brothers, attempted a *coup* that would permit him to become regent or guardian until his nephew Sancho reached his majority as stipulated in the *Partidas*.[25] It was, however, a solution not acceptable to *infante* Sancho who thus complied with his father's order to suppress it.

Infantes Felipe and Manuel

Alfonso X's family conflicts did not end with the two cases of the *infantes* Enrique and Fadrique. There were also "misunderstandings" between him and his brothers Felipe and Manuel. We have briefly referred to Felipe earlier. Just as Fernando III had appointed Sancho to the see of Toledo, he had also decided that Felipe should be archbishop of Seville. This explains why Felipe studied in Paris where he was known to Albert the Great. A few months after the conquest of Seville in June 1249, he was appointed *procurador* or administrator of the see

---

22 "E ben com' ard estadal // Ardeu a carne daqueles que non querian moller." Kinkade, p. 315; O'Callaghan, *Learned King*, p. 241.

23 A later text, the so-called "Silos Annals," states that "meterlo en una arca que estava llena de fierros agudos e allí murió." Quoted in González Jiménez, "Alfonso X y sus hermanos," p. 210; Linehan, p. 177.

24 Jesus Montoya Martínez, "La gran venganza de Dios y Alfonso X," *Cantigueiros de Santa María*, 3 (1990), pp. 53–9. See also Joseph F. O'Callaghan, *Alfonso X and the Cantigas de Santa Maria: A Poetic Biography* (Leiden: Brill, 1998), pp. 144–51.

25 Samuel Parsons Scott (trans.), *Las siete partidas*, ed. Robert I. Burns (5 vols, Philadelphia, PA: University of Pennsylvania Press, 2001), vol. 2, pp. 367–8, *partida* II, *título* XV, *ley* III, declares that a guardian should be appointed "until the king attains the age of twenty years." The same law also explains that a guardian and young king should rule when the old king "happens to lose his mind, until he regains his senses, or dies." In 1277 Sancho was 19. See González Jiménez, *Alfonso X*, p. 492.

in Seville by the pope. Two years later, he entered the clergy and, as anticipated, was elected archbishop by the canons of the cathedral.[26]

Fernando III died, however, before Felipe took the final steps of being ordained a priest and consecrated bishop. It is possible that he received no more than the tonsure and minor orders. With his father gone, Felipe no longer felt the call to the priesthood and wanted to abandon the Church. Despite his initial opposition, Alfonso X finally consented and authorized him to give up his clerical studies. But the archbishopric of Seville had been intended to give the *infante* sufficient income to live in accordance with his rank. Instead, the king was now obliged to supply his brother with rents and lordships. This he did with great generosity in 1258 on the occasion of Felipe's marriage to Princess Kristin of Norway. Alfonso granted Felipe all royal revenues in the city of Ávila, the payments owed to the crown from the archbishopric of Toledo in addition to the bishoprics of Ávila and Segovia, the estate of Valdecorneja (comprising the towns of El Barco de Ávila, Piedrahita, la Forcajada and Almirón), and the rents paid by the Moors in the valley of Purchena in Almería.[27]

Despite Alfonso's generosity, in 1272 *infante* Felipe allowed himself to be convinced by a group of nobles headed by Nuño González de Lara to take part in a plot against the king. The nobles, unhappy with the authoritarian policies of Alfonso, elected Felipe to head their revolt, which almost led to a civil war. The king did everything in his power to appease them but could not prevent Felipe and a large number of important nobles going into exile in Granada where they remained for almost a year in the service of the Nasrid king. Finally, after long and arduous negotiations, they returned to Castile, more as victors than as vanquished.[28] Felipe died soon after in 1274. He was buried in the church of Santa María in Villasirga (Palencia) in a magnificent sarcophagus beside his third wife, Leonor Ruiz de Castro.

If the life of Felipe was short and of little relevance, we cannot say the same about *infante* Manuel, the youngest son of Fernando III. Born c.1234, he was about 18 years old when his father died. He was left in the care and tutelage of his eldest brother Alfonso X, under whose protection he occupied important positions at court including that of *alferez real* between 1258 and 1274 and *mayordomo* from the year 1278. In 1256 he married Constanza, daughter of

[26] Julio González, *Repartimiento de Sevilla* (2 vols. Madrid: Consejo Superior de Investigaciones Científicas, 1951), vol. 1, pp. 350–51.

[27] Thacker and Escobar, chap. 29, pp. 109–10; González Jiménez, *Crónica*, pp. 96–7.

[28] O'Callaghan, *Learned King*, pp. 223–9.

Jaime I of Aragon and sister of Violante, Alfonso's wife. Alfonso arranged the marriage in order to ratify a peace agreement with Aragon.[29]

During these years, Manuel accumulated a solid fortune. In 1253, with the distribution of land in Seville, he received the hamlet of Heliche. Later he was given the towns of Ágreda, Santa Olalla (Toledo), Cuéllar, Peñafiel, and Villena. The grant of Villena, at the time part of the kingdom of Murcia, was his first step towards the accumulation of an enormous lordship. In 1262 Manuel became provincial governor (*adelantado mayor*) of the kingdom of Murcia, which included the towns of Elche, Crevillente, Aspe, Elda and Novelda.[30]

Manuel remained loyal to his brother the king, who in 1272 employed him as an intermediary in negotiations with *infante* Felipe and the nobles who had gone into exile in Granada. In 1274, Manuel accompanied Alfonso on his journey to Belcaire, on the banks of the Rhone, where the monarch met with Pope Gregory X (1271–76) to discuss the renunciation of his claim to the imperial crown. At the pope's request, Manuel, whose influence over Alfonso X must have been considerable, attended the interviews, after which the king renounced his right to the title of emperor.

On the return journey, Manuel's only son from his marriage to Constanza of Aragon died in Montpellier. Constanza herself had died in 1266. In the hope of having another son who would inherit his estates and continue his lineage, Manuel married Beatrice, daughter of Amadeo IV of Savoy (1233–53), a former vassal of Alfonso X. A son was born to them in 1281 who grew up to be the writer and politician known as *infante* Juan Manuel. The godfather to the child was *infante* Sancho, the future Sancho IV.

Manuel had early on shown himself to be an ardent supporter of his nephew Sancho. According to the royal chronicle, in the aftermath of the death of Fernando de la Cerda in 1275, Manuel emerged as an advocate of Sancho's right to succeed instead of the *infantes* de la Cerda. In the spring of 1276, at a meeting the royal chronicle places in Toledo, Manuel addressed the king and insisted that any previous agreement to recognize Fernando's children needed to be ignored:

> Lord, one is not cut off from the tree of the kings by an agreement; nor is the one who comes according to nature disinherited thereby. If the oldest who comes from the tree dies, the branch under him ought to rise to the top. Three things

---

29 González Jiménez, *Alfonso X*, p. 89.

30 Derek W. Lomax, "El padre de don Juan Manuel," in *Don Juan Manuel: VII centenario* (Murcia: Academia Alfonso X el Sabio, 1982), p. 167.

> there are that are not under agreement: law, king and kingdom. Anything that is done against any one of these is not valid and ought not to be held nor observed.[31]

His support for Sancho and the fact that Sancho later became his son's godfather may explain, or at least partly justify, Manuel's later betrayal of his brother. In 1281 Alfonso proposed providing for his grandsons, the *infantes* de la Cerda, by bestowing on them the kingdom of Jaén. Objecting to any diminishment of his inheritance, Sancho rebelled and called an assembly at Valladolid in April 1282 to hear grievances against his father. That assembly dispossessed Alfonso X of all his rents and power, with the exception of the title of king. The person who pronounced those terrible condemnatory words was none other than *infante* Manuel, Alfonso X's favorite brother.[32] It is hard to imagine what Manuel's state of mind must have been as he read out point by point, in front of an expectant audience, the sentence that justified the destitution of the "Learned King."

Manuel's presence at Valladolid legitimized a revolt that should never have taken place. It was there that he experienced his greatest moment of glory, pathetic glory, by publicly betraying the person who for 30 years had treated him like a son. His enormous fortune, accumulated under the protection of Alfonso, was now safeguarded under Sancho, tutor to his son Juan Manuel. Manuel died in Peñafiel in December 1283, just four months before Alfonso.[33]

Conclusion

We have seen the disastrous relationships that existed between Alfonso X and his brothers and attempted to discern what motivated his brothers. But what do we know about Alfonso X himself? Were the bad relationships with his family members in part due to traits in his personality?

Alfonso valued friendship and greatly enjoyed the company of poets, intellectuals and men of science. If we are to believe the testimony of the time, in particular that of court poets, the king was generous, witty and brilliant. He enjoyed taking part in poetic discussions (*tenções*) and the over two dozen profane *Cantigas d'escarnho* which he is believed to have written show a man

31 As translated in O'Callaghan, *Learned King*, p. 238; cf. Thacker and Escobar, chap. 67, p. 217, González Jiménez, *Crónica*, pp. 190–91.

32 Thacker and Escobar, chaps 75–6, pp. 238–49; O'Callaghan, *Learned King*, pp. 260–61.

33 Lomax, pp. 163–76.

with a keen sense of humor. Though this humor at times was acidic and merciless, these poems reveal a sensitive man who fostered friendship. He perhaps trusted his friends more than he should have and this led to many deceptions, which he voiced in texts that are well known to us.[34]

He was, without doubt, an intellectual and endowed with an inquisitive mind. But he was conscious of his intellect and of the fact that all the prestigious lineages of Christianity converged in his person. While learning, power and lineage could lend him self-assurance, he frequently experienced doubt and indecision. Yet once he had made a decision he was capable of maintaining it, irrespective of the cost, even if it entailed conflict with his closest collaborators or his own family. This complex combination of self-esteem and affectivity, of sensitivity and reflection, was undoubtedly misunderstood by his contemporaries. His conceit and intellectual superiority were considered to be a sign of satanic pride, his reflective character a sign of weakness, his decisions as authoritarian and his artistic sensitivity as frivolous and unfit for a king.

It is undeniable that Alfonso X failed to maintain a normal relationship with his immediate family and historians have generally failed to explain why. For them, his reign is a complex succession of family break-ups: with his brothers the *infantes*, with his wife Violante of Aragon and with his sons. His illegitimate children escaped this disaster—Beatriz, Queen of Portugal, and Alfonso Fernández, *el Niño*, were his favorites, especially Beatriz, as they were children born of love and not of political convenience. Likewise he remained on good terms with his sister Berenguela, Abbess of Las Huelgas in Burgos, and her daughter, also Berenguela, Lady of Guadalajara. Ultimately, the only way to explain the problem of Alfonso's bad relationship with his brothers is to attribute it to a combination of his errors, their errors and their individual characters. After all, they were brothers and, as with all families, it is not fair to lay the blame for tragedy on one member alone.

[34] José Pardes (ed.), *Cancionero profano de Alfonso X el Sabio* (L'Aquila: Japadre Editiore, 2001).

Chapter 6

The *Siete partidas* and the Law of Charity in Thirteenth-Century Castile

James William Brodman

Charity, while a part of Christian practice since the Apostolic Age, was not a subject of much discussion in western Europe between the end of the patristic era and the onset of the Gregorian Reform movement of the late-eleventh century. This latter era saw new efforts to define and refine the role of the clergy in a society that was becoming larger, more prosperous and somewhat less rural. Structurally, this age saw the birth of many new institutions of charity: hospitals and shelters for the sick, the elderly, the dying, abandoned children and pilgrims; agencies that dispensed food and clothing to those suffering famine or episodic economic difficulties; religious orders that ransomed captives, tended to the victims of ergotism or aided reformed prostitutes; and countless laic confraternities that saw to the needs of neighbors. The resulting system of charity had to be supported both ideologically and financially. Canon lawyers and moral theologians of the twelfth and thirteenth centuries sought to define society's obligation toward the unfortunate, the so-called "miserable people." At the same time, a mechanism for supporting these works had to be created. For example, in an important treatise on alms-giving written c. 1202–3, during a time of severe famine, Pope Innocent III stresses the universality of the obligation to give alms, their importance as a tool for achieving salvation and the role that the Church plays as intermediary between donors and the recipients of charity.[1] From this perspective arose an infrastructure for alms collection that was supported by a combination of local social responsibility, a belief that such work was meritorious in the eyes of God, and spiritual rewards in the form of indulgences meted out by popes and bishops.

1 Innocent III, "Libellus de eleemosyna," in J.P. Migne (ed.), *Patrologiae cursus completus, series latina* (221 vols, Paris: Migne, 1844–65), vol. 217, pp. 752–62. See further James W. Brodman, *Charity and Religion in Medieval Europe* (Washington, DC: Catholic University of America Press, 2009), pp. 21–4.

In the Spanish kingdoms and elsewhere, secular law before the thirteenth century took scant notice of charity. Traditional peninsular law descends from the *Forum Iudicum*, based upon the Visigothic code issued by King Chindasuinth in 642/43. While this early medieval code takes cognizance of "miserable persons" such as widows and orphans, it does so only from the perspective of their legal status. New legislation arose during the twelfth and early-thirteenth centuries in the form of *fueros* or charters issued to new town settlements in León, Castile, and the other peninsular realms. In this municipal or foral legislation, the topic of charity does arise. The intent of the law, however, is not its promotion but rather its limitation.[2]

Consequently, the *Siete partidas* of King Alfonso X of Castile (1252–84) breaks new ground by approaching charity and society's obligations toward the unfortunate from a positive perspective. It takes an ideology and practice of charity already associated with the medieval church and co-opts it into the ideology and policy of the medieval state. While scholars debate fine points about this code's composition and promulgation, most agree that intellectually it is a product of the late 1250s and early 1260s.[3] It belongs roughly to the same era during which the great Dominican theologian Thomas Aquinas sought to refine in his *Summa theologiae* Christianity's understanding of charity and the Christian's obligation to give alms.[4] As such, then, the *Siete partidas* is a window on how the Church's teaching on charity was received by a lay audience and on how medieval rulers interpreted these admonitions to be generous within the context of Christian governance.

The Alfonsine code addresses both the nature of charity and the character of the poor. As one would expect, much of the discussion of the practice of charity focuses upon the obligations of the king toward the poor and also upon forms of charitable giving that would be in the public interest. Less directly, the code endorses the spiritual regime of the medieval Church by promoting specific acts of charity as beneficial for the salvation of the soul. As for the poor, the code not only echoes earlier statements by canon lawyers and moral theologians concerning the rights of the poor and the categorization of their need but also

---

2 For a discussion of the limitations placed upon charitable giving in foral law, see James W. Brodman, "What is a Soul Worth? *Pro anima* Bequests in the Municipal Legislation of Reconquest Spain," *Medievalia et Humanistica*, n.s., 20 (1994): pp. 15–24.

3 On the dating of the *Siete partidas*, see Joseph O'Callaghan, *The Learned King: The Reign of Alfonso X of Castile* (Philadelphia, PA: University of Pennsylvania Press, 1993), pp. 36–7.

4 Brodman, *Charity*, pp. 25–7.

reflects particular social needs within Iberia by promoting specific charities, such as aid to captives and pilgrims.[5]

While the *Siete partidas*, at least by implication, sees charity as the obligation of all citizens, it places a special responsibility upon those in power, particularly the king and the clergy. First and foremost is the king, who has a special duty to protect those incapable of defending themselves against the powerful. These include children, widows, orphans and foreigners (2.10.2).[6] Thus, lawsuits brought against a minor child, a pauper or anyone in "great affliction"—that is, those incapable of mounting a proper defense—are to be heard in the first instance in the king's court (3.3.5). Further, there is a ban against anyone bringing suits against minors, widows, the elderly or the very poor in courts outside the area of their residence due to the difficulty these persons would have answering such summons. Those under royal protection, however, are not bound by this limitation and could thus bring claims of their own in other courts if they so desired (3.18.41). Whatever the venue, the king also insists that the weak have proper legal representation. Thus, royal judges are instructed to appoint a lawyer to act on their behalf. Such an attorney is obligated to serve for whatever amount of money the individual was able to pay. If the person were entirely without resources, then such service would be *pro bono*, "for the love of God" (3.6.6). Furthermore, this category of litigant has the right to appeal any decision to a royal court, and only to this court. This provision includes within its protection any individual with a net worth of less than 20 *maravedis*, the very old and the so-called "shame-faced" poor, namely those of higher estate newly degraded by poverty (3.23.20).

Besides the king, the clergy are singled out by the *Siete partidas* as having a special obligation toward the poor. In a law regarding qualifications for the episcopacy, for instance, avarice, defined as niggardliness or an absence of generosity, appears among the sins that could disqualify an individual from office (1.5.33). Another law encourages bishops to emulate their forebears

5 For an overview of canonistic and theological perspectives on the poor, see Brodman, *Charity*, pp. 14–19, 28–9.

6 There are several accessible editions of the *Siete partidas*. In Spanish, there is *Las siete partidas del rey don Alfonso el Sabio* (3 vols, Madrid: Real Academia de la Historia, 1801); José Sánchez-Arcilla Bernal (ed.), *Las siete partidas: El libro del fuero de las leyes* (Madrid: Reus, 2004). In English, Samuel Parsons Scott (trans.), *Las siete partidas* (Chicago, IL: Commerce Clearing House, 1931) is now superseded by Samuel Parsons Scott (trans.), *Las siete partidas*, ed. Robert I. Burns (5 vols, Philadelphia, PA: University of Pennsylvania Press, 2001). For the convenience of the reader who can use any of these editions, references to the laws are given in the text parenthetically. Thus, 2.10.2 refers to the second *partida*, the tenth *título*, and the second *ley*.

depicted in the Acts of the Apostles, who shared their goods in common. A generation earlier, scholars at the University of Paris had debated the extent of the Church's obligation toward the poor.[7] The Alfonsine code reflects the eventual consensus arising from that debate, namely that the Church has an obligation to assist paupers only with its surplus. So, prelates and other clergy were not required to sacrifice by skimping on their own needs, but anything over and above what was necessary for their sustenance or for the maintenance of their churches should be given to the poor. Thus, the code rather grandly asserts that the houses of bishops should be "like hospitals" (1.5.40). In the context of the thirteenth century, this reference is to shelter and alimentation, not to any form of medical or nursing care. Similarly, those who have the office of preaching must be motivated by a love of God and of neighbor and lead a good life (1.5.42). Priests, therefore, should be hospitable and generous with their possessions and avoid the sin of covetousness (1.6.34).

Generally, the code does not allow clergy to apply the incomes or endowments of their churches to poor relief, but there are exceptions. Parish clergy, for example, could dip into the till in certain emergencies: to liberate a poor parishioner from captivity, to feed people in times of famine, and to purchase property to enlarge the parish cemetery—presumably during times of plague (1.15.2). Privileged individuals also had a special claim upon parochial resources: a church's patron who has fallen upon hard times or a parish priest incapacitated on account of leprosy or illness (1.15.2; 1.16.18).

The *Siete partidas* also addresses charitable giving by members of religious orders who, bound by the vow of poverty, had nothing of their own to bestow as alms. The principal concern seems to prevent monks, nuns and friars from disposing of property belonging to their religious corporation without proper permission. Thus, there is no prohibition against one giving away income earned in an outside job. Similarly, a religious given leave to travel or to attend school has the discretion to assist any needy person encountered en route with the travel funds provided by his order. As with the parish priest, religious clergy could bypass normal restrictions upon giving in emergency situations. For example, in dire circumstances where a failure to act might mean death, a monk or a friar can grant alms even over the objections of his superiors since surely God would wish such alms to be bestowed (1.23.11).

Like the king, clergy have an obligation toward the poor that transcends their own personal obligation to give alms. The *Siete partidas* echoes the position expressed by Pope Innocent III in his treatise on alms by recognizing

[7] Brodman, *Charity*, pp. 16–19.

the importance of the Church in the distribution of alms that are granted by the laity.[8] Thus, if a donor or testator does not specify how or to whom his gift be distributed, then the responsibility for this rests with the clergy. Furthermore, money left for the ransoming of captives but not designated for any particular individuals was to be turned over to the bishop of the locality where the testator died so that the prelate could distribute the funds to deserving captives (6.10.5). Bishops could also sequester the property of any captives whose children refused to attempt a ransoming. In this case, the resulting funds would be used by the bishop to free the captive or, if that proved impossible, be used to buy the freedom of other Christians (6.7.6). Similarly, the personal effects of deceased pilgrims were the bishop's responsibility, either to turn over to heirs or, in their absence, to support works of piety favored by the bishop (6.1.31).

Besides the special responsibilities of king and clergy toward the poor, the second broad theme taken up in the *Siete partidas* is how aid should be prioritized among the poor. The ideal is that everyone in need should be helped and so the clergy should make no distinction among the poor (1.5.40). But, in the real world, even a wealthy individual could not assist each and every poor person. Thus, the Alfonsine code cautions: "he who cannot bestow alms on all persons should make a distinction" (1.23.7). The discrimination outlined in several laws takes into account the worthiness of the recipient, the nature of his need, and the proximity in relationship between grantor and grantee.

The practice of charity recommended in the Alfonsine code privileges locals over foreigners, neighbors over strangers, and the good over the wicked. Such a sense of priority is typical in this era. For example, Pope Innocent III, in his treatise on alms, established concentric circles of obligation that radiated outward from the individual. Interestingly, he observed that one should first be generous with oneself since the miser or ascetic is not likely to feel much empathy for others. After attending to one's own needs, then those of family, dependents, neighbors and other honest individuals should be addressed.[9] Similar ideas are also found in the *Siete partidas*. First of all, it distinguishes between the act of giving and the motives which underlie the act. The latter are labeled as spiritual alms, and the former as corporeal. Spiritual alms are defined as the essential prerequisite to the corporeal because they not only encourage material generosity but ensure that charity is given from a proper motivation.

---

8 In his treatise, Innocent III repeatedly states: "Keep your alms in your sweaty palms until you find the man to whom you can give them." Until such an individual is identified, the pope advises that the alms be entrusted to priests whose office is deemed by scripture to be just. Brodman, *Charity*, pp. 22–3.

9 Brodman, *Charity*, p. 22.

An objectively good act—for example, throwing coins at a beggar—is without merit if not done out of love but merely to avoid an unpleasant confrontation. Similarly, a public generosity that seeks merely the praise of the community has no redemptive quality (1.23.9; 1.23.13).

Law 1.23 addresses the helping of neighbors and so contains specific priorities in the allocation of charity. Unique to Iberia was the role played by religious identity, which was a fundamental discriminator for dispensing any alms. Thus, one is admonished to prefer Christians over Muslims or Jews, even if the latter were residents of one's own community. Christian captives are also singled out, but these are a special case that will be discussed below. Within one's confessional community, one should help relatives before non-family members. Disabled individuals have priority over those not handicapped. This includes not only those with physical handicaps—such as the blind, lame, elderly and sick—but also those of fallen social status, the so-called "shamefaced poor." Those imprisoned for debt are worthy of assistance but criminals are not. The code argues that it is better to help many than just a few and so recommends small gifts over a few large donations.[10] Outside of the family, but within the community, the seriousness of need seems to have been the controlling factor. It was common in the wills of the thirteenth century for individuals to leave whatever residual funds that remained in an estate to the "poor of Christ," typically to be distributed either by the individual's executors or parish priest. Law 6.3.20 indicates how these funds should be distributed. Priority should be given to inmates of the local hospital or shelter because, presumably infirm, these lacked the mobility to beg personally for their own food. Throughout, however, it is understood that even those judged as less than worthy—because of religion, status, profession, manner of life—deserve some help in desperate situations when their life hung in the balance (1.5.40, 1.23.8, 1.23.11, 1.23.12).

One category of vulnerable person receives especial attention in the *Siete partidas*—children. Who is responsible for their care? The primary obligation was that of parents toward their biological offspring. Law 4.19.4 rules that if one parent cannot support the child, then the other parent, if she or he possesses the means, incurs the obligation. If mothers and fathers cannot adequately care for their children, then the obligation passes to the extended family, beginning with grand- and great-grandparents. Fathers of natural children, that is, those born out of wedlock, however, have fewer responsibilities. If the child is the fruit of an openly acknowledged relationship, then the father incurs the obligation of

---

[10] All of the other criteria are congruent with those cited in ecclesiastical sources. See Brodman, *Charity*, pp. 22–3, 27–9.

support. However, if the father is a cleric, who has taken vows of poverty and chastity, then there is no personal obligation toward the child (4.19.5). Instead, the child seems to become a dependent of the ecclesiastical institution to which the cleric belonged and, presumably in return for support, the child is then bound to its service. Such children, however, are not to be regarded as slaves and could inherit property from their mothers (4.21.4). Children, on the other hand, who are the product of adultery, incest or some other illicit relationship are entirely the responsibility of their mothers and, if they have such resources, her family (4.19.5).[11] Because many poor women, particularly prostitutes or female slaves, lacked the ability to raise children unwanted by their fathers, their children were abandoned. The Alfonsine code, while condemning the practice of abandonment as evil and wicked, nonetheless recommends church doors and hospitals as proper sites for depositing unwanted children. If a child is abandoned without the consent of a parent, however, the latter has the right to reclaim the child but only if he or she pays reimbursement for any care not rendered to the child as an act of charity (4.20.4). To forestall the exploitation of such children, the code recommends that those who take in abandoned children do so out of either kindness or pity (4.20.1) and not as a source of free labor. Those who claim charitable motivations are then barred from demanding any repayment from the child or from anyone else at a later date. Those whose motives are not charitable must make clear at the onset the financial or service claims that they hold against the child and/or his family (4.20.3).

Understandably the Alfonsine code gives special attention to two categories of the needy: captives and pilgrims. With an extensive land and sea frontier with Muslim lands and a long tradition of raiding and piracy by both sides, Christian Spain suffered the scourge of captivity and human enslavement in a particularly acute way. Thus, the protection of the rights of captives and encouragement for their liberation is the most important topic under the rubric of charity within the entire *Siete partidas*. It argues that the liberation of captives has a dual purpose, one religious and the other secular. As a work of piety toward a neighbor, the act pleases God; through winning the release of one's own valuable soldiers, it also inflicts harm on the enemy (2.29.2). Given the military implications of the act of redemption, however, the code specifically excludes from assistance those who failed to resist capture and those who as renegades went over to the enemy (2.29.9).

11 This mirrors the status of children born of a free man and a slave woman who are held to be slaves, since children acquire the status of their mothers. See 4.21.2.

Ties of both family and friendship obligate individuals to assist in the liberation of captives. The code places a particular responsibility upon wives, sons and adopted sons, who can be disinherited if they fail in their obligation to ransom a captured husband or parent (6.7.6). In addition, lords who neglect to ransom a vassal forfeit any future claims against that individual. Friends who fail to assist in a ransoming suffer a loss to their reputation and can be denounced before the king (2.39.3). For those outside the bonds of kinship or friendship, the law provides a financial incentive to cooperate in the work of ransoming. For example, Muslim captives or goods acquired as the spoils of war, if used as all or part of a ransom, were exempted from the 20 percent royal tax normally owed on all booty (2.26.8).

The code also seeks to preserve the legitimate rights of those held in captivity by sanctioning relatives who attempt to take unfair advantage of these circumstances. Relatives thus have an affirmative obligation to preserve a captive's property; if the captive lacks close relatives, then the king is to appoint responsible trustees. Those whose negligence causes any loss to a captive's assets are obligated to make restitution; those who defraud a captive are liable to pay double indemnity (2.29.4). These rights to property persist as long as the captive remains alive; there is no statute of limitation. Any wills, moreover, executed during a period of captivity are held to be invalid in the absence of sworn testimony from relatives that the instrument was in no way coerced and that it was carried back home by a trusted envoy (2.29.6). Children born to female captives are guaranteed their share in the family's property (2.29.7). Presumably any claims arising from these rights would have to be lodged by the captive himself. Thus, the code permits all liberated individuals four years in which to reclaim property and raise issues of malfeasance and fraud (2.29.5).

The final topic concerning captives in the code is the payment of the ransom. As the work of Jarbel Rodriguez and others have shown, ransoms could be sizeable in amount and consequently difficult to raise.[12] The process of amassing adequate funds could stretch out for many years. To protect the captive's interest during this process, the law addresses several issues. The first of these is who is the captive obligated to reimburse for the ransom. According to the *Siete partidas*, the freed Christian is not required to repay a wife, sons or any who contributed toward the ransom as an act of charity. Further, non-family members forfeit any right to reimbursement if they in any way mistreated the captive as, for example, by raping a freed woman. Those legitimately owed reimbursement, such as those

---

[12] Jarbel Rodriguez, *Captives and Their Saviors in the Medieval Crown of Aragon* (Washington, DC: Catholic University of America Press, 2007), pp. 149–74.

who merely lent funds to the captive, must make their demand for repayment within a year of the ransoming (2.29.12). Failing such a prompt claim, the captive presumably could then regard his liberation as an act of charity.

Three laws (2.30.1–3) describe the office of *alfaqueque*, the professional agent entrusted by many captives or their families with the negotiation of the ransom and the conduct of the ransoming. The first of these laws sets out the basic requirements necessary for the agent to act appropriately: honesty, compassion, fluency in language, ownership of property. The second describes their selection and licensing, generally by municipal councils but also by the king. The final discusses the conduct of the ransoming itself. Unlike foral law, which compensated the agent with a tenth of the ransom,[13] the Alfonsine code specifies no fixed remuneration. Instead, it seems to see the work less a commercial venture than a work of mercy and places the burden of paying the *alfaqueque* upon the king or the town council. Captives, of course, have an obligation to reimburse the *alfaqueque* for the actual amount of the ransom; those who do not pay can be held for up to five years and required to perform service. Under no circumstances, however, can an *alfaqueque* enslave one whom he has liberated (2.29.11). The agents are advised to act prudently when in the lands of enemies; they are sanctioned if they cause injury or loss of property to the captive or even if they needlessly delayed his liberation.

Another category of needy individuals singled out for special attention in the code is that of pilgrims. The kingdom of León-Castile was home to the second most important site of pilgrimage in western Europe, the shrine of St. James or Santiago at Compostela in the northwestern corner of the peninsula. Thus, because the peninsula played host to thousands of pilgrims each year drawn from the far corners of Europe, the law seeks to protect the legitimate rights of these religious travelers.

In general, pilgrims are to travel under a safe conduct, and the code provides royal sanctions against those who do them violence. Pilgrims are exempted from any toll for their livestock and their property is to be protected (1.24.1–2). They cannot be denied passage on ships or shelter in inns. Vendors are warned not to cheat these outsiders by using false measures or charging prices above those paid by local residents (5.8.27). Since the journey was dangerous and many who went were in ill-health, a principal concern of the code is how to deal with individuals who die en route to or from the site of their devotion. Innkeepers are charged with collecting the effects of the dead pilgrim and handing them over to

13 See James W. Brodman, "Municipal Ransoming Law on the Medieval Spanish Frontier," *Speculum*, 60 (1985): p. 328.

the bishop without any deduction for food or lodging. The bishop is entrusted with locating the pilgrim's heirs or, lacking any, using his property for pious purposes. Furthermore, pilgrims about to die are not to be kept from making a final declaration or will by those who might covet their property, perhaps an unscrupulous innkeeper or traveling companion. Pilgrims who do not die, but instead suffer an injury of any sort, are promised a quick hearing by local judges and officials (6.1.30–2).

Foral legislation anterior to the *Siete partidas* placed limitations upon the amount of money town residents could give to the Church or devote to works of charity. Generally, individuals were barred from passing on any real property, i.e., land or buildings, or more than a fifth of their personal property for such uses.[14] The Alfonsine code is less restrictive. In general, it holds that a free man over the age of 25 can give away any amount of his property to whomsoever he wishes, as long as the recipient is not barred by law from receiving gifts (5.4.1). The only group specifically forbidden to make charitable gifts are heretics (5.4.2). Even the wages of sin—for example, the earnings of a prostitute—can be given as alms so long as the income does not result from outright theft (1.23.10). While presumably only the king had absolutely no restrictions upon his ability to give gifts, everyone else is specifically permitted to give without any limit for the purposes of ransoming captives or the construction of a church. Gifts to hospitals or churches or religious communities, furthermore, were exempted from the requirement that any gift worth more than 500 *maravedis* had to be recorded in a written document (5.4.9). Since much charity is the product of old age, the law discusses deathbed gifts. These presumably are subject to the same restrictions as any other gift but, because the donor cannot himself oversee the execution of his benefaction, the *Siete partidas* insists upon their validity unless revoked by the testator prior to death (5.4.11). In wills, moreover, bequests made to specific individuals or institutions had priority over more generalized gifts, such as to "the poor of Christ," and had to be paid out first (6.10.3). In the end, however, any bequest that promoted a work of mercy had to be honored. Executors were empowered to sue in court for custody of any property necessary to fulfill such a bequest (6.10.4).

In this important thirteenth-century law code, therefore, King Alfonso X of Castile asserts both his own responsibility to be generous toward the poor and his obligation to oversee and regulate the generosity of others. In an earlier legal text issued in 1255 by Alfonso, the *Fuero real*, the king emphasizes the congruence and harmony of spiritual and temporal authority since both derive

---

14 Brodman, "What is a Soul Worth?," pp. 15–24.

from God.[15] This attitude carries over into the *Siete partidas*. Here the king accepts the jurisdiction of the pope in spiritual matters (2.1.1) but also sees his role as king (or emperor) as having a religious dimension: "The emperor is the vicar of God in the empire, in order to dispense justice in temporal matters, just as the pope does in those which are spiritual (2.1.1)." For Alfonso, then, charity, because it transcends the boundary between the spiritual and secular, logically fell within the king's purview. Theologically, Alfonso steps on no hierarchical toes. His justification for alms in the religious sense—they are pleasing to God, they atone for sin, they require a proper intent (1.23.7, 9–10)—mimic the writings of contemporary canonists and theologians. His ideas about the proper distribution of alms—generosity to self and discrimination based upon relationship and worthiness (1.23.7, 12)—reflect those of Pope Innocent III and Thomas Aquinas.

Alfonso X, however, was not merely a passive recipient of the Church's teachings for he clearly shaped their implementation to emphasize his power as king and to promote acts of piety of particular importance within the realm of León-Castile. Particular classes of subjects—widows, orphans, the elderly, the indigent—are placed under immediate royal jurisdiction, presumably even those who do not reside in royal territory (*realengo*). These are the same classes of individuals that canonists had already identified as being the special responsibility of the Church and particularly of bishops, as fathers of the poor.[16] In the *Siete partidas*, however, the king appears to replace the bishop in this role. Indeed, Alfonso goes so far as to remind bishops, monks and other clergy of their own charitable responsibilities, although the king is careful to respect the limitations imposed in canon law upon the alienation of ecclesiastical property and acknowledges the continuing role of the clergy in the distribution of alms. Alfonso also refines the definition of need, giving priority to special needs within his realms. Captives, a consequence of the ongoing conflicts with Muslim lands to the south, are given a privileged position as are pilgrims who traversed the northern roads of the kingdom en route to Santiago de Compostela. Thus, if some areas of the church-state divide in medieval Europe fostered rivalry and conflict, charity, as reflected in the laws of Alfonso X, represents one area where ecclesiastical and secular authorities could cooperate in relative harmony.

---

15 Gonzalo Martínez Diez (ed.), *Leyes de Alfonso X*, vol. 2, *Fuero real* (Avila: Fundación Sánchez Albornoz, 1988), p. 198, *ley* 1.5.3; O'Callaghan, pp. 22–3.

16 On the role of the bishop toward the poor, see Brodman, *Charity*, p. 12, p. 18, pp. 46–7, pp. 81–2.

Chapter 7

Towards a Symbolic History of Alfonso XI of Castile: Power, Ceremony, and Triumph

Teofilo F. Ruiz

Alfonso XI's reign (1312–50) coincided with one of the most pivotal periods in Castilian medieval history. The barely 1-year-old monarch rose to the throne following a debilitating period of civil war under his rather incompetent father, Ferdinand IV (1296–1312). A rapid decline in population, a severe reduction in royal income, and the unrestrained ambitions of the regents presented almost insurmountable difficulties for the young king. Many of these long-term and systemic problems would plague the history of Castile for the next two centuries and trouble the realm until the Catholic Monarchs' reforms at the end of the fifteenth century. That Castile did not sink into a period of anarchy in the first half of the fourteenth century was due in great part to Alfonso XI's remarkable abilities and policies. Yet for a king of such historical importance who achieved a fair amount of success against considerable odds, his rule has received no full treatment from historians. We do not yet have a biography of the king, nor do we have a full study of his reign.[1]

[1] For the history of the reign of Ferdinand IV and Alfonso XI's minority, see Peter Linehan, *Spain, 1157–1300: A Partible Inheritance* (Oxford: Blackwell, 2008), pp. 210–34; Teofilo F. Ruiz, *Spain's Centuries of Crisis: 1300–1474* (Oxford: Blackwell, 2007), pp. 1–71; Joseph F. O' Callaghan, *A History of Medieval Spain* (Ithaca, NY: Cornell University Press, 1975), pp. 407–14. For the social and economic crisis, see Julio Valdeón Baruque, "Aspectos de la crisis castellana en la primera mitad del siglo XIV," *Hispania*, 111 (1969), pp. 5–24. The main sources for the reign of Alfonso XI are "Crónica del rey don Alfonso el Onceno," in Cayetano Rosell (ed.), *Crónicas de los reyes de Castilla*, vol. 1, Biblioteca de autores españoles, vol. 66 (1875; reprint, Madrid: Ediciones Atlas, 1953), pp. 171–392 (hereafter cited as "Crónica Alfonso el Onceno"); Yo Ten Cate (ed.), *El poema de Alfonso XI* (Madrid: Anejo de la Revista de Filología Española, 1956) (hereafter cited as *El poema*); Esther González Crespo, *Colección documental de Alfonso XI* (Madrid: Universidad Complutense, 1985). On the authorship and dating of both the chronicle and the poem, see Peter Linehan, *History*

An article is not the place to attempt such a study, but perhaps one may start with what I have described in the title as a symbolic history of Alfonso XI's rule. Alfonso XI's conscious deployment of gestures of power filled with symbolic value signaled different stages of his personal rule. They also clarified and asserted (to the crown's benefit) the complex relations between the king and his subjects. But the acts I discuss here were not fully symbolical in the sense that they stood as signifiers for something else. They were real political deeds. Nonetheless, since we know of Alfonso XI's deeds through the narrative of the chronicles, they have come down to us as literary representations of historical events. I would argue, however, that beyond their face or literary value, these dramatic performances of royalty had a symbolic valence that shaped Alfonso XI's rule and his contemporaries' perception of that rule. Because of the limitations of space, I focus here on four specific events that mark different stages of the king's reign. Together, they constitute a thread that linked Alfonso XI's projection of his royal authority with his claims as sole leader of the reconquest in Castile-León.

These four events are as follows: (1) Alfonso XI's emancipation from his regents in 1325 while still an adolescent; (2) his ceremonial entry into Seville in 1327; (3) his peculiar knighting and coronation in 1332; (4) finally, the ceremonial and symbolic gestures that accompanied his victory at the river Salado over Muslim forces in 1340. These four highly ritualized events, spread over 38 years of his rule, would dominate the subsequent history of Castile and Spain. One word of caution, however, is necessary. As noted earlier, our information for these events comes almost exclusively from the royally sponsored chronicle of Alfonso's reign and the contemporary *El poema de Alfonso XI*. Although the elusive historical reality of these particular political deeds may sometimes be verified by additional sources, the literary representations of what happened allows us to enter into the mental world of those who described the king and his actions and what they understood to be the political value of these four markers in Alfonso XI's long reign.

Becoming a King

In 1325, when Alfonso XI reached his fourteenth birthday, the young king assumed his personal rule and freed himself from the nefarious ambitions of his

---

and Historians of Medieval Spain (Oxford: Clarendon Press, 1993), pp. 614–18; *El poema*, pp. xix–xxxii.

tutors and regents. The chronicle of his reign describes in laconic but descriptive words the conditions of the realm at the beginning of Alfonso's personal rule. Magnates and knights lived by robbing those below and oppressing them without mercy. Castile, the chronicler tells us, was deeply torn by social tension and violence, the villages deserted and the fields abandoned. Some of the king's subjects had fled to nearby kingdoms to escape the social, economic, and political ills plaguing the land.[2]

Becoming king, however, required more than just announcing the assumption of his personal rule. Alfonso XI also needed the regents' acknowledgment of the end of his tutelage in a public ceremony. After announcing his intention of ruling on his own in Valladolid in 1325, the king rested in that city, heard the pleas of his subjects, and rendered justice to those who came to him. Meanwhile, the regents—most of them the young king's uncles and other princes of royal blood—and their retinues gathered outside the city walls. The young king came out of the city with royal banners aloft and, meeting the regents outside the walls of Valladolid, accepted—or more likely wrested—their resignation, allowing him to assume direct rule over the realm. The king's march outside the city with the colors and emblems of the monarchy held high, served as a reminder of his power over the gathered princes and nobility outside the city, but it was also a performance for his urban supporters in Valladolid. It reiterated his willingness and ability to ascend to the throne.

Valladolid was just one of the cities that stood for the monarchy and against the anarchy imposed on the realm by the regents and magnates. Elsewhere, as the chronicle does not fail to inform us, the most important cities in northern Castile-León (Burgos, Toro, Segovia, and others) closed their gates to the regents and joined the royal cause in the hope that a new king would restore order. The symbolic capital that Alfonso XI accumulated outside the walls of Valladolid and his forceful actions against the *malfechores* (evil doers) throughout the realm would eventually pay political dividends.

Many of the former regents left Valladolid bent on creating mischief and resisting Alfonso XI's rule. The most active among the dissident royal princes were two cousins of the king both named Juan. The *infante* Don Juan Manuel was a noted literary figure and a perennial trouble maker.[3] The other *infante* Don Juan was known as *el Tuerto* or the One-Eyed. Together they were ready to oppose the young king by force of arms if necessary. Luring Don Juan Manuel

---

2 "Crónica Alfonso el Onceno," p. 192; *El poema*, pp. 29–31, see also pp. 47–9, 198 for how the king dealt with those disrupting the peace elsewhere in the realm.

3 Linehan, *Spain*, p. 59.

into cooperation by promising to marry his daughter, the young Alfonso XI broke the alliance between these two powerful aristocrats, allowing him to deal with each individually. Don Juan *el Tuerto* was then enticed to come to the city of Toro in the fall of 1326 to reconcile with the king. In Toro, on the feast of All Saints, the king ordered his assassination and that of two of his knights. *El poema de Alfonso XI* puts it in the most dramatic of fashions: "And the king when he was a child/Killed Don Johan, the one-eyed/Toro (the city) is the fountain of wine/Where Don Juan was killed."[4] Murder is a very real and material deed, but murder at this level, particularly considering the manner in which it was carried out and the day it was undertaken, provide an opportunity for a symbolic reading of the king's action.

In choosing to follow this course, Alfonso XI engaged in two distinct types of action. The first involved deceitfulness and served as a clear message to all his opponents that the king was willing to act swiftly, violently, and even illegally against his enemies. The king lured Juan *el Tuerto* to Toro with promises of reconciliation and a pardon. He broke bread with him but, once he had the *infante* in his grip, ordered his murder even though it was an important Church holiday. The second and far more significant gesture took place following the assassination. Alfonso XI sat on a stage in the midst of Toro's main square, summoned all the nobles then at Toro as well as others to his side, and explained the reasons for Don Juan's murder. Alfonso's presented his audience with a list of the *infante*'s treacherous acts (essentially a bill of indictment), detailing his alliance with the king's enemies. Alfonso's violent, one may even say treacherous, actions, became fully justified. The *infante* had risen in rebellion and consorted with other rulers in Portugal and the Crown of Aragon against his own king. Don Juan *el Tuerto* therefore was a traitor to his king and realm. This discourse on power provided a salutary lesson to all. The murder of Don Juan must have sent chills down the spine of other rebellious nobles.

Alfonso did not rest, however. He marched out of Toro, claiming and taking control of the 80 castles that had been in Don Juan *el Tuerto*'s possessions. A bigger prize fell when his *merino mayor* in Castile, Garcilaso de la Vega (who would also later succumb to the king's anger), forced Don Juan's mother to sell the lordship of Vizcaya to the king.[5] With just a few strokes, Alfonso had dealt with his main enemy, restored important lordships that had been pilfered from

---

[4] "Crónica Alfonso el Onceno," pp. 202–3; *El poema*, pp. 59–71. The poem offers a long explanation of the discussions preceding the actual murder of Don Juan, placing it within a prophetic tradition dating back to Merlin and comparing Alfonso XI to a lion.

[5] "Crónica Alfonso el Onceno," p. 203.

the royal domain, and taken the newly invested power of the monarchy on a tour of Castile-León.

The chronicler does not always provide a clear sense of Alfonso's movements throughout the realm, nor of the chronological sequence. Fortunately, the documents issued by the royal chancery provide a rough itinerary, allowing us to trace the king's trajectory from Valladolid to Seville. In 1325 and part of 1326, he was mostly in Valladolid. By early 1326 he was in Burgos where he remained until probably late June. From Burgos, Alfonso and his court traveled to Medina del Campo for July and August, reaching Toro in September. Returning to Valladolid in December for the Christmas festivities, the king was already in Segovia in January 1327, before his entry into Seville in the fall of 1327.[6]

The king's peripatetic sojourns sought to firm up his allies and deal with his enemies. Moreover, while these actions asserted the primacy of the crown over a selfish magnate class, the symbolic valance of these acts, undertaken as they were with the support of the ruling urban oligarchies of most Castilian cities (almost always supportive of royal authority against noble anarchy), was a powerful reminder to the population at large and, most of all, to an unruly nobility that the new king, young as he was, meant business. Alfonso was swift to order the execution of other enemies and rivals. In Segovia, to provide just one example, shortly after his killing of Don Juan *el Tuerto*, Alfonso XI ordered that those responsible for burning the cathedral (partly a result of factional conflicts raging in the city during the king's minority) were to be dragged on the ground, their bones broken, their extremities cut, and their bodies burned. He would act as swiftly and as harshly throughout the rest of his rule.[7] Political violence from the throne forcefully reminded Alfonso XI's subject of the power of kings, but it also served as a lesson on what was expected from all—whether high nobility or urban oligarchs—and the consequences of disobedience and treason.

Alfonso XI's Royal Entry into Seville (1327)

In the fall of 1327, Alfonso XI, after a fairly successful campaigns to restore royal authority, came to Seville, one of the most important cities in Castile-León and

6 González Crespo, pp. 127–223.

7 Political violence, royal murders and other highly dramatic forms of asserting the right to rule had a long history in medieval Spain harkening back to the Visigoths. See Teofilo F. Ruiz, "Unsacred Monarchy: The Kings of Castile in the Late Middle Ages," in Sean Wilentz (ed.), *Rites of Power: Symbolism, Ritual & Politics since the Middle Ages* (Philadelphia, PA: University of Pennsylvania Press, 1985), pp. 132–3.

the unofficial capital of western Andalusia. Although *El poema de Alfonso XI* does not mention the king's ceremonial entry into Seville, as does the king's chronicle, it provides us with three significant clues about his time in Andalusia that help set his royal entry into the city in a political context. According to the poem, first the young king continued his efforts to rid the land of rebellious nobles and their retinues. Second, Alfonso rejected the matrimonial alliance with Constance, the daughter of Don Juan Manuel (to which he had agreed as a way of weakening Don Juan Manuel's opposition) in favor of marriage to his cousin María of Portugal. Don Juan Manuel left Seville, now threatened by the royal armies, and fled to his own lands in Murcia. There he continued to plot against the king as he would do for most of the next two decades. Third, and most significant in the symbolic articulation of royal power, the king led a raid on the Granada frontier. Leadership in the reconquest, the so-called *ida contra los Moros* (raid against the Moors), formed an integral part of the qualities that defined a king in Castile.[8]

It is in this context of military success and the restoration of order that we are to read the chronicler's description. Alfonso XI's chronicle dedicates a very short chapter (less than a page) to the king's entry into Seville. Nonetheless, the account is novel in its detail and unparalleled in any of the chronicles covering the reigns of Alfonso XI's father, grandfather, and great-grandfather. The chronicler writes that the coming of the king was ardently wished for and that his formal entry into the city pleased many since he was well beloved by both *ricos hombres* (the magnates) and the commons or community (*comunidades*). One must rightly be wary of the chronicler's partisan description for, as we know, Alfonso XI's forceful administration and reforms were based, to a large extent, on curtailing the power of the high nobility. We are also explicitly told that the general pattern of the king's entry into Seville did not differ much from how other Castilian kings had entered other towns in the realm for the first time. (*Et como quier que lo ficieren en algunas villas del regno.*) Seville, the chronicle adds, "being one of the noblest cities in the world, having always [among its inhabitants] men of great nobility, and suffering greatly during the king's minority," organized an entry worthy of its citizens' love for the king, knowing, as they did, that they were now safe from anarchy after a long period of troubles.

8 "Crónica Alfonso el Onceno," p. 204; *El poema*, pp. 73–83. The poem describes a procession undertaken by the young king in Seville after his arrival there following a successful (though very minor) campaign against Granada, but it does not describe his initial entry. Peter Linehan, *History and Historians*, pp. 572–3; 635–6, addresses aspects of this royal entry and its place in medieval historiography.

The king was thus received into the city with much happiness and many dances. The city commissioned many sculptures of beasts that were done so well that "they seemed to be alive." As the king approached Seville, he was escorted into the city by many knights who, with lance and shield, came out "bohordando" (engaging in equestrian demonstration). Other nobles and members of the urban elite played martial games riding "a la gineta" or in the Moorish style. On the river Guadalquivir, a mock battle of barges, re-enacting the conquest of Seville by Ferdinand III in 1248, provided entertainment to the king and crowds alike. All these events played out while accompanied to the loud and festive music of trumpets, drums, and other instruments. Before the king entered the gates, "the best men, knights, and citizens," jumped off their mounts and brought the king into the city under a rich gold cloth canopy (a *palio*) held by poles carried by Seville's leading nobles. The city streets (as were the walls of the houses along his ceremonial route from the main gate to the cathedral) were covered with clothes of gold and silver. The chronicler adds almost as an afterthought that the king was now escorted by a mounted Moorish guard.

In Alfonso's triumphal entry into Seville in 1327 we find almost all of the main elements of Spain's future royal entries. But Alfonso XI's fabled entry has also a special place in the long history of Iberian royal entries because of one special detail. The young king entered the city under a cloth of gold, a *palio* or *baldachin*. In the festival of Corpus Christi, the Body of Christ also perambulated through cities and towns of western medieval Europe under a *baldachin*. The symbolic implication of Alfonso's use of the device is unmistakable. In the next three centuries, his Trastámara and Habsburg descendants would deploy the *palio* only on their most notable royal entries.[9]

Alfonso XI's entry into Seville stands as one of the most important events in the political history of his reign and as one of Castile's most signal political symbols. Although the chronicle alerts us to a pre-existing tradition of royal entries, its mention of a *palio* at this particular entry is the first in the late medieval period.[10] It seems clear that Alfonso's coming to Seville marked a new stage in the representation of regal power. The city had been in the hands of Don Juan Manuel only a few short weeks before and it was crucial for his control of

---

[9] "Crónica Alfonso el Onceno," p. 204.

[10] Teofilo F. Ruiz, "The Symbolic Meaning of Sword and *Palio* in Late Medieval and Early Modern Ritual Entries: The Case of Seville," *Memoria y Civilización: Anuario de Historia, Universidad de Navarra*, 12 (2009), pp. 13–48; Teofilo F. Ruiz, *A King Travels: Festive Traditions in Late Medieval and Early Modern Spain* (Princeton, NJ: Princeton University Press, 2012), chapter 4.

all of al-Andalus, serving as a staging point for campaigns against Granada. He therefore entered the city under a *palio* only *after* he had met the Moors in battle for the first time. The ceremonial entry, symbolic, and ritual gestures, and the chronicle's description of the king's visit reaffirmed Alfonso XI's new claims to power and his control of the realm (and of the people of Seville) against his still resilient magnate enemies. It was of course a physical act: entering a city. It was undertaken within a ceremonial tradition known to his contemporaries in Iberia and elsewhere in the medieval West, but the use of the *palio* raised the stakes and the role of the monarch to a level unprecedented within the political history of Castile. And Alfonso XI was not yet done.

Knighthood, Coronation, and Anointment

In 1332, a mere five years after his spectacular entry into Seville, Alfonso orchestrated a series of ceremonies that were also unprecedented in Castile's symbolic and ritual history. Two distinct though related ceremonies deserve special mention. The first was his elaborate knighting by a mechanical statue of St. James at the cathedral dedicated to the apostle at Santiago de Compostela; the second consisted of his crowning and anointment at the monastery of Las Huelgas outside the city of Burgos. Both rituals were accompanied by numerous festivities and celebrations, especially in Burgos.[11]

The king officially became a knight at the age of 21. By then he had been king for 20 years and had assumed sole rule seven years earlier. He had confirmed the uniqueness of his royal prerogatives through his ceremonial entry into Seville under a *palio* five years earlier. Why did he wait so long to be formally invested with arms? Why did he wait so long to be formally crowned and anointed? Linehan is absolutely right in connecting these ceremonial acts to the pregnancy of the queen. Although Alfonso XI had already fathered children with his mistress, he lacked a legitimate heir. The expectation of a child must have prompted the king to now claim the knightly attributes incumbent in his position. The chronicle's version of the event is succinct and to the point, but its description allows us insight into the uniqueness of the ceremony and its highly charged symbolism.

[11] Elsewhere I have examined Alfonso XI's coronation (or in this case self-coronation) as a significant departure from the Castilian practice of eschewing coronation or anointment. Ruiz, "Unsacred Monarchy," pp. 109–10. Peter Linehan, who is the foremost scholar of the ceremonial history of Castile in general and of these events in particular, has also examined them in detail. Linehan, *History and Historians*, pp. 567, 584–601.

The king left Burgos—where he had called a meeting of the *cortes* and where preparations were under way for his coronation and anointing—and traveled to Santiago de Compostela. He traveled as a pilgrim to visit the body of Saint James (*et fué por sus jurnadas en romerías a visitor el cuerpo sancto de Sanctiago*), entering the city on foot. That night he kept vigil over his arms at the main altar of the cathedral. The following morning, after the archbishop offered a mass and blessed Alfonso's weapons and armor, the king took the weapons from the altar himself (*él por si mismo*) and girded them on without any help. Approaching a mechanical statue of Saint James, he received the dubbing on his shoulder from the saint himself. As the chronicler insists, Alfonso XI received the order of knighthood directly from the apostle.[12]

By these actions, Alfonso XI reiterated his unique position as king and the distance that separated him from other knights. What makes his self-knighting even more striking is that it was unprecedented. The ceremony as well as the representation of it in his very partisan chronicle sent a message to all the kingdom of the unique relation that existed between the king and the Apostle James.

As peculiar as his self-knighting was, the king's crowning and anointment were also quite different from Castile's royal practices. Although self-crowning was not unique and can be found in Sicily, Portugal, and the Crown of Aragon, what Alfonso XI did during the ceremonies held at Las Huelgas in 1332 was a departure from the agreed protocol and ritual that existed between Church and crown. An *ordo* had been commissioned for the ceremony written, strangely, by the Bishop of Coimbra. As Linehan has shown, it followed papal examples and a tradition of crowning and anointment well known throughout the medieval West.[13] It did not reference any Castilian tradition as, for example, the Toledan coronation *ordo*.[14] While this is already peculiar, the king's control over the ceremony was also unprecedented, though very much in line with the general attitude of Castilian monarchs towards the Church.

The chronicle of Alfonso XI carefully describes the king's slow progression from Burgos to the monastery of Las Huelgas in the outskirts of the city. The king's clothes are described in detail, as are his horse and the expensive adornments that covered his mount's saddle, reins, and halter. Gold, silver, and precious jewels shone in the sunlight. Don Alfonso de la Cerda, once a pretender

12 "Crónica Alfonso el Onceno," p. 234; *El poema*, pp. 109–11, mentions that the king went to take "his sword to Santiago" without elaborating as the chronicle did. Linehan, *History and Historians*, pp. 592–3, dates the first use of the mechanical statue of St. James to 1332.

13 For self-crowning or the absence of crowning for most kings of late medieval Castille, see Ruiz, "Unsacred Monarchy," pp. 109–44.

14 Linehan, *History and Historians*, pp. 584–7.

to the throne of Castile (he was, in fact, the only real legitimate claimant to the office, but had settled his differences with the king in return for a substantial lordship) put one of the spurs on the king's foot. Don Pedro Fernando de Castro, a representative of one of the highest and oldest noble houses in Castile, girded the other foot with the other spur. Surrounded by all the magnates and high nobility on foot, the king made his way to Las Huelgas in a slow procession, followed by the queen. At Las Huelgas, the altar was crowded with the highest dignitaries of the Castilian Church. They blessed the crowns (for the king and queen) on the altar and anointed the king on his right shoulder. Having done this, the archbishops and bishops sat on their respective chairs while the king climbed the altar alone, took the crowns, placed one on his wife's head, and the other on his own. No ecclesiastical coronation had taken place. The deed, both in its physical gesture and symbolical valence, spoke volumes as to the power of the king, his relations with the Church, and his relation with the sacred.

Alfonso XI's dramatic and symbolic act of self-knighting and self-crowning followed closely on Alfonso IV of Aragon's (1327–36) own self-knighting and self-crowning in Zaragoza in 1327, but there were important differences in intent and in the symbolic meaning of these two events.[15] In *El poema de Alfonso XI*, the author associates the great festivities and lavish displays seen in Burgos that accompanied the self-coronation with the preparations for a campaign against Granada. The ceremonies and the king's new stature, according to the anonymous author of *El poema*, threw fear into the heart of his Moorish rivals. Alfonso XI's crowning and knighthood served therefore as a rallying point for a new military campaign in the south. His heir, born shortly after his self-knighting and coronation (but soon to die) served as a confirmation of the king's ability to produce a legitimate successor to his rule.[16] In 1332, the king basked in the glory of the lavish ceremonies that confirmed him as the true king of Castile against the pretensions of his noble adversaries and relatives. This final symbolic claim to adulthood also gave his rule the patina of knighthood and the sacred. *El poema de Alfonso* XI continuously describes him as a rampant lion.

The frontier, where the kings of Castile-León made their reputation and their money, now beckoned. There the Marinids, a new invading group from

---

15 Ruiz, *A King Travels*, chapter 9.

16 *El poema*, pp. 109–25. Alfonso XI had one legitimate son who succeeded to the throne after all, the ill-fated Pedro I (1350–66/1367–69), and a host of illegitimate children, the oldest one gaining the throne as Enrique II (1366–67/1369–79) after a devastating civil war. But that was later. For the context of the period and the reigns of Pedro I, Enrique II and the civil war, see O'Callaghan, pp. 403–27; Ruiz, *Spain's Centuries of Crisis*, pp. 51–84.

North Africa and allied to Granada, presented a challenge to Alfonso and to the Christian conquests of the mid-thirteenth century in western Andalusia.[17]

The Victory of the River Salado

If we follow the high points of Alfonso XI's reign as a series of deeds invested with symbolic value, his great victory at the Salado River against the Marinid armies represents the apex of his long and eventful stewardship of the kingdoms of Castile and León. More than the actual events of the battle, however, I am interested here in its literary representations. How did the chronicle and the poem attempt to portray Alfonso XI's feats of arms?[18]

The chronicle of Alfonso XI provides a long prelude to the description of the battle. The encounter at the Salado River, close to besieged Tarifa, took place in the context of a series of skirmishes, attacks and counterattacks south of Seville. The Castilian fleet had been decisively defeated by the North African navy. The Marinids, led by their king Albohacen, and the armies of the king of Granada (who had finally allied with the invading Muslims), pressed hard even to the outskirts of Seville. The naval defeat in the Straits of Gibraltar led Alfonso XI to seek an alliance with the Genoese, known for their seafaring prowess, and to reconcile with the king of Portugal and other Christian rulers in the peninsula. On October 30, 1340, the Christian armies (Castilian and Portuguese) met the Muslims in battle by the Salado River. The encounter ended with a convincing Christian victory, the capture of much booty, and a short respite from the Marinid threat.[19] The battle was followed by another triumphal entry into Seville with Muslim captives trailing banners on their necks. This is the same manner in which the *infante* Don Fernando, later Fernando I of Aragon (1412–16), returned to Seville after his victory over Granada's armies at Antequera in 1410.[20]

As O'Callaghan notes, the chronicler sought to parallel Alfonso XI's victory at the Salado River with that of Alfonso VIII at Las Navas de Tolosa in 1212.[21] This glowing literary representation of Alfonso XI's military victory (gained

[17] On the meaning of the ceremonies of 1332 in the context of Castilian ideological history, see Linehan, *History and Historians*, pp. 592–613; Ruiz, "Unsacred Monarchy," pp. 109–44.

[18] For an account of the Battle of the River Salado and its aftermath, see O'Callaghan, pp. 411–14.

[19] "Crónica Alfonso el Onceno," pp. 328–9.

[20] Ruiz, *A King Travels*, chapter 3.

[21] O'Callaghan, p. 413.

with the support of the Portuguese king) in 1340 served to legitimate the claims the king had been making from the moment of his majority onwards. Important as well in this construction of Alfonso XI as a lord of hosts and a Christian king is the chronicle's careful description of the treasure captured at the battle, and how it was distributed by the king. That Alfonso XI sent some of the banners captured from the Muslims to the pope only added to his heightened representation.[22]

El poema de Alfonso XI, contemporary with the actual events of Alfonso XI's reign, follows along the lines already seen in the chronicle. The battle of the Salado River is also prefaced by a long account of the conflict between Castilians, North Africans, and Granadan Muslims in southwestern Andalusia. *El poema* provides careful details of the diplomatic negotiations between the warring parties before the battle even took place. It describes, indirectly praising Alfonso XI's chivalrous behavior, the king's challenge to the king of Morocco for a single combat to decide the struggle and avoid the carnage that was to be inflicted on both armies. The poem, as the chronicle does, depicts in a fairly neutral, though sometimes positive, tone Muslim actions in North Africa. (It was of no use to lessen an enemy soon to be defeated.) Emphasizing Alfonso XI's Christian fortitude throughout, the poem builds dramatic tension page after page as we wait for the battle's denouement. The king takes communion. The archbishop of Toledo blesses the king's weapons that, in imitation of his self-knighting, had been placed on top of the altar. The battle is represented as a crusade and those who fall will "be saved." The Muslims are also to provide their own dramatic space. Their speeches and fortitude mimic that of the Christians. It is a crusade, but it is a crusade against worthy adversaries. Then the armies meet, and the author of the poem puts his remarkable poetical and descriptive powers to a dramatic re-enactment of the battle.[23]

Many elements of the poem's narrative are worth highlighting for they fall into the category of symbolic or ceremonial gestures that allowed for the fashioning of the king. As was the case in earlier parts of the poem, the author places the battle within the context of Merlin's prophecies. The king is, once again, described as a lion while the Muslims are represented as pigs. (This is one section of the poem that employs the usual pejorative descriptions of Muslims.)[24] The Virgin Mary appears in battle and intercedes in favor of the Christians. The Knights of the Order of la Banda, a chivalrous order founded by Alfonso XI in 1330, also play a prominent role.[25] As noted, the king's piety and the crusading

22 "Crónica Alfonso el Onceno," pp. 329–30.

23 *El poema*, pp. 343–503.

24 Ibid., pp. 505–17.

25 On the Order of la Banda, see Ruiz, *A King Travels*, chapter 2.

aspects of the battle are duly emphasized. The poem then recounts a series of minor conquests or reconquest which halt the Marinids, at least temporarily. The narrative of the battle, its prelude and aftermath, takes a substantial portion of the poem's entire text. Clearly, although certainly not as important as other Christian victories, the battle represented a high moment in Alfonso XI's reign for contemporaries.

Conclusion

What has been discussed above is, at best, a very selective and impressionistic glance at Alfonso XI's rule. I would argue that these four episodes permit us to read his years as king in terms of highly symbolic gestures or deeds, captured as literary efforts to create an image of the king for ideological purposes. These were not, of course, the only highlights of Alfonso XI's 30-year rule, but they were highly significant in contributing to the effectiveness of his power. More than the king's actions, these small vignettes are also about how the two partisan authors of the chronicle and the poem respectively represented the king and his power.

The events I have described involved elements of performance and theatricality, both important aspects of ruling in medieval political life. Castile faced severe crises in the first half of the fourteenth century. These crises (for we must describe them in the plural) affected the social, economic, cultural, and political life of the realm. The minority of Alfonso XI, the period between 1312 and 1325, was the nadir of the deteriorating conditions of the realm. In the face of these crises, the young king's actions were dramatic indeed. He assumed his majority through highly ceremonial demonstrations of power and by graphic deeds of violence. The latter was a reminder to all his enemies that the new king was willing to act swiftly and harshly against his opponents, a pattern of behavior that was to be re-enacted throughout his reign.

The chronicle of Alfonso XI is an endless tale of rebellious nobles, besieging of castles, noble treachery, and royal punishment. If Alfonso XI restored some order, it was a difficult struggle throughout most of his reign and not always successful. His battles against a selfish nobility took most of his energies. When Don Juan Alfonso de Haro continued to plague the land and rob peasants instead of going to the frontier to fight the Moors as ordered, Alfonso XI sought him in his stronghold in Agunciello, took him prisoner, accused him of treason and executed him.[26] The town of Lerma, controlled by his enemies, drew a great deal of the king's attention, as he laid siege to the city, eventually captured it, and destroyed its walls. When refused admittance to the castle of Iscar by its castellan, the king met the lord of Iscar, Juan Martínez de Leyva, took him by his hair, and dragged him to his lodgings. Under questioning, Juan Martínez affirmed that he had ordered his squire (the castellan) to admit the king. The squire was forcefully brought into the king's presence and summarily executed after admitting that he had disobeyed the order of his lord. Most fortresses and castles, the chronicle added, were willing to accept the king after that.[27] Violence as part of the king's policies had been formalized by the events that followed Alfonso XI's personal assumption of the throne.

Alfonso XI's reception in Seville, a reception that must have been carefully scripted, fulfilled a different purpose, though the aims—to enhance the king's power—were one and the same as his use of violence. In Seville, the king began a tradition that would play a central role in the festive history of Castile. The *palio* granted him an authority beyond the always troublesome, unrestricted and swift use of violence. It connected him with the Corpus Christi and with Jesus' entry into Jerusalem. The symbolic meaning of his ceremonial entry must have resonated throughout the realm. It was not to be repeated in his reign, but this example serves as a powerful reminder of the symbolic capital that only kings could deploy. In doing so, he imitated the ceremonial patterns just deployed by Alfonso IV of Aragon in Zaragoza but with the importance addition of the *baldachin*. The Castilian monarch was to be more than that of Aragon.

That was also the case with his self-knighting and self-coronation (and more significant, his crowning of the queen). While these ceremonies imitated those of Alfonso IV in Zaragoza in 1327, they nonetheless established the Castilian royal claim that its kings were not to be knighted by another man but only by St. James, conflating and weaving together a series of sacral and courtly elements while leaving the Church fairly out of the picture. The special *ordo* that had been commissioned for the ceremony was set aside. It was replaced by the king's ad hoc decision to follow his own wishes as to what the coronation ceremony should be. The fact that, as the chronicler tells us, the archbishops and bishops withdrew to their seats while Alfonso XI crowned his wife and himself reveals a whole host of symbolic messages aimed at the dignitaries in attendance and, through the chronicle, to the people of Castile.

---

26 "Crónica Alfonso el Onceno," p. 263.

27 Ibid., p. 265.

The prelude and follow up to the victory at the Salado River marks the zenith of Alfonso XI's rule. He died 10 years afterwards of the plague, the only king to do so in western Europe, but never in those 10 years would he again reach such a pinnacle. The long descriptions of both the chronicle and the poem, their representations of the king's piety and courage, and the implied comparison with the victory at Las Navas de Tolosa reaffirmed connections between power, feats of arms, and legitimacy. In doing so, these symbolic (and actual deeds)—represented in the sources for Alfonso XI's reign in such dramatic fashion—strengthened Alfonso as king and aided future monarchs in the art of ruling.

Chapter 8

The Castilian Navy in the Reign of Alfonso XI

Nicolás Agrait

The images most associated with Alfonso XI (1312–50) have always been triumphant: a tough monarch who subdued the aristocracy and defeated the Muslims and was only deprived of more victories by his inopportune death of plague at Gibraltar in 1350.[1] One of Alfonso's principal methods in asserting his will was the use of force. The Castilian navy formed a fundamental component of his military complex, especially in the south where he struggled for control of the Strait of Gibraltar with the Nasrid emirate of Granada and the Marinids, a Muslim dynasty controlling swaths of North Africa as well as some fortified ports on the Iberian southern shores. In the Strait and elsewhere, the Castilian fleets not only protected shipping and coastal areas but also gathered intelligence on enemy movements, supplied and complemented land forces, and confronted enemy forces at sea. Yet the impact of the Castilian navy reached well beyond its immediate activities. Its development stimulated the growth of the Castilian state by forcing Alfonso to make existing taxation more efficient, find new revenue streams and institute new fiscal mechanisms to exploit them.

---

[1] Salvador de Moxó was the principal proponent of this view. See his "La sociedad política en la época de Alfonso XI" in Salvador de Moxó (ed.), *Estudios sobre la sociedad hispánica en la Edad Media* (Madrid: Concejo Superior de Investsigaciones Científicas, 1975), pp. 187–326. See further Salvador de Moxó, "Relaciones entre la corona y las órdenes militares en el reinado de Alfonso XI" in Manuel Espadas Burgos (ed.), *VII Centenario del infante d. Fernando de la Cerda: Jornadas de estudio, Ciudad Real, abril 1975* (Ciudad Real: Instituto de Estudios Manchegos, 1976), pp. 117–58, and, most importantly, the synthesis in Salvador de Moxó, "Época de Alfonso XI" in Juan Torrres Fontes et al. (eds), *La expansión peninsular y mediterránean (c.1212–c.1350)* (2 vols, Madrid: Espasa-Calpe, 1990), vol. 1, pp. 279–428. His line of thought is followed in general works such as Joseph F. O'Callaghan, *A History of Medieval Spain* (Ithaca, NY: Cornell University Press, 1975) and, more recently, in Jose Sánchez-Arcilla Bernal, *Alfonso XI: 1312–1350* (Palencia: Diputación Provincial de Palencia, 1995).

By the fourteenth century, the Castilian crown had to defend two shorelines, north and south, but the locus of naval activity was in the latter. The Castilian sources use the expression *guarda de la mar* (safeguard of the sea) or *guarda del Estrecho* (safeguard of the Strait) to refer to missions intended to impede supplies and forces from Morocco or Granada from reaching fortified locales such as Algeciras and, after 1333, Gibraltar. The presence of the fleets in the area also protected Christian mercantile shipping from piracy.[2] While most naval activity took place in the area between the ports of Tarifa, Tangier and Ceuta, Castilian fleets at times ventured as far east as Almería and beyond.[3]

Because of their constant presence, these ships formed part of the first line in Alfonso's intelligence-gathering apparatus in the Strait. The military buildups to the battle of Salado (1340) and the siege of Algeciras (1342–44) were undertaken because of ships' reports to the crown of increased activity in the Moroccan ports. During the Algeciran blockade itself, maritime intelligence regarding Muslim fleets became even more important as a contingent of the Castilian navy was devoted to observing activity in Ceuta and Tangier. Such surveillance led Admiral Egidio Boccanegra to inform Alfonso that the combined Granadan and Marinid fleet in the Strait numbered more than 80 galleys and *naos* (round ships).[4] Another common method of acquiring intelligence was by capturing enemy vessels. In some very lucky instances, ships carrying important messages were intercepted. In addition to letters, the vessels' crews provided, voluntarily or otherwise, whatever information they had.[5] Although getting meaningful intelligence using this method was in all likelihood difficult, any news, even if suspect, was welcome.

Another crucial service performed by the Castilian navies was the transport of troops and supplies.[6] As land routes remained dangerous due to Castile's instability in the first half of the fourteenth century, sea and river transit, despite its inherent dangers, could be more reliable. Supplies intended for a Castilian

---

2 Jean Gautier Dalché, "A propos d'une mission en France de Gil de Albornoz: Operations navales et dificultés financières lors du siège d'Algeciras," in Evelio Verdera y Tuells (ed.), *El Cardenal Albornoz y el colegio de España* (3 vols, Bolonia: Real Colegio de España, 1972–73), vol. 1, p. 255.

3 The conflict in the strait stretched back to the mid-thirteenth century. The best general treatment remains Miguel Angel Manzano Rodríguez, *La intervención de los Benimerines en la península ibérica* (Madrid: Concejo Superior de Investsigaciones Científicas, 1992).

4 "Crónica del rey don Alfonso el Onceno," in Cayetano Rosell (ed.), *Crónicas de los reyes de Castilla*, vol. 1, Biblioteca de autores españoles, vol. 66 (1875; reprint, Madrid: Ediciones Atlas, 1953), chap. 263, p. 338.

5 "Crónica Alfonso el Onceno," chaps 282, 300, 317, pp. 354, 356, 376.

6 Gautier-Dalché, pp. 258–9.

army on campaign near the Strait of Gibraltar arrived by two different routes. The first started in Seville, where grain and other supplies gathered from the vicinity were loaded and transported down the Guadalquivir River to the port of Sanlúcar on the Atlantic coast. From there a supply fleet continued to Puerto de Santa María, which also served as a depot for victuals and materials coming by sea from Vizcaya, Asturias and Galicia. The last link in this supply chain was the fortified port of Tarifa on the Strait of Gibraltar itself. The second route involved ships traveling in a westerly direction from Cartagena, Murcia, Aragon and Genoa, bypassing the hostile Granadan ports, and docking at Tarifa, Cádiz or other Castilian havens.[7]

During the siege of Algeciras, this port network became even more important. In addition to victuals, Castilian vessels transported the materials and experts necessary to assemble more than 20 siege engines such as trebuchets and catapults.[8] Finally, these galleys and round ships brought food and fresh water to the blockading ships and relieved them every few months. Even if we only considered its role in the logistical aspects of campaigns, it is clear that the navy formed an integral part of Alfonso's military operations.

Castilian fleets also assisted ground forces and often engaged in joint military operations.[9] For instance, during Alfonso's march through Portuguese territory in 1336, he had a navy shadow his host's progress. On one occasion when he found his army's route blocked by the Guadiana River, he ordered some of his galleys to travel upriver to form a bridge for his land forces.[10] Coordination between naval and ground forces continued during Alfonso's successful relief of Tarifa and victory over the Muslims in the battle of Salado and in the siege of Algeciras. In the former, the Castilian navy not only dispersed the Muslim blockade of Tarifa, but also prevented supplies from easily reaching the Moroccan armies.[11] During the Algeciran campaign, Alfonso situated his fleet as close as he could to his ground forces so they could easily assist each other.[12] In the summer of 1343, crossbowmen drawn from the Castilian naval contingent helped drive back a Muslim attempt to break through the siege lines. The following December,

---

7 Antonio Torremocha Silva, *Algeciras entre la Cristiandad y el Islam: Estudio sobre el cerco y la conquista de Algeciras por el rey Alfonso XI de Castilla, así como de la ciudad y sus términos hasta el final de la Edad Media* (Algeciras: Instituto de Estudios Campogibralteños, 1994), pp. 195–6.

8 "Crónica Alfonso el Onceno," chap. 277, pp. 350–51.

9 Gautier Dalché, p. 256.

10 "Crónica Alfonso el Onceno," chap. 183, p. 291.

11 Ibid., chap. 242, p. 318.

12 Ibid., chap. 270, p. 344; Torremocha Silva, p. 186.

the Castilian navy, acting in concert with Alfonso's ground forces, engaged and scattered a Granadan fleet as it headed toward Algeciras. By neutralizing the ability of the Granadan army and fleet to support each other, the Castilian navy helped the king garner a significant victory.[13]

The navy's most important role was pursuit of enemy ships. While most encounters between vessels outfitted for war during the Middle Ages consisted of small skirmishes,[14] Alfonso's reign witnessed several large naval clashes. One such battle occurred in 1337 when the navies of Castile and Portugal fought near Gibraleón. The Castilian fleet boarded and captured the Portuguese admiral's galley and caused the other enemy ships to retreat, though bad weather was also a factor. The considerable victory helped Alfonso assume a dominant position in his conflict with Portugal.[15] Castile's luck, however, changed three years later when a Marinid flotilla surprised the fleet while it was anchored off the beach at Getares, near Algeciras. The Castilian flagship was taken and the admiral and his standard captured. With only a fraction of the vessels able to escape, most of the navy ended up captured, wrecked or sunk. The defeat left Castile dangerously exposed in the Strait, forcing Alfonso to take drastic steps. To ensure a naval presence in the area, he quickly contracted ships from Genoa and Aragon and asked Portugal for aid.[16]

---

[13] "Crónica Alfonso el Onceno," chaps 310, 325–31, pp. 371–2, 381–5.

[14] Ian Friel, *The Good Ship: Ships, Shipbuilding and Technology in England 1200–1520* (London: British Museum Press, 1995), p. 187.

[15] "Crónica do rei Afonso IV"in Carlos de Silva Torouca (ed.), *Crónicas dos sete primeiros reis de Portugal* (3 vols, Lisbon: Academia Portuguesa da História, 1952–53), vol. 2, chaps 37–9, pp. 258–65; "Crónica Alfonso el Onceno," chap. 181, pp. 289–90.

[16] "Crónica Alfonso el Onceno," chaps 209, 212, 264, pp. 307–9, 338; Diego Catalán (ed.), *Gran crónica de Alfonso XI* (2 vols, Madrid: Editorial Gredos, 1977), vol. 2, chap. 281, pp. 316–18; "Crónica do rei Afonso IV," chap. 55, p. 314. See Pere IV of Aragon's instructions to Juan Escrivá, ambassador to Alfonso XI, and his letter to Alfonso XI sending ten galleys to the Strait in Próspero Bofarull y Mascaró (ed.), *Colección de documentos inéditos del Archivo General de la Corona de Aragón*, vol. 7 (Barcelona: D. José Eusebio Monfort, 1851), p. 102, no. 11 (1/8/1341), pp. 168–9, no. 46 (7/1/1343). See also Pere IV's letter to Juan Manuel in Andrés Giménez Soler, *Don Juan Manuel: Biografía y estudio crítico* (Zaragoza: La Académica de F. Martínez, 1932), p. 636, no. 561 (4/10/1340). See further Manuel López Fernández, "Del desastre de Getares a la victoria del Salado: La crítica situación en la zona del Estrecho en 1340," *Espacio, Tiempo y Forma*, 3rd ser., *Historia Medieval*, 20 (2007): pp. 145–8; Manuel López Fernández, "La actuación de las flotas de Castilla y Aragón durante el cerco meriní a Tarifa en el año 1340," *Aljaranda: Revista de Estudios Tarifeños*, 64 (2007): p. 4.

During the siege of Algeciras, the primary function of the navy was to blockade the city, but the large fleet also actively sought battle.[17] The Muslim ships, however, avoided direct engagements, denying the Christian fleet the opportunity to determine the outcome of the operation at sea.[18] In spite of the many problems faced by the navy at Algeciras—loss of ships during storms, the need for vessels to be relieved and repaired, the difficulty in preventing enemy ships from skirting the blockade at night—it reduced the flow of foodstuffs entering the city through its port to a trickle. Even so, success in closing off the city was not assured until January 1344 when an elaborate artificial barrier was arranged.[19] By March 1344, the immense naval effort bore fruit and Alfonso took possession of Algeciras after its negotiated capitulation.[20] While one must be careful not to belittle the land campaign, without the naval blockade the Castilian forces would have never taken the city.

The Castilian navy, in order to be effective, marshaled resources from both the north Atlantic and the Mediterranean. It was one of the few institutions that could integrate such disparate areas. In the north, Burgos acted as an administrative center overseeing the Cantabrian ports and served as a link to the commercial network of the rest of Castile.[21] The main royal shipyard was located in the port of Castro Urdiales in the Basque Vizcaya region.[22] Other Vizcayan towns enjoyed royal patronage that allowed them to solidify their position in the burgeoning northern European trade. They consolidated their interests by

---

17 Gautier Dalché, p. 255; Carlos Martínez Valverde, "La campaña de Algeciras y la conquista de esta plaza (1342–44)," *Revista de Historia Militar*, 25 (1981): pp. 24–6; Torremocha Silva, pp. 155–9, 182–4.

18 "Crónica Alfonso el Onceno," chaps 338–42, 370, 382, pp. 263–5, 370, 382.

19 The barrier was constructed out of weighted barrels chained to masts and lowered into the water. It incorporated the small Isla Verde as well as some ships for surveillance. "Crónica Alfonso el Onceno," chaps 285, 333–5, pp. 287, 386–8.

20 See Mateo Mercer's letter to Pere IV of Aragon announcing the capitulation of the city in Giménez Soler, p. 642, no. 572 (3/26/1344).

21 Lawrence V. Mott, "Iberian Naval Power, 1000–1650," in John B. Hattendorf and Richard W. Unger (eds), *War at Sea in the Middle Ages and Renaissance* (Rochester: Boydell & Brewer, 2002), p. 108. The main difference between the northern and Mediterranean maritime traditions was in ship construction. Northern shipyards in the fourteenth century used the clinker process, as opposed to the frame first construction used in the Mediterranean, because it produced sturdier ships more suitable for the difficult conditions in the northern seas. See Felipe Fernández Armesto, "Naval Warfare after the Viking Age," in Maurice Keen (ed.), *Medieval Warfare: A History* (Oxford: Oxford University Press, 1999), pp. 231, 234; N.A.M. Rodger, *The Safeguard of the Sea: A Naval History of Britain*, vol. 1, *600–1649* (New York: W.W. Norton & Company, 1998), p. 62.

22 Castro Urdiales is located on the Bay of Biscay northwest of Bilbao and San Sebastián.

lobbying the monarchy for privileges, mainly freedom from taxation on the transport of their cargoes.[23] The crown was generally happy to confirm their liberties so as to benefit from the growth of trade. While their autonomy limited royal authority, their naval power freed the crown from spending to protect the northern coast. More importantly, the Basque towns constantly provided naval support beyond Cantabria; their vessels were present in every significant Castilian naval operation during Alfonso's reign and beyond.[24]

Because of the pressing demands of the Strait of Gibraltar, Alfonso concentrated his naval resources almost exclusively in the south, especially after 1330. Seville, the principal port, boasted the massive *El Arenal* shipyard, built upon an existing Almohad foundation. A rectangular structure 182 meters long, it faced the Guadalquivir River and was divided into 17 naves of varying dimensions to accommodate ships during construction or repair.[25] With royal patronage since Alfonso X's (1252–84) reign, *El Arenal* was intended to produce a constant supply of armed ships.[26] Seville, the surrounding towns of Cádiz, Rota, Sanlúcar, Puerto de Santa María, Tarifa, and others, served as the loci of southern Castilian maritime and naval operations.[27] Cádiz and Tarifa were especially important because of their unimpeded access to the Strait.

The difficult task of gathering and administering Castilian naval resources fell upon the *almirante mayor* or high admiral. As the theoretically undisputed naval commander, it was the *almirante*'s duty to prepare a fleet when necessary. He presided over a naval hierarchy of *cómitres* (captains), *naucheres* (skippers) and others.[28] He gathered the ships, outfitted them, recruited crewmen, kept a

---

[23] See, for example, Pedro I's confirmation in 1351 of Alfonso XI's privileges to the Navarrese port of Fuenterrabía in 1329 in Luis Vicente Días Martín (ed.), *Colección documental de Pedro I de Castilla, 1350–1369* (4 vols, Salamanca: Junta de Castilla y León and Caja Duero, 1997–99), vol. 2, p. 91, no. 368 (10/15/1351).

[24] José Cervera Pery, *El poder naval en los reinos hispánicos* (Madrid: Editorial San Martín, 1992), pp. 129–30.

[25] Cesáreo Fernández Duro, *La marina de Castilla* (Madrid: El Progreso Editorial, 1894), p. 39; Florencio Pérez-Embid, "La marina real castellana en el siglo XIII," *Anuario de Estudios Medievales*, 6 (1969): p. 159.

[26] Joseph F. O'Callaghan, *The Learned King: The Reign of Alfonso X of Castile* (Philadelphia, PA: University of Pennsylvania Press, 1993), p. 39.

[27] Fernández Duro, pp. 42–3.

[28] See *partida* 2, *título* 24, *leyes* 3–6 in *Las siete partidas del rey don Alfonso el Sabio* (3 vols, Madrid: Real Academia de la Historia, 1801), vol. 2, pp. 259–63. The first evidence for the position of admiral is Fernando III's (1217–52) appointment of Ramón Bonifaz durirng the Sevilla campaign of 1248. However, there is no evidence of an official royal office until the Ruy López de Mendoza confirming as *Almirage de la mar* in a privilege of Alfonso X of 1254. *Memorial histórico español: colección de documentos, opúsculos y*

written record of the state of the royal fleet and, in most cases, personally led the navy. He was also responsible for the operation of the royal shipyards in Seville and Castro Urdiales, the shipwrights who worked them, and the town quarters where the shipyard workers lived. In times of peace, he secured the legal, efficient and safe operation of the kingdom's ports.[29]

In compensation for these duties, the high admiral enjoyed many privileges. He took a share of all booty from naval operations, received payment for the transport of goods in all ships under his personal authority and, especially in the fourteenth century, collected taxes such as the *almirantazgo* on merchandise transported through Castilian ports and the *ancoraje* levied on ships dropping anchor at Castilian docks.[30] Alfonso XI rewarded his high admirals, especially Juan Jofre Tenorio and Egidio Boccanegra, with grants of land and lordships.[31] Even though the post was much sought after by his aristocracy, Alfonso looked for naval expertise and competence when filling it and refused to rely strictly on privilege or even nationality. He further strengthened the office in his *Ordenamiento de Alcalá* (1348), which established a hierarchy of authority for Castile's manifold legal codes. As such, the naval and maritime sections in the *Siete Partidas,* including the duties and privileges of the *almirante mayor*, were given the force of law as long as they did not interfere with subsequent royal statutes.[32]

---

antigüedades (Madrid: Real Academia de la Historia, 1851), p. 21, no. 10. See further José Manuel Calderón Ortega, *El almirantazgo de Castilla: Historia de una institución conflictiva (1250–1560)* (Alcalá de Henares: Universidad de Alcalá, Servicio de Publicaciones, 2003), p. 168; Pérez-Embid, "El almirantazgo de Castilla hasta las capitulaciones de Santa Fe," *Anuario de Estudios Americanos* 1 (1944): p. 10, 86.

29 Calderón Ortega, p. 221.

30 Cervera Pery, pp. 219–25, 232.

31 In 1333, Alfonso XI granted Juan Jofre Tenorio the village of Moguer in Niebla in return for his services. Two years later he ordered the *alcaides* of Niebla, Almonte and Palos to safeguard the privileges of the lordship of Moguer that belonged to Alfonso Jofre Tenorio. In a series of privileges Alfonso granted Egidio Boccanegra the castle and village of Palma de Río in Córdoba, the *alcázar* of Manifle in Algeciras and two houses in the parish of Santa María, Seville. See Manuel García Fernández, "Regesto documental andaluz de Alfonso XI (1312–1350)," *Historia, Instituciones, Documentos,* 15 (1988), p. 51, no. 229 (10/3/1333), p. 58, no. 259 (5/1/1335), p. 81, no. 363 (7/22/1342), p. 87, no. 389 (5/25/1344), p. 88, no. 391 (5/2/1344).

32 Ignacio Jordán del Asso y Miguel de Manuel Rodríguez (ed.), *El ordenamiento de las leyes que don Alfonso XI hizo en las cortes de Alcalá de Henares* (Madrid: D. Joachim Ibarra, 1774), pp. 65–9, título 27, ley 3, cf. *Cortes de los antiguos reinos de León y de Castilla*, vol. 1 (Madrid: M. Rivadeneyra, 1861), pp. 595.

The *almirante mayor* relied on three methods for obtaining ships: requisition, construction and contraction from foreign sources. Requisition, also practiced by the English crown, was a galling procedure for merchants and ship owners, who had little or no guarantee of the return of their ships or compensation in the event of damage or destruction.[33] They also lost any profit that would have derived from their use. Though most of the documents regarding this practice are complaints or royal grants of exemption from it, the practice was widespread before and during Alfonso's reign.[34] Vessels also could be built at one of the royal shipyards at Castro Urdiales or Seville. Even so, Castile's resources proved insufficient for Alfonso's needs, especially after the aforementioned naval disaster of 1340. At this junction, he was forced to contract vessels from outside the realm.[35]

Irrespective of method, assembling a fleet was expensive. If a vessel came from the royal shipyards, there were substantial costs in material and labor. It had to be equipped with oars, sails and rope, weaponry, and supplies like fresh water, biscuit, oil and other foodstuffs.[36] Officials then had to recruit its crew: sailors to work its sails and navigational instruments, oarsmen to propel the ship, and a contingent of soldiers.[37] There were also the constant repairs needed to assure a vessel's seaworthiness, unforeseen emergencies, and the replacement of lost weaponry and equipment. As for foreign ships, Alfonso could expect not to pay for construction, but still had to provide payment and supplies.

---

[33] Timothy J. Runyan, "'Naval Logistics in the Late Middle Ages: The Example of the Hundred Years' War," in John Albert Lynn (ed.), *Feeding Mars: Logistics in Western Warfare* (Boulder, CO: Westview Press, 1993), pp. 79–80, 82–3, 89; Gillian Hutchinson, *Medieval Ships and Shipping* (London: Leicester University Press, 1997), p. 149; Michael Prestwich, *Armies and Warfare in the Middle Ages: The English Experience* (New Haven, CT: Yale University Press, 1996), pp. 269–70.

[34] See Fernando IV's charter to San Sebastián ordering that no more of its ships be requisitioned for the royal navy and Alfonso XI's subsequent confirmation in Gonzalo Martínez Díez et al. (eds), *Colección de documentos medievales de las villas guipuzcoanas (1200–1369)* (San Sebastián: Diputación Foral de Gipuzkoa, 1991), pp. 135–6, no. 134 (1318), pp. 246–7, no. 232 (5/23/1345). See also Pedro López de Ayala, "Crónica de don Pedro I" in José Luis Martín (ed.), *Crónicas* (Barcelona: Planeta, 1991), p. 199.

[35] See n. 16 above.

[36] See the *cuaderno* of Juan Matheo de Luna to King Sancho IV (1293–1294) in Mercedes Gaibrois de Ballesteros, "Tarifa y la política de Sancho IV de Castilla," *Boletín de la Real Academia de la Historia*, 77 (1920): p. 193.

[37] Gaibrois de Ballesteros, p. 215; Asunción López Dapena (ed.), *Cuentas y gastos (1292–1294) del rey d. Sancho IV el Bravo (1284–1295)* (Córdoba: Monte de Piedad y Caja de Ahorros de Córdoba, 1984), pp. 662–4.

The exact cost for Alfonso to maintain his navy is difficult to determine. Due to the lack of chancery accounts, historians must rely on references from chronicles and other documentation. All point to very high costs. For instance, the royal chronicle tells us that after Alfonso Jofre Tenorio's defeat in 1340, Alfonso hired 14 galleys from Genoa at a price of 800 florins (16,000 *morabetinos*) per month, plus the Genoese admiral's galley at 1,500 florins (30,000 *morabetinos*) a month. In addition, the admiral was to receive 1,500 florins for himself and the whole fleet was entitled to sufficient biscuit each month. The total cost of the fleet, then, not counting the price of biscuit, was 14,200 florins (284,000 *morabetinos*) per month.[38] The chronicler's account, however, may be exaggerated. A ledger drawn up in Aragon tabulating Alfonso's debts to Pedro IV (1336–87) from 1339 to 1344 contains one of the most detailed accounts of the Castilian king's naval efforts. The original agreement called for Aragon to provide galleys—20 during the years 1339–41 and then 10 during the Algeciran operation 1342–44—for Castile at the rate of 9,000 *morabetinos* a month per ship, almost half of the reported price of the Genoese galleys. While one must treat these figures skeptically, they tend to point to the conclusion that sustained operations by the Castilian navy were astronomically expensive.[39] In fact, the projected costs of the massive naval operation at Algeciras—over 100 ships—could have reached over 14 million *morabetinos* for one year and 22 million *morabetinos* over its entire 20 months. To put this in context, this expense could be one to two times Alfonso's royal annual budget, judging by the claim in 1316–17 that the crown's expenditures amounted to 9.6 million morabetinos.[40] Although Alfonso's administration had access to further resources and it passed some of the direct supply costs—food, fresh water, repairs—unto its subjects, this outlay must have strained the royal treasury to the breaking point.

Considering this heavy burden, Alfonso used several mechanisms to generate the necessary revenue. First, he relied on traditional rents like the *galera*, a tribute meant to provide outfitted ships whenever the monarch assembled a

---

38 "Crónica Alfonso el Onceno," chap. 212, p. 309. I use an exchange rate of 20 morabetinos to the florin as calculated by Peter Spufford, *Handbook of Medieval Exchange* (London: Royal Historical Society, 1986), p. 158.

39 The crowns of Castile and Aragon argued over who owed money to whom for the Algeciran operation (1342–44). In a letter dated August 30, 1349, Alfonso XI demanded that Pere IV reimburse him for Castile's support of the Aragonese contingent. Francisco de Moxó y Montoliú, "Cartas reales de Alfonso XI a Pere IV en el Archivo de la Corona de Aragón," *Anuario de Estudios Medievales*, 18 (1988): p. 287, no. 34 (8/30/1349).

40 "Crónica Alfonso el Onceno," chap. 10, pp. 180–81.

fleet.[41] Santander, for example, was required to arm a *nao* and a galley when the king went on campaign. Castro Urdiales similarly was obligated to produce a sailing ship or galley for three months' service after which the vessel passed to the king. While the ship was being built and used, the city would be exempt from all other taxes. Laredo in the Basque country, in lieu of other privileges, provided the crown with an armed galley outfitted with 60 oars, 60 armed men, 6 crossbows, a few dozen lances, and bolts. After three months service, the men could return home or continue in the royal fleet.[42] The *galera* appears to not have been widespread as references to its existence come almost entirely from the kingdom's northern regions. While Algeciras after 1344 was required to outfit two galleys whenever a royal fleet was assembled in Seville,[43] it is not clear that such obligations extended to the rest of the southern ports.

Since the *galera* and other traditional sources of income were never enough, the crown was forced to borrow heavily to sustain the navy, especially during complex military operations. In 1329, Alfonso repaid a loan of 20,000 *morabetinos* to the archbishop of Seville borrowed for the royal fleets.[44] In September 1342, with the siege of Algeciras barely off the ground, Alfonso dispatched diplomatic missions to secure loans from several foreign rulers. His delegation succeeded in the papal court where Clement VI agreed to lend him 20,000 florins in May 1343.[45] He also received a loan of 50,000 florins from Philip VI of France (1328–50). Alfonso devoted nearly all of it to pay his fleets, even arranging for the papal portion to be sent directly to his Genoese naval officers.[46]

As Alfonso's military expenditures increased he was plagued by serious budgetary deficits and forced to develop more creative methods of extracting

---

[41] Miguel Angel Ladero Quesada, *Fiscalidad y poder real en Castilla (1252–1369)* (Madrid: Editorial Complutense, 1993), p. 45.

[42] Gonzalo Martínez Díez (ed.), *Libro becerro de las behetrías* (León: Centro de Estudios e Investigación "San Isidro," 1981), vol. 2, pp. 180–81, no. 108, pp. 567–9, nos 328, 330.

[43] Pedro López de Ayala, "Crónica del rey don Enrique," in Martín, *Crónicas*, chap. 7, p. 441.

[44] See Alfonso XI's instructions to the executors of the *tercias reales*, *décimas* and crusading bulls granted by Pope John XXII in 1328 ordering them to allow the archbishop and cathedral chapter of Seville to collect 20,000 morabetinos as payment for the sums they had lent Alfonso in support of the Castilian fleet. García Fernández, "Regesto," p. 34, no. 146 (4/28/1329).

[45] Luciano Serrano, "Alfonso XI y el Papa Clemente VI durante el cerco de Algeciras," *Cuadernos de los Trabajos de la Escuela Española de Arqueología e Historia de Roma*, 3 (1912): pp. 27–31, no. 4 (5/14/143).

[46] "Crónica Alfonso el Onceno," chap. 303, pp. 367–8.

revenue from his subjects.[47] One way was to appeal to the papacy for access to Castilian ecclesiastical income.[48] Another was the appropriation of the income from local taxation. In 1338, Alfonso imposed new regulations upon the sale of salt in Burgos and diverted some of its income for the maintenance of ships in his service.[49] In other instances, he directed the revenue from *escribanías*, fees levied on local public notaries, toward naval expenses.[50] While overall sums collected cannot be quantified, they appear substantial since the royal treasury only reluctantly returned them to the respective urban councils. In 1340, for example, the council of Briviesca provided 160,000 *morabetinos* to the crown for the return of its *escribanía*, but access to its income remained out of reach until five years had passed.[51] Most significantly, Alfonso imposed extraordinary tributes upon his subjects like *servicios* and *alcabalas*. The former were implemented so many times during his reign that they became habitual.[52] The utility of these

---

[47] Hilda Grassotti, "Los apremios fiscales de Alfonso XI," in Manuel J. Peláez (ed.), *Historia económica y de las instituciones financieras en Europa* (Málaga: Universidad de Málaga, 1990), p. 3445. I discuss the funding of military expenditures more in depth in "Castilian Military Reform under the Reign of Alfonso XI (1312–50)," *Journal of Medieval Military History*, 3 (2005): pp. 88–126 and in "El asta de la lanza: Mecanismos de financiación de la guerra durante el reinado de Alfonso XI (1312–50)," *Gladius*, 32 (2012): pp. 103–20.

[48] Alfonso could access ecclesiastical income in several ways. First, he could ask the papacy to declare his operation a crusade and then collect money from the faithful in the process of preaching the crusade. Secondly, the king could seek the pope's permission to claim the *tercias reales*, that is a third of the church's tithe. Or, he could persuade the pope to allow him a tenth (*decima*) of the yearly income of the Church in his realm. See José Goñí Gaztambide, *Historia de la bula de la cruzada en España* (Vitoria: Publicaciones de Vitoria, 1958), p. 133; Ladero Quesada, pp. 191, 195–201, 203–7; Joseph F. O'Callaghan, *The Cortes of Castile-León, 1188–1350* (Philadelphia, PA: University of Pennsylvania Press, 1989), pp. 132–3.

[49] Esther González Crespo (ed.), *Colección documental de Alfonso XI: Sección del clero* (Madrid: Universidad Complutense,1985), p. 435, no. 257 (4/28/1338).

[50] O'Callaghan, *Cortes*, pp. 164–5.

[51] In 1351 Pedro I confirmed a grant of Alfonso XI done in May 1345 recognizing the right of the council of Briviesca to the income from its public notary. Días Martín, *Colección*, vol. 2, pp. 229–31, no. 488 (5/2/1345).

[52] *Servicios* (or *ayudas*) were extraordinary taxes approved by the Castilian *cortes* or regional *ayuntamientos*. *Servicios* at times took the form of a tax on movable property while in other instances appear to be a simple head tax. The *alcabala* was a sales tax collected in theory at 5 per cent, but during Alfonso's reign it was collected at 3.33 per cent. See O'Callaghan, *Cortes*, pp. 142–3; Ladero Quesada, pp. 180, 189. *Servicios* were collected 15 times during Alfonso's reign. The *alcabala* was collected kingdom-wide for the first time in 1342 and then renewed for the following six years. Agrait, "Castilian Military Reform," pp. 116–19.

taxes was twofold: a larger portion of the citizenry was subject to them and the royal treasury wielded more control over their collection.

Alfonso's ambitious development of his navy contributed to the development of a new and more efficient fiscal structure for the crown. It would be inaccurate to say that Alfonso was the first monarch to use the Castilian navy, but he was astute enough to recognize its potential in furthering both his military and political ambitions. By the time of his death in 1350, it was an important part of the kingdom's military machine. In the Mediterranean, fleets continued to transport troops and supplies, engage in joint operations with land armies and patrol the Strait of Gibraltar. In the northern seas, Vizcayan ships played a crucial role in Castile's developing commercial rivalry with England, culminating in their victory over English ships at the Battle of La Rochelle in 1372.[53] In the fifteenth century, Castile was among the first states to adopt the caravel and turn its attention to Atlantic exploration by journeying to and colonizing the Canary Islands.[54] Under Isabel and Fernando (1474–1516), the joint naval forces of Castile and Aragon helped conquer the Nasrid emirate of Granada and ultimately helped establish an empire in the Americas.[55]

53 Ricardo Cerezo Martínez, *La proyección marítima de España en la época de los Reyes Católicos* (Madrid: Instituto de Historia y Cultural Naval, 1991), pp. 82–3.

54 Felipe Fernández Armesto, *Before Columbus: Exploration and Colonization from the Mediterranean to the Atlantic, 1229–1492* (Philadelphia, PA: University of Pennsylvania Press, 1987), pp. 207–12; Eduardo Aznar Vallejo, "La colonización de las Islas Canarias en el siglo XV," *En la España Medieval*, 5 (1986): pp. 195–218.

55 John Lynch, *Spain 1516–1598: From Nation State to World Empire* (Cambridge: Wiley-Blackwell, 1991), pp. 116–22, 329–41.

Chapter 9

Shifting Alliances: The Unstable Bond between Castile and Aragon in the Late-Fourteenth Century

Donald J. Kagay

As a land born in war, the medieval Iberian Peninsula was composed of polities that fought each other because of religious differences and for territorial aggrandizement. Thus besides the struggles of Christian against Muslim that comprise the reconquest (*reconquista*), the medieval centuries also witnessed episodes of warfare between Spain's Christian states.[1] Wars between the Crown of Aragon and Castile-León, though sometimes sparked by dynastic rivalries, normally originated with disagreements over tracts of land conquered or to be conquered from the Muslim south.[2] Relations were exacerbated by the extremely porous borders that separated the territories taken from Islam.[3] These "regions

1 Francisco García Fitz, *Castilla y León frente al Islam: Estrategias de expansión y tácticas militares (siglos xi–xiii)* (Seville: Universidad de Sevilla, 1998); Donald J. Kagay, "Reconquest, Concept of," in Clifford J. Rogers (ed.), *The Oxford Encyclopedia of Medieval Warfare and Military Technology* (3 vols, Oxford: Oxford University Press, 2010), vol. 3, pp. 157–9; J.M Lacarra (ed.), *La reconquista española y la repoblación del pais* (Zaragoza: Instituto de Estudios Pirenaicos, Consejo Superior de Investigaciones Científicas, 1951); Derek W. Lomax, *The Reconquest of Spain* (London: Longman, 1978); Joseph F. O'Callaghan, *Reconquest and Crusade in Medieval Spain* (Philadelphia, PA: University of Pennsylvania Press, 2003); Joseph F. O'Callaghan, *The Gibraltar Crusade: Castile and the Battle for the Strait* (Philadelphia, PA: University of Pennsylvania Press, 2011).

2 Eloy Benito Ruano, "El problema sucessorio de la Corona de Castilla a la muerte de don Fernando de la Cerda," in Manuel Espadas Burgos (ed.), *VII centenario del infante don Fernando de la Cerda. Jornadas de estudio Ciudad Real, abril 1975* (Ciudad Real: Instituto de Estudios Manchegos, 1976), pp. 217–25; Donald J. Kagay, "The Dynastic Dimension of International Conflict in Fourteenth-Century Iberia," *Mediterranean Studies*, 17 (2008): pp. 78–9.

3 José Enrique López de Coca Castaner, "Institutions on the Castilian-Granadan Frontier 1369–1482," in Robert Bartlett and Angus MacKay (eds), *Medieval Frontier Societies* (Oxford: Clarendon Press, 1996), pp. 141–5; Manuel Rojas Gabriel, *La frontera*

of peril" were often dominated by marcher lords who played the neighboring Christian sovereigns off one another.[4]

To demonstrate the complex military and diplomatic mechanisms of intra-Christian warfare during the later Middle Ages, this chapter addresses the shifting personal and dynastic relationships that bound Castile to Aragon between 1356 and 1379. It will concentrate on the trio of determined, but flawed, rulers who directed the fates of the two realms. While the half-brothers Pedro I (1350–66/1367–69) and Enrique II (1366–67/1369–79) struggled for control of Castile, nearly ruining it in the process, Pere III (1336–87) of Aragon-Catalonia fought to protect the territorial integrity of his realms while simultaneously engaging in bold diplomacy designed to hamstring his Castilian enemies.[5] The result of these intertwined rivalries led Castile into a century marked by weak kings and over-mighty aristocrats while providing Aragon with a model for survival and advancement based more on diplomatic guile than military strength. To understand how diplomacy shaped the conduct of late-medieval, Iberian warfare and broad-based combat propelled diplomatic aims and methods, this chapter will focus on the 10-year border war between Castile and Aragon (the so-called War of the Two Pedros), the bitter Castilian civil war, and the final reluctant rapprochement between Pere III and Enrique II.

Combat and Diplomacy during the War of the Two Pedros (1356–1366)

War broke on the major states of the Iberian Peninsula in the fall of 1356 when an Aragonese privateer attacked two Piacensan vessels allied to both Genoa and Castile.[6] Enraged, Pedro I of Castile berated Pere III and encouraged his people

---

entre los reinos de Sevilla y Granada en el siglo XV (1390–1481): Un ensayo sobre la violencia y sus manifestaciones (Cadiz: Servicio de Publicaciones Universidad de Cadiz, 1995); Juan Torres Fontes, *Instituciones y sociedad en la frontera murciano-granadina* (Murcia: Real Academia Alfonso X el Sabio, 2001).

4 Robert I. Burns, "The Significance of the Frontier in the Middle Ages," in Bartlett and MacKay, pp. 322–3; Kagay, "The Dynastic Dimension," pp. 80–82.

5 Pere III of Aragon-Catalonia is also known by his Aragonese name and number, Pedro IV. See Thomas N. Bisson. *The Medieval Crown of Aragon: A Short History* (Oxford: Clarendon Press, 1986), pp. 191–2, 200–201.

6 For background of the conflict, see Pedro López de Ayala, *Corónica del rey don Pedro*, ed. Constance L. Wilkins and Heanon M. Wilkins (Madison, WI: Hispanic Seminary of Medieval Studies, 1985), p. 83; Pere III of Catalonia (Pedro IV of Aragon), *Chronicle*, trans. Mary Hillgarth, ed. J.N. Hillgarth (2 vols, Toronto, ON: Pontifical Institute of Mediaeval Studies, 1980), vol. 2, pp. 495–6; Jerónimo Zurita y Castro, *Anales de la Corona de Aragón*,

"to commit crimes and dangers in ... [Aragonese] lands." Claiming complete innocence, the Aragonese sovereign responded by declaring war on Castile.[7] For the next 10 years, the two rivals fought a bitter frontier and propaganda war. As the years passed, however, neither of the combatants could live without allies. Pedro had an easier task in this regard. The advisers of the young Nasrid king, Muhammad V of Granada (1354–59/1362–91), were happy to buy peace by supporting Castile's war effort. The Portuguese kings, Afonso IV (1325–57) and his son Pedro I (1357–67), were drawn into the war on Castile's side by the long-standing marital bonds between the two kingdoms.[8]

For his part, Pere quickly called on "the intimate benevolence and friendship" owed him by his Pyrenean vassal Gaston III "Phoebus" of Foix, whose control of the Pyrenean pass of Roncesvalles was of crucial importance.[9] Gaston, however, proved an unfaithful ally who betrayed his allegiance to Aragon, Castile, and England to maintain control over his Pyrenean lands. Aragon's greatest supporter, Enrique de Trastámara, was one whose service Pere had purchased. Enrique, the illegitimate son of Alfonso XI (1312–50), had served his half-brother, Pedro I, for some years before breaking with him and entering into the military employment of King Jean II of France (1350–64).[10] To reward his new captain, Pere settled on Enrique a large annual subsidy drawn from the revenues of several important Aragonese and Valencian border towns. This first grant was made in the fall of 1356 and was reissued with varying stipulations several times over the next six years.[11]

ed. Ángel López Canellas (9 vols, Zaragoza: Institución Fernando el Católico, Consejo Superior de Investigaciones Científicas, 1967–85), vol. 4, pp. 292–3; Maria Teresa Ferrer i Mallol, "Causes i antecedents de la guerra dels dos Peres," *Boletín de la sociedad Castellonense de cultura*, 63 (1987): pp. 445–67.

7 Arxiu de la Corona d'Aragó [ACA], Cancillería real, Registro [R.] 1148, fols 104v; R. 1379, fols 13v–15v; Ramon Gubern (ed.), *Epistolari de Pere III* (Barcelona: Editorial Barcino, 1955), pp. 123–7, no. 17; Pere III, *Chronicle*, vol. 2, pp. 500–503.

8 L.P. Harvey, *Islamic Spain 1250 to 1500* (Chicago, IL: University of Chicago Press, 1992), pp. 208–9; Hugh Kennedy, *Muslim Spain and Portugal: A Political History of al-Andalus* (London: Longman, 1996), pp. 288–9; A.H. De Oliveira Marques, *History of Portugal* (2 vols, New York: Columbia University Press, 1972), vol. 1, pp. 122–4.

9 ACA, Cancillería real, R. 1293, fols 43v–5. For Gaston's life, see Pierre Tucoo-Chala, *Gaston Fébus: Prince des Pyrénées (1331–1391)* (Pau: J&D éditions, 1991); Richard Vernier, *Lord of the Pyrenees: Gaston Fébus, Count of Foix (1331–1391)* (Woodbridge: Boydell, 2008).

10 ACA, Cancillería real, R. 1293, fols 43, 50.

11 ACA, Cancillería real, R. 1293, fols 84v–5v; Varia, R. 68, ff. 69–74; Ángeles Masiá de Ros, *Relación castellano-aragonesa desde Jaime II a Pedro el Ceremonioso* (2 vols, Barcelona: Consejo Superior de Investigaciones Científicas, 1994), vol. 2, pp. 444–51, no. 213/78bis.

The long border war between Castile and Aragon that faded away in 1366 was marked by military and diplomatic strategies that changed drastically during the course of the war. In the first eight years, Pedro I continually took the offensive and, as a result of several major invasions, won a great deal of Aragonese and Valencian territory.[12] He manipulated alliances with Granada and Portugal to expand his military and naval forces and so was not overly troubled by repeatedly violating peace accords with Aragon negotiated by the papacy. Pere III used diplomacy, most especially with the pope, in an effort to bring hostilities to an end, even if this cost him in territorial terms.[13] At the same time, he utilized a defensive military strategy to maintain, at least partially, his exposed frontiers. In the last two years of the war, however, the tables turned. The Aragonese ruler took the offensive on many occasions while his Castilian counterpart, now worried by the threat posed by Enrique de Trastámara and other Castilian aristocrats who had defected to the Aragonese side, increasingly assumed a defensive posture.[14]

Combat and Diplomacy during the Castilian Civil War (1366–1369)

After Enrique almost killed Pedro in a border skirmish in 1360, Pere was convinced that his principal captain was more valuable as a raider into Castile than as a garrison commander on the Aragonese frontier. From 1363, he

pp. 533–6, no. 233/162; Pere III, *Chronicle*, vol. 2, p. 510; Zurita, *Anales*, vol. 4, pp. 306–7. The sites that Trastámara was given control over were Tamarite de Litera, Ricla, and Epila in Aragon; Montblanch, Tarrega, and Vilagrasa in Catalonia; and Castellón and Villareal in Valencia. Rents were drawn from Jativa, Alcira, Murviedro, Morella, and Calatayud.

12 For Pedro's victories, see Antonio Gutiérrez de Velasco, "La conquesta de Tarazona en la guerra de los dos Pedro," *Cuadernos de historia Jeronimo Zurita*, 10–11 (1960): pp. 70–98; Antonio Gutiérrez de Velasco, "Las fortalezas aragonesas ante la gran ofensiva castellana en la guerra de los dos Pedros," *Cuadernos de historia Jeronimo Zurita*, 12–13 (1961): pp. 7–39; María Teresa Ferrer i Mallol, "The Southern Valencian Frontier during the War of the Two Pedros," in L.J. Andrew Villalon and Donald J. Kagay (eds), *The Hundred Years War: A Wider Focus* (Leiden: E.J. Brill, 2005), pp. 90–94.

13 For the peace treaties of Terrer (1361) and Murviedro (1363) arranged by the papal envoys, see Ferrer i Mallol, "Southern," pp. 106–7; María Teresa Ferrer i Mallol, *Entre La paz y la guerra: La corona catalano-aragonesa y Castilla en la baja edad media* (Barcelona: Consejo Superior de Investigaciones Científicas, 2005), pp. 396–9, 409–10.

14 Donald J. Kagay, "Battle-Seeking Commanders in the Later Middle Ages: Phases of Generalship in the War of the Two Pedros," in L.J. Andrew Villalon and Donald J. Kagay (eds), *The Hundred Years War (Part 3): Further Considerations* (Leiden: E.J. Brill, 2013), pp. 63–83.

bankrolled Enrique's plan for a major invasion of Castile.[15] This raid did not become a reality until 1366 when Enrique entered Castile with a force of 5,000 men and forced Pedro off the throne almost without a fight. The defeated king escaped to Aquitaine where he threw himself on the mercy of a heretofore lukewarm ally, Edward, the Black Prince of England (b. 1330–76).[16] After buying the support of Carlos II of Navarre (1349–87), Pedro was able to bring a multinational force across the Pyrenees in early spring of 1367, and sought out his hated rival, now crowned King Enrique II. On April 3, the armies of the two siblings confronted each other along the banks of the Najarilla River near the town of Nájera where Enrique's army eventually collapsed under a brutal frontal attack led by the Black Prince.[17]

Despite Pedro's victory, the seeds of his ultimate defeat were sown by Enrique's escape into France. Gaining support from the French monarch, Charles V (1364–80) and Duke Louis of Anjou, Enrique quickly assembled an army composed of Castilian survivors of the Battle of Nájera and French troops under the command of Constable Bertran de Guesclin. With these 3,000 troops, he re-entered his homeland in late 1367 passing through Andorra and northern Aragon.[18] After a year of small-scale operations in which he slowly reduced his half-brother's territory, Enrique personally killed Pedro on March 23, 1369 outside Montiel (southwest of Ciudad Real).[19] The conflict

[15] For Enrique's raid of 1360, see Kagay, "The Dynastic Dimension," p. 85. For Pere's agreement of support, see Ayala, pp. 141–2; Zurita, *Anales*, vol. 4, pp. 499–504; Pere, *Chronicle*, vol. 2, pp. 548–50.

[16] ACA, Cancillería real, R. 1214, fol. 78; Mildred K. Pope and Eleanor C. Lodge (eds), *Life of the Black Prince by the Herald of Sir John Chandos* (Oxford: Clarendon Press, 1910), p. 150; Ayala, pp. 156–7; Benjamin Frederick Taggie, "The Castillian Foreign Policy during the Reign of Pedro I, 1350–1369," Ph.D. diss., Michigan State University, 1972, pp. 282–3; P.E. Russell, *The English Intervention in Spain and Portugal in the Time of Edward III and Richard II* (Oxford: Clarendon Press, 1955), pp. 58–63. Joaquín Miret y Sans, "Négociations de Pierre IV d'Aragon avec la cour de France (1366–1367)," *Revue Hispanique*, 13 (1905): pp. 81–3, 85–7.

[17] Chandos Herald, p. 164; L.J. Andrew Villalon, "Spanish Involvement in the Hundred Years War and the Battle of Nájera," in Villalon and Kagay, *A Wider Focus*, p. 46.

[18] Ayala, pp. 167, 180–83; Clara Estow, *Pedro the Cruel of Castile* (Leiden: E.J. Brill, 1995), pp. 250–51.

[19] Ayala, pp. 196–8, Estow, pp. 258–9; L.J. Andrew Villalon, "Pedro the Cruel: Portrait of a Royal Failure," in Donald J. Kagay and Joseph T. Snow (eds), *Medieval Iberia: Essays on the History and Literature of Medieval Spain* (New York: Peter Lang, 1997), p. 201.

between Enrique's supporters, the *enriqueñistas*, and Pedro's adherents, the *petristas*, however, would continue for some two years.[20]

During the intense struggle between Enrique de Trastámara and Pedro I, Pere had stood as both a witness and a possible ally to each. Enrique had served the Aragonese king for over a decade, but with the successful invasion of 1366 their relationship drastically changed. When Enrique refused to turn over the towns and properties promised for Pere's material support, the Aragonese king attempted to reclaim the frontier towns and villages granted to Enrique in 1356. In addition, he tried to restrict free passage through Aragon and Catalonia to both sides.[21] Toward this end, he re-garrisoned some strongholds that had been left under-manned from the start of the Castilian civil war. To meet these new expenses, he ordered his minter (*moneder*) of Barcelona to produce secretly in the castle of Murviedro a debased counterfeit version of the "silver money that King Enrique makes." Pere apparently hoped to pay off some of his rising expenses in these debased coins but the scheme was, as far as we know, never put into operation.[22]

After the Battle of Nájera put Pedro back on the Castilian throne in 1367 and sent Enrique into exile, Pere, ever the realist, had no option but to deal with his old enemy. Thus a week after the battle he received Pedro's envoys at Zaragoza and quickly agreed to a year-long truce.[23] This instrument freed Pedro to wreak bloody vengeance on his perceived enemies inside Castile while forcing Pere to curtail pro-Enrique allegiances among his own people.[24] For his part, Enrique viewed Aragon's pact with his half-brother as the worst type of perfidy; he had, after all, militarily won back from Pedro over a hundred Aragonese and Valencian towns and fortresses and Pere, the beneficiary of this service, now refused to allow

20 Joseph F. O'Callaghan, *A History of Medieval Spain* (Ithaca, NY: Cornell University Press, 1975), pp. 524–6; Julio Valdeon Baruque, *Enrique II de Castilla: La guerra civil y la consolidación del regimen (1366–1371)* (Valladolid: Universidad de Valladolid, 1966), pp. 228–34.

21 Antonio Gutierrez de Velasco, "Molina en la corona de Aragón (1369–1375)," *Teruel*, 6 (1951): p. 77; ACA, Cancillería real, R. 1217, fol. 57; Miret y Sans, pp. 84–5.

22 ACA, Cancillería real, R. 1551, fol. 25v; Gutierrez de Velasco, "Molina," pp. 111–12; Miret y Sans, pp. 102–3.

23 Ayala, p. 182; Russell, p. 123; Taggie, p. 354.

24 Luis Vicente Díaz Martin, *Itinerario de Pedro I de Castilla: Estudio y regesta* (Valladolid: Universidad, Secretariado de Publicaciones, 1975), p. 433, no. 953, p. 434, no. 959, p. 437, no. 966. A group of Castilian nobles led by the former chancellor and chronicler, Pero Lopez de Ayala, escaped Pedro's wrath, but the master of Calatrava, Martin López de Córdoba, was not so fortunate. For Pere's attempts to prevent his subjects from acting for Enrique and against Pedro, see ACA, Cancillería real, R. 1387, fols 183v–4v.

him to bring his troops across any part of the Crown of Aragon.[25] These actions clouded the relationship between the two men for the next decade, a period during which Enrique repeatedly had to fight for his own survival against his own countrymen as well as foreign invaders while Pere conspired with England, Navarre, and Portugal to weaken and possibly dismember Castile.

The Foreign Encirclement of Castile after Nájera

While Pedro struggled with his half-brother for the Castilian throne, Pere of Aragon pursued two interconnected goals: the survival of his own realms and the systemic weakening of his Castilian enemies. As an experienced opportunist, he attempted to utilize every opportunity, no matter how unexpected, to attain these objectives. In the period after Pedro's victory at Nájera and the civil war that followed it, the Aragonese king began to see Castile less as a military threat and more a possibility for territorial aggrandizement. This view was not conceived by Pere alone but was brought about through negotiations with representatives of other European powers who stood to gain from the struggle between the royal siblings. Pere, however, stood as the senior member in a group of conspirators attempting to fashion a final solution for a severely weakened Castile.[26]

Pere's relationship with this coterie of ambitious leaders was complicated by their political connections to the two contenders for Castile's throne. His aims, however, were generally consistent: the capture of Castilian territory promised him by Enrique de Trastámara before the 1366 invasion of his homeland and then the encouragement of Castile's political weaknesses. To accomplish these goals, he turned from Enrique and toward Pedro's English handlers. After the truce talks in May, 1367, Pere began to view an English alliance in a favorable light. Though initially rebuffed by John of Gaunt, duke of Lancaster, he worked behind the scenes and eventually began to see the possibility of an alliance.[27] In early June, Pere sent ambassadors to a site near Calatayud while Pedro set up his delegation of Castilian and English representatives near Ariza.[28] Despite

---

25 Ayala, pp. 181–2; Miret y Sans, p. 127; Russell, pp. 119–20, 129.

26 Miret y Sans, p. 121, n. 2. These leaders included the Edward, the Black Prince, his younger brother, John of Gaunt, duke of Lancaster (b. 1340–99), Charles V of France, Carlos II of Navarre, Pedro I of Portugal and his son Fernão I (1367–83).

27 Zurita, *Anales*, vol. 4, p. 562. The two Aragonese ambassadors were Ramón de Peguera and Jaime de Ezfar.

28 Zurita, *Anales*, vol. 4, p. 562; ACA, Cancillería real, R. 1217, f. 193; Miret y Sans, p. 116; Russell, p. 124. The Aragonese delegation consisted of Bishop Romeo of Lerida,

widespread rumors that the English army "had entered the hamlets of Calatayud and inflicted great damage," Pere supported negotiations that continued at Tarazona in August.[29] Accomplishing a truce with Castile, Pere's ambassadors worked for "peace and friendship between Pere and Edward (the Black Prince)."[30] This would come into effect only when Aragonese protection of Enrique ended and Pedro made good on territorial promises and unpaid military salaries to the English crown prince. To bring stability to this fluid situation, Edward suggested that Pedro marry again to produce a legitimate male heir and offered to serve as a regent for any offspring from such a union.[31] As a result of the secret talks within the conference, a coalition hostile to both Castilian contenders now emerged. Edward, Pere and the sovereigns of Navarre and Portugal seemed ready to overthrow a balance of power that had been in place within Castile for decades, but was now sorely tested by the civil war.

As civil war spread across Castile in late 1367, Pere and Edward remained committed to the accords of Tarazona, commencing negotiations again in October, 1367 at the French city of Tarbes. Though Pedro's ambassadors were present, they had little effect on the talks that first focused on a betrothal between Pedro's daughter, Constanza, and Pere's first-born, Joan. The Aragonese, English, and Navarrese envoys then conducted secret talks to determine Castile's ultimate fate, ordering the warring half-brothers to submit to their arbitration. If they did not agree to do so, the envoys established a contingency plan for the "conquest [and division] of the lands and kingdoms of Castile."[32]

English and Aragonese representatives continued the discussion of this fantastic plan in December, 1367 at Bordeaux.[33] To formalize these accords, they submitted them to Edward III of England (1327–77) for his approval,

---

Count Pere I of Urgel, Viscount Hug Folç of Cardona and Juan Fernández de Heredía, Castellan of Amposta and Prior of San Gil.

29 ACA, Cancillería real, R. 1221, fol. 17v; Antonio Gutiérrez de Velasco, "Los Ingleses en España (siglo xiv)," *Estudios de Edad Media de la corona de Aragón*, 4 (1951): pp. 250, 253–4.

30 Zurita, *Anales*, vol. 4, p. 563.

31 Taggie, p. 349. Pedro had married his first wife, the French princess Blanche de Bourbon, in 1353 and, after quickly deserting his new bride for his mistress María de Padilla, kept her incarcerated until her death in 1361. Though Pedro apparently consummated the union, no children were born to the couple.

32 Luis Suárez Fernández, "Política internacional de Enrique II," *Hispania*, 16 (1956): pp. 18–20; Russell, pp. 134–7; Taggie, 364–5, 367; Zurita, *Anales*, vol. 4, pp. 572–4.

33 Zurita, *Anales*, vol. 4, p. 576; Russell, p. 137; Gutiérrez de Velasco, "Ingleses en España," pp. 263–4.

but the English king showed little of his son's enthusiasm for Iberian affairs.[34] In the next year, however, he was called to answer for his son's sworn agreements when Pedro's ambassador presented the English king a number of "petitions and requests." Pedro, it seems, was worried about what the Black Prince and Pere were up to. His envoy called for Edward's approval of all the agreements the Black Prince had made with the current Castilian sovereign. Edward assured Pedro's minion that this relationship remained solidly in force but refused to commit to marriage negotiations. When Pedro's envoy asked for money to continue his war on Enrique, Edward responded that he had already sent his sons into Iberia "for the recovery of [Pedro's] realms and lands" and they were yet to be paid for their service.[35]

Even after Pedro's bloody demise at Montiel, the Castilian civil war raged on and English-Aragonese plans for the partition of the central Iberian realm continued. Under the cover of marriage negotiations between Aragon and England in September 1369, envoys of the two powers considered proposals for a final Castilian settlement.[36] Pere, clearly shaken by the great influx of French and English mercenaries across the Pyrenees, insisted that the Black Prince agree to a "good confederation and love" with the Aragonese ruler. The formal alliance that tied Pere, Prince Edward, and Carlos II of Navarre forbade them or their subjects from attacking each other's territories "by land or sea." This alliance of convenience clearly attempted to weaken Castile by allowing none of the signatories to make agreements with Enrique without the consent of the others. In reality, the triumvirate planned to eliminate Enrique, divide between themselves much of Castile, and force the remaining population to accede to the rule of Pedro I of Portugal. The new Iberian suzerains established by the agreement would be responsible for the conquest and the defense of the land assigned them but could call on each other for help in carrying out these lofty goals. Once the final victory against Enrique had been attained, the new masters of Spain could claim "right of conquest" or arrange for a "friendly concord" with the Castilian nobility. Yet the troop levels assigned to each of the

---

34 ACA, Cancillería real, R. 1082, fol. 12; Russell, p. 137; Gutiérrez de Velasco, "Ingleses en España," pp. 264–5. The Aragonese envoys were Francesç de Santclement and Bertran de Vall.

35 Gutiérrez de Velasco, "Ingleses en España," pp. 268–70; Taggie, pp. 379–82. The Castilian envoy was Juan Gutiérrez.

36 ACA, Cancillería real, R. 1293, fol. 205v; Michael Prestwich, *The Three Edwards: War and State in England 1272–1377* (London: Routledge, 1996), p. 282. This marriage, which did not take place, was to link the Aragonese princess, Joanna, and the English prince, Edmund of Langley, Earl of Cambridge.

confederates—between 1,000 and 1,500 men-at-arms and archers—reveal how unrealistic the entire project was.[37] The marriage alliances designed to underpin the confederation proved as chimerical as the political agreements themselves since none of them was ever carried out. The only union of any importance for English–Iberian relations was that of John of Gaunt to the Pedro I's orphaned daughter, Constanza, in 1371.[38] Supposedly acting for his bride, Gaunt assumed the Castilian royal title and spent much of the next decade-and-a-half trying to make good his claim.[39]

Enrique II and the Diplomacy of Survival

As Castilian affairs took their first step toward resolution in 1369 with Pedro's death and Enrique's survival as Castile's only king, Pere continued to spin complex webs of diplomacy in hopes of profiting from his weakened rival who still had strong domestic enemies. While surrounding Castile through several treaties with foreign partners, the Aragonese king proved unwilling to engage in open warfare even when frontier violence intensified in the district around Molina.[40] Instead, he turned to negotiations with Enrique as the best way of

---

37 ACA, Cancillería real, R. 1293, fols 206–11; Gutiérrez de Velasco, "Ingleses en España," pp. 266–7, 270–75. Pere was to get Murcia, Alicante, Velez, Riquea, Moya, Conca, Huepre, Corita de las Canes, Valldolinas, Saliners, Pareja, Alcocer, Penyalver, Penyalen, Fita, Guadalfarara, Brihuega, Les Penyes de Viana, Tihuencas, Siguença, Molina, Medinaceli, Atiença, Barlanga, Santestrena, Gormaç, Ahylon, Cararena, Madervolo, Aranda de Duero, Osma, Almanzan. Benamaça, Moros, Seron, Montagut, Deça, Cihuels, Gomera, Alcacer, Soria, Cabreras, Sant Leonard, Agreda, Cervera, and Cernago. This grant included the "castles, villages, and hamlets" connected to the larger settlements.

38 Sydney Armitage-Smith, *John of Gaunt: King of Castile and León, Duke of Aquitaine and Lancaster, Earl of Derby, Lincoln, and Leicester, Seneschal of England* (London: Constable and Co., 1904), pp. 92–3; Anthony Goodman, *The Exercise of Princely Power in Fourteenth-Century Europe* (New York: St. Martin's Press, 1992), pp. 48–51; Jennifer Goodman Wolloch, "Medieval England and Iberia: A Chivalric Relationship," in María Bullón Fernández (ed.), *England and Iberia in the Middle Ages, 12th to 15th Centuries: Cultural, Literary, and Political Exchanges* (New York: Palgrave, 2007), p. 19.

39 Anthony Goodman, "England and Iberia in the Middle Ages," in Michael Jones and Malcolm Vale (eds), *England and Her Neighbours, 1066–1453* (London: The Hambledon Press, 1986), pp. 86–7; Anthony Goodman, "Before the Armada: Iberia and England in the Middle Ages," in Nigel Saul (ed.), *England in Europe 1066–1453* (London: Collins & Brown, 1994), pp. 114–15; Anthony Goodman, *John of Gaunt*, pp. 111–43; Armitage-Smith, *John of Gaunt*, pp. 260–74, 301–11.

40 Suárez Fernández, pp. 19–20.

regaining the Castilian territory owed him. To reaffirm their earlier relationship, Pere, on January 24, 1369, assured his fellow monarch that he still had great concern "for ... [his] honor and advantage."[41]

Pere thought the time auspicious to reopen formal diplomatic relations with Enrique.[42] The negotiations conducted for Aragon by the cagey military and diplomatic veteran Archbishop Lope of Zaragoza were hardly designed to implement equity between the parties but instead sought to reestablish the former Aragonese–Castilian relationship in a way that rendered Pere's position greater than that of Enrique's. To personalize their mutual trust, a marriage was proposed between their oldest children. Once these diplomatic niceties were attended to, Pere was prepared to swear that he "would not wage war nor consider waging it" against the Castilian king. This vision of a blissful future depended, of course, on Enrique's willingness to comply with earlier treaties and surrender to Aragonese control the Castilian towns Molina, Soria, and Almazan. Despite the possibility of further dispute, the Aragonese envoys assured their Castilian counterparts that Aragon's sovereign "would honor all agreements ... [with Enrique] in such a way that God and man ... will have proof."[43] This pledge of good faith seemed to portend better diplomatic relations between the two realms. After months of negotiation, Enrique triumphantly announced on December 17, 1369 a truce with Aragon until the upcoming feast of Pentecost.[44] Despite this apparent end to their era of bad feelings, Pere still openly demonstrated his fear of Castilian attack. Warning his officials that "many [of Enrique's] ... men-at-arms from Castile and France are threatening to enter into our realms,"[45] Pere sought to surround his new ally with the members

[41] ACA, Cancillería real, R. 1293, fols 167r–v.

[42] Masiá de Ros, vol. 1, pp. 331–2.

[43] ACA, Cancillería real, R. 1293, fols 212–13v. The marriage was supposed to tie Enrique's daughter Eleanor to Pere's first-born son, Joan, Duke of Gerona, but it did not take place. For political aspects of marriage negotiations in the later Middle Ages, see Georges Duby, *The Knight, the Lady, and the Priest: The Making of Modern Marriage in Medieval France*, trans. Barbara Bray (New York: Pantheon Books, 1983), pp. 189–209; Anthony Molho, *Marriage Alliances in Late-Medieval Florence* (Cambridge, MA: Harvard University Press, 1994); Rafael Olivar Bertrand, *Bodas reales de Aragón con Castilla, Navarra y Portugal: Relación cortesana de los enlaces matrimoniales que en el siglo XIV cimentan los pilares de unidad nacional* (Barcelona: Editorial Alberto Martín, 1949); Rafael Olivar Bertrand, *Bodas reales entre Francia y la corona de Aragón y Cataluña con respecto a Francia nacional* (Barcelona: Editorial Alberto Martín, 1949); S.J. Payling, "The Economics of Marriage in Late Medieval England: The Marriage of Heiresses," *The Economic History Review*, 54 (2001): 413–29.

[44] Masiá de Ros, vol. 1, p. 332.

[45] ACA, Cancillería real, R. 1228, fol. 66; R. 1230, fols 6v, 21v–2; Valdeon Baruque, pp. 260–63.

of the old conspiracy, thereby severely weakening his position and forcing him to turn over the Castilian territory promised since 1366.[46]

Enrique was well aware of Pere's interlocking agreements with England, Granada, Navarre, and Portugal and offset them with a skillful combination of military bluff and diplomatic openness. As a result, the Castilian king repeatedly blocked his rival's plans. In 1370 and 1371, having made an alliance with France, he used threat and accommodation to pull the new Portuguese king, Fernão (1367–83), out of Pere's orbit and into his own.[47] He did much the same thing with Carlos II of Navarre in October 1371 when he bound their families in a marriage alliance that ultimately restored to Castile lands taken by Navarre in the past decade.[48] He had already cleared the field for these diplomatic victories by concluding an eight-year truce with Muhammad V of Granada in the spring of 1372.[49]

Faced with Enrique's skill as a diplomat, Pere had no choice but to repeat his desire for peace, using the apostolic legates named by Pope Gregory XI (1370–78) to further this end. The Aragonese king appointed a distinguished delegation that conferred throughout 1371 with a Castilian embassy.[50] After a summer of high-level talks, peace was declared between Aragon and Castile at Toro on September 12 and then again at Tortosa on October 13. The treaty was formally confirmed by both sides on December 8 in the Catalan city of Tortosa and in the Valencian town of Castelhabib.

Besides the formal cessation of hostilities, the new agreement attempted first to pacify the Castilian-Aragonese frontiers by outlawing all "raids, reprisals, and damages" conducted or allowed by either of the signatories. The unsafe nature of their borderlands was addressed by the signatories who guaranteed the safety of their merchants as well as the merchandise they transported. To make amends for confiscated goods or incarcerated traders, the principal architects of the pact were appointed as commissioners who would use funds from tolls or "arbitrary exactions" (*questiae*) to pay off claims of merchants from either side of the border who had suffered losses during

46 Valdeon Baruque, pp. 250–51; Masiá de Ros, vol. 1, p. 333.

47 Masiá de Ros, vol. 1, p. 388; Suárez Fernández, pp. 38–43, 62–4 no. 3; Valdeon Baruque, pp. 260–63.

48 Valdeon Baruque, p. 266; O'Callaghan, *History*, 527; Suárez Fernández, pp. 32–3, 64–77, no. 4, pp. 117–18, no. 12.

49 Suárez Fernández, pp. 61–2, no. 2; O'Callaghan, *History*, p. 525.

50 Masiá de Ros, vol. 1, pp. 335–6; Valdeon Baruque, p. 267; Russell, pp. 162–3. The Aragonese delegates were the bishop of Lerida and Ramón Almany de Cervelló; the Castilian envoys were the bishop of Burgos and the royal chamberlain, Alvar García de Albornoz.

the war. To close the many gaps in borders from either direction, the treaty proposed the immediate confiscation of contraband of all types. This order included counterfeit "money of gold or silver," much of which Pere had been guilty of putting into circulation over the past decade.[51]

The Nagging Details of a Final Peace

Even after Pere received the new agreement from the hands of the papal legate at Alcañiz on January 4, 1372 and acted to "confirm, ratify, and strengthen" the pact, "questions, claims, and debates" remained to be settled.[52] Appointing new procurators on April 16, the Aragonese king told his Castilian counterpart and the legate that he was willing to see all these outstanding matters settled.[53] After another year of intermittent negotiations, the two monarchs announced a truce at Burgos and Barcelona in September 1373, to remain in effect until the feast of Pentecost the following spring. The rulers would observe this agreement "with good faith and without deceit," not allowing any damage to be inflicted on the other's territory. An accused counterfeiter, Pere swore that he would not allow the striking of money "on which the name or insignia of the lord king of Castile was imposed." The new agreements were again witnessed and sworn to by the royal agents responsible for the negotiations.[54]

The differences between Aragon and Castile had proven so intractable that even given two major treaties after Montiel, Pere and Enrique demonstrated very little trust of each other in the years that followed. On December 21, 1373 (less than a year after their second proclamation of mutual friendship), Pere received alarming news. Through his spy network, the Aragonese king heard that Enrique was considering renouncing the throne in favor of his first-born, Juan. To Pere, the reason for such a move was obvious. It allowed the Castilian monarchy to wriggle out of the recent peace initiatives and be free to launch

---

[51] ACA, Cancillería real, R. 1543, fol. 81v; Masiá de Ros, vol. 2, pp. 576–7 no. 251/15.

[52] ACA, Cancillería real, R. 1543, fol. 91. Masiá de Ros, vol. 1, pp. 336–7; vol. 2, pp. 583–4, no. 253/18. The apostolic legate in this case is referred to as "Cardinal Bertrand."

[53] ACA, Cancillería real, R. 1543, fols 95v–6; Masiá de Ros, vol. 1, pp. 337; vol. 2, pp. 584–5, no. 254/19. The new Aragonese envoys were Pere's "beloved counselors," Francisco Roma, "knight, doctor of laws, and vice-chancellor," and Bernat Olives, Archdeacon of Lerida.

[54] ACA, Cancillería real, R. 1543, fols 114v–22; Masiá de Ros, vol. 1, p. 340; vol. 2, pp. 585–90, no. 255/28; Suárez Fernández, pp. 31–2.

yet another surprise attack on Pere's exposed frontiers.[55] None of this fanciful Aragonese "intelligence," however, proved accurate. In reality, Enrique, still surrounded by enemies, could no longer afford the luxury of international warfare. After solidifying his ties to Navarre and Portugal through marriage alliances, he confirmed the truce with Aragon on January 11, 1374.[56]

Despite Enrique's bold move toward peace, Pere's fear of surprise attacks was often borne out by lingering instability along the Aragonese and Valencian frontiers. In November 1373, the Aragonese king wrote to his Castilian counterpart that a large number of armed men—surely mercenaries—had crossed out of Castile into Aragon. The raiders, led by a captain nicknamed Rechon, still held "a number of castles and villages ... by fierce and traitorous means."[57] This clearly violated the peace accords and Aragonese raiding parties eventually crossed the Castilian border in retaliation. Pere's concern seemed to have some effect on the Castilian ruler who agreed to a 30-day truce during the spring of 1375. During this period, however, Pere was forced to write to the Castilian crown prince, Juan, and impatiently point out that two of his Valencian merchants had been captured in Murcia by the count of Carrión, one of Enrique's captains in the region. Since this had occurred during the truce, Pere angrily requested the crown prince to free the traders with "their shipments and other goods."[58] Even though the Castilian and Aragonese rulers had twice proclaimed peace between themselves, direct diplomatic efforts were apparently still necessary to maintain it.

In the midst of truces and complaints concerning their violation, Pere and Enrique turned again to finding a viable peace that would eventually make amends for the "great damages, evils, discords, and wars" they had for so many years unleashed on each other and their lands.[59] This drive for a final settlement was almost derailed in the first months of 1375. The two kings seemed unable to put aside personal disputes and renewed war on the southern frontier seemed

55 ACA, Cancillería real, R. 1543, fol. 122; Masiá de Ros, vol. 1, p. 341; vol. 2, pp. 595–6, no. 257/32.

56 ACA, Cancillería real, R. 1543, fols 123r–v; Masiá de Ros, vol. 1, pp. 340–41; vol. 2, pp. 594–5; Suárez Fernández, pp. 77–81, no. 5. Enrique betrothed his daughter Leonora to the Navarrese crown prince, Carlos, as part of the treaty with Navarre. In connection with the accord with Portugal, the Castilian king married his sons Fadrique and Alfonso to the Portuguese princesses Isabel and Beatriz.

57 ACA, Cancillería real, R. 1543, fol. 125v; Masiá de Ros, vol. 2, pp. 596–7, no. 258/35.

58 ACA, Cancillería real, R. 1543, fol. 148v; Masiá de Ros, vol. 2, pp. 605–6, no. 260/37.

59 ACA, Cancillería real, R. 1543, fols 157–66.

a real possibility. Pere was certain that Enrique had "arrogantly" rejected the peace and was planning to fall back on the tested Castilian strategy of attacking Murcia and southern Valencia. But the Aragonese king hedged his bet once again in the late spring and received Enrique's ambassadors.[60] With war looming through the first months of 1375, Castilian and Aragonese negotiators produced yet another "perpetual peace and concord" between Enrique, his son Juan, and Pere and his son Joan, as well as all future Aragonese and Castilian rulers. This new statement of friendship would allow nobles of the two states to serve in the armies of either king and would see to the final settlement of all "suits, pleas, claims, grants, oaths, and obligations of whatever manner or condition" between Pere, Enrique, and their people. Because of the general nature of the treaty with Castile, Pere had to explain away his other pacts with England, France, Navarre, and Portugal, all of which were openly or covertly inimical to Castile. He eventually attempted to do so by saying that each was designed to establish peace, "a thing that will be pleasing to God." He also stated that these accords would promote "public faith and ... the public good."[61]

The general treaty, confirmed in the monastery of San Francisco at Almazan on April 12, 1375 and in the royal palace at Soria on June 20, was fulfilled in personal terms with the betrothal of Pere's 17-year-old daughter, Leonore, to Enrique's 15-year-old son, Juan. The terms of their nuptial agreement were generous to both sides. Leonore, characterized by her father as "a most beautiful creature," brought a dowry of 200,000 florins and received as a gift from the groom's family full control of the Castilian towns of Almazan and Atienza, sites that Enrique had granted Pere in 1366 in exchange for his support of the invasion of Castile.[62]

---

60 ACA, Cancillería real, R. 1543, fol. 125v; Ferrer i Mallol. *Entre*, pp. 494–6; Masiá de Ros, vol. 2, pp. 596–7, no. 256/35. The Castilian envoys were Bishop Alfonso of Salamanca and the knight Juan Ramírez de Arellano. They were received by the sub-chamberlain Simon de Empuries.

61 Suárez Fernández, pp. 50–53. The Aragonese envoys were Ramón Almany de Cervelló, Dalmacio de Muro and Ramón de Cervera, doctors of law. The Castilian envoys were Bishop Gutierre of Palencia and Bishop Martin of Plascencia.

62 E.L. Miron, *The Queens of Aragon: Their Lives and Times* (London: Stanley Paul and Company, 1913), p. 191. ACA, Cancillería real. R. 1543, fols 171–7; Pere III, *Chronicle*, vol. 2, pp. 578–83, 587–91. The marriage was first agreed to in 1366 at Burgos immediately after Enrique was crowned Castilian king. Pere had delayed the betrothal because of Enrique's failure to turn over the territories he had promised his prospective father-in-law before his first invasion of Castile. Juan had apparently fallen in love with Leonore during his stay at the Aragonese court in the first year of the Castilian civil war. When Enrique again insisted that

At the heart of this new era of amity between Aragon and Castile was Pere's drive to realize the many territorial promises Enrique had made to him from 1363 onward. To clarify this extremely complex history of Castilian promises made but never kept, the father of the new bride, in March 1378, had a long list of Enrique's grants to him from the past 15 years drawn up. Whether this was a prelude to litigation concerning the undelivered land or not, it showed clearly that the Castilian king had pledged more to his intermittent Aragonese ally over the years than he had "given to the city of Seville."[63] Despite repeated promises, Enrique proved unwilling or unable to make good his word even after 1366 when he had the power to do so. Instead, as in the 1375 accord, he began to promise the payment of revenues that would eventually compensate Pere for the loss of the territory.[64] Unfortunately, this monetary compensation would also fail to materialize.

The land that stood at the core of their relationship was the strategically placed fortress/town of Molina due south of Calatayud. With the death of Pedro in 1369, Enrique had rewarded his French captain Bertran Du Guesclin with the site and several other neighboring towns.[65] Angered at the prospect of formerly Aragonese lands being subjected to the rule of a foreigner, Molina's ruling council voted to surrender their town to Pere's control. Putting Molina under the command of a local captain, Diego García de Vera, the Aragonese king spent the next several years attempting to safeguard the outpost from Castilian or French attack.[66] By 1375, the Aragonese king removed García de Vera from power and, looking to escape from the responsibility of the expensive Castilian enclave, deeded Molina back to Enrique after guaranteeing the personal safety and fortunes of the town residents who preferred to cross the border to make a new life in Aragon. The foreign stumbling block to these settlements, Du Guesclin, was removed in the early 1370s when the French constable sold his rights to Molina back to Enrique and those in Valencia back to Pere.[67]

The pressure that had brought Pere to the bargaining table in 1375 moved him in succeeding years to attempt a final solution concerning Aragonese and

---

the nuptials take place in 1375, Pere resisted but, "weighed down by evils and troubles and toils," finally gave in.

63 ACA, Cancillería real, R. 1543, fol. 178v; Masiá de Ros, vol. 1, pp. 342–3.

64 ACA, Cancillería real, R. 1543, fols 158r–v.

65 Richard Vernier, *The Flower of Chivalry: Bertrand Du Guesclin and the Hundred Years War* (Woodbridge: D.S. Brewer, 2003), pp. 145–6, 154.

66 Gutiérrez de Velasco, "Molina," pp. 82–3, 88–90, 94–5, 115; ACA, Cancillería real, R. 1551, fols 73v–4.

67 ACA, Cancillería real, fols 138r–v, 142v–4; Gutiérrez de Velasco, "Molina," pp. 98, 122–5; Vernier, *Flower*, p. 154; O'Callaghan, *History*, p. 525.

Castilian merchants and their freedom of movement within the two states. Addressing this issue on April 30, 1378, Pere re-stated the general principles of Aragonese-Castilian trade laid out by the treaty of 1375. He declared that Aragonese and Valencian merchants should be safe while trading in Castile as would Castilians doing business in the Crown of Aragon. He also re-affirmed for his own people the right of salvage in regard to Castilian ships sinking off the Valencian or Catalan coasts. If Castilian merchants managed to off-load their cargoes from such vessels, they were free to sell their goods within his lands once they had paid the requisite imposts and tolls. If ecclesiastical institutions, Aragonese or Castilian, entered into such international salvage for profit, they also had to pay all the applicable tolls. If they engaged in trade only to support their communities, however, their trade would be free of taxes within Aragon. Disputes emanating from "frauds and scandals" that accompanied trade across Iberian borders would be settled according to the letter of the treaty of 1375.[68] This economic pacification of international frontiers was an ingenious solution, but did not always function as intended. Thus on July 15, 1378, Pere had to write one of his commissioners at Valencia instructing him to reimburse two Valencian merchants who had recently suffered damages in Castile. He assured his official that these outlays would duly be reimbursed by the Castilian ruler, but there is no record they ever were.[69] Peace had come to the monarchs of Aragon and Castile, but it would apparently take a little longer to descend on their frontiers.

Conclusion

The long and stormy relationship between Pere III and Enrique II ended with the latter's death in 1379. The turbulent period of open warfare and intrigue between Iberia's largest states, which actually commenced with the accession of Pedro I in 1350, had also come full circle. At the beginning of this time frame, Aragonese and Castilian rulers utilized alliances much as a traveler might a bridge, not thinking again of its importance after crossing it. Despite the sacral nature of the treaties they signed and swore to uphold, Pere, Pedro, and Enrique took up or abandoned diplomatic bonds as present concerns demanded and without a hint of compunction at violating the terms of agreements that bound them. The military drive to expand their territory and extend royal

68 ACA, Cancillería real, R. 1543, fol. 180v.

69 ACA, Cancillería real, R. 1543, fol. 181.

power overshadowed the conservative goals of such diplomacy. As the conflict between Aragon and Castile continued, Pere, an adept practitioner of defensive survival, began to utilize every economic means available to keep troops in the field.[70] Eventually he saw the border war he had grown used to fighting morph into an international conflict as Enrique fought his way to temporary control of the Castilian crown in 1366. In the three-year civil war that followed, Pere refused to remain a mere onlooker but instead utilized the political, economic, and social instability caused by Enrique's struggle with Pedro to engineer a set of interlocking alliances with England, Navarre, and Portugal that had as their principal aim the lethal weakening of Castile. Pere's ambitions, however, soon faded before Enrique's talent as a commander who encircled and killed Pedro as well as his accomplishment as a forceful negotiator who methodically dismantled the confederation of foreign powers surrounding him. In the end, Pere's diplomatic endeavors that were laid out in such ambitious terms proved to be little more than "generalities and [mere] words."[71] Enrique's triumphs, on the other hand, came about from a much simpler combination of war and diplomacy.

The period between 1356 and 1379 witnessed the brutal and self-seeking interchange of three royal egos, each seeking to gain control of Castile or bring about its ultimate dismemberment. In geopolitical terms, however, it points back to the desperate frontier disputes between Aragon and Castile in the

---

[70] For Pere as war financier, see Donald J. Kagay, "War Financing in the Late-Medieval Crown of Aragon," *Journal of Medieval Military History*, 6 (2008): pp. 119–48; Donald J. Kagay, "A Government Besieged by Conflict: The Parliament of Monzón (1362–1363) as Military Financier," in Villalon and Kagay, *A Wider Focus*, pp. 117–48. For the estimates of the costs of war in France and England, see K.B. McFarlane, "War, the Economy and Social Change: England and the Hundred Years War," *Past and Present*, 22 (1962): p. 6; M.M. Postan, "The Costs of the Hundred Years War," *Past and Present*, 27 (1964): p. 40; Richard Bean, "War and the Birth of the Nation State," *Journal of Economic History*, 33 (1973): pp. 215–17. The estimate for French expenses cannot be as accurate as that of the English because of the many breaks in French accounts of the era and the great proliferation of tax collection areas. For war financing in the heartlands of the Hundred Years War, see John Bell Henneman, *Royal Taxation in Fourteenth Century France: The Development of War Financing 1322–1356* (Princeton, NJ: Princeton University Press, 1971), pp. 5–10, 126, 155–6, 250, 285–6, 292, 322–3; John Bell Henneman, "Financing the Hundred Years War: Royal Taxation in France in 1340," *Speculum*, 42 (1967): pp. 15–43; J. Russell Major, *Representative Government in Early Modern France* (New Haven, CT: Yale University Press, 1980), pp. 14–17; G.L. Harriss, *King, Parliament, and Public Finance in Medieval England to 1369* (Oxford: Clarendon Press, 1975), pp. 231–69; Chris Given-Wilson, *The Royal Household and the King's Affinity: Service, Politics, and Finance in England 1360–1413* (New Haven, CT: Yale University Press, 1986), pp. 121–30.

[71] Miret y Sans, p. 120.

twelfth and thirteenth centuries and forward to modern episodes such as the Revolt of the Catalans (1640–52) and the nationalist uprising among the realms of the defunct Crown of Aragon during the Spanish Civil War (1936–39). The political instability wrought by these struggles is obvious. Only after the death of Francisco Franco in 1975 would this long tradition of regional warfare be abandoned for true nation building.[72]

[72] For the issue of nation building in post-Franco Spain see Francesc Hernandez, "Cataluña y España," in Cristina Dupláa and Gwendolyn Barnes (eds), *Las nacionalidades del estado español: Una problemática cultural* (Minneapolis, MN: Institute for the Study of Ideologies and Literature, 1986), pp. 137–60; Angel Smith and Clare Mar-Molinero, "The Myths and Realities of Nation-Building in the Iberian Peninsula," in Angel Smith and Clare Mar-Molinero (eds), *Nationalism and the Nation in the Iberian Peninsula: Competing and Conflicting Identities* (Oxford: Berg, 1996), pp. 1–30.

Chapter 10

Trastámara Kings, Queens, and the Gender Dynamics of Monarchy

Theresa Earenfight

The Trastámara name dominates the history of fourteenth- and fifteenth-century Spain. The family's rise to prominence was a result of the messy personal life of King Alfonso XI of Castile (1312–50), who bequeathed a violent legacy to his children, legitimate and illegitimate. Alfonso's son Pedro I (1350–66/1367–69) was murdered by his half-brother Enrique Trastámara, who as Enrique II (1366–67/1369–79) established the Trastámara dynasty in Castile-León. Enrique's own family history was just as complicated as Alfonso XI's, with three legitimate children from his wife Juana Manuel and at least 12 illegitimate children with as many as eight women. Enrique made sure that his children of various mothers married into royal and noble families and in so doing created a network of competing allegiances. Squabbles over land and lordship were exacerbated by European-wide social, medical, political, and religious tensions—sporadic outbreaks of plague, economic upheaval, social unrest, religious persecution, papal schism, and the Hundred Years War. Although Enrique II's son and heir, Juan I (1379–90), was a model of marital stability, with two legitimate wives (Leonor of Aragon and Beatriz of Portugal) and four children (only one of whom may have been illegitimate), the tensions continued. The succession after Juan's death was peaceful. His eldest son inherited and ruled Castile as Enrique III (1390–1406). His second son inherited the duchy of Peñafiel, county of Mayorga, and lordship of Lara, and then extended Trastámara hegemony when he succeeded to the Crown of Aragon as Fernando I (1412–16). Still, the sons of Enrique and Fernando continued to jockey for power, a struggle ultimately resolved when Isabel I of Castile (1474–1504) married Fernando II of Aragon (1479–1516), thus uniting the two branches of the family.[1]

---

1 Joseph F. O'Callaghan, *A History of Medieval Spain* (Ithaca, NY: Cornell University Press, 1975), pp. 553–5; J.N. Hillgarth, *The Spanish Kingdoms, 1250–1516* (2 vols, Oxford

The events of this tumultuous period have been studied almost entirely through the framework of kingship. Whereas this approach makes sense, it diminishes the importance of the Trastámara queens who were central to the events and constricts our understanding of medieval monarchy. Monarchy in medieval Europe was an institution structured entirely around the family, and although premised on the patriarchal ordering of society with the king as head of the royal household, the queen was fundamental to its operation. In late medieval Spain, queens were not shadowy side notes to war and diplomacy but active participants in governance.[2] This is particularly true for the queens who were wives and daughters of Enrique III and Fernando I. Enrique married Catalina of Lancaster (b. 1372–1418), the daughter of John of Gaunt, Duke of Lancaster, and granddaughter of Pedro I. The union was meant to forge enduring links between Castile and England but was overshadowed by Gaunt's pretensions to the throne of Castile through his wife, Constanza, and anxieties about English overlordship. Fernando married Leonor of Albuquerque (b. 1374–1435) who, as daughter of Count Sancho of Albuquerque (an illegitimate son of Alfonso XI) and Beatriz of Portugal, had vast wealth and prodigious regional connections. Catalina and Leonor, and their daughters, also queens—María of Castile (b. 1401–58) and María of Aragon (b. 1403–45)—worked closely alongside their husbands, Alfonso V of the Crown of Aragon (1416–58) and Juan II of Castile (1406–54) governing either in an official capacity as regent or queen-lieutenant, or as an unofficial adviser.

These four queens may not be household names to modern scholars, but they were well known to contemporary chroniclers who documented their actions. Those chronicles and the queen's own letters to one another as well as to secular and religious figures inside and outside their realms demonstrate their importance in the politics of the day.[3] These sources permit a close analysis of

Clarendon Press, 1978), vol. 2, pp. 300–314; Luis Suárez Fernández, Ángel Canellas López, and Jaime Vicens Vives, *Los Trastámaras de Castilla y Aragón en el siglo XV: Juan II y Enrique IV de Castilla (1407–1474): El compromiso de Caspe, Fernando I, Alfonso V y Juan II de Aragón (1410–1479)*, vol. 15 of *Historia de España*, ed. Ramón Menéndez Pidal (Madrid: Espasa Calpe, 1964), pp. 85–94; Eloy Benito Ruano, *Los infantes de Aragón* (Pamplona: Escuela de Estudios Medievales, 1952). For genealogy, see Figure 10.1.

2 Theresa Earenfight, "Preface: Partners in Politics," in Theresa Earenfight (ed.), *Queenship and Political Power in Medieval and Early Modern Spain* (Aldershot: Ashgate, 2005), pp. xiii–xxviii.

3 The letters are official chancery copies contained in the Arxiu de la Corona d'Aragó in Barcelona [hereafter ACA], in the registers of two sections, the Curie [C] and Domine Reginale [DR]. "Crónica del serenísimo príncipe don Juan, segundo rey deste nombre en Castilla y en León" in Cayetano Rosell (ed.), *Crónicas de los reyes de Castilla*, vol. 2, Biblioteca

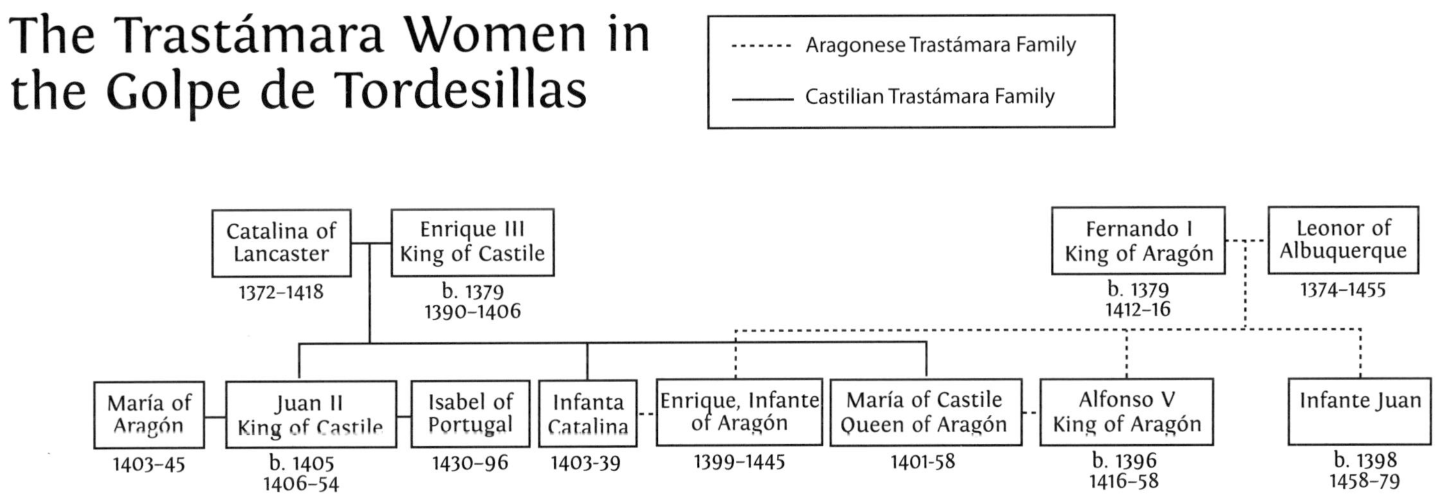

Figure 10.1 Geneaology: The Trastámara Women in the Golpe de Tordesillas

one particular event, a coup d'état known as the *golpe de Tordesillas* of 1420. Viewing the *golpe* from the vantage point of the queens rather than simply that of the kings allows us to better understand the masculine and feminine aspects of monarchy and gain a much fuller picture of the events themselves.

Rival Sisters-in-Law: Catalina of Lancaster and Leonor of Albuquerque

Catalina of Lancaster, born and raised in England, was a well-educated and worldly woman of 16 in 1388 when she married her half-cousin, the future Enrique III, seven years her junior. Enrique was 11 in 1390 when he succeeded to the throne, so Catalina governed as his regent with a council until 1393, when he turned 14.[4] The chroniclers were uneasy about Enrique's minority not solely because the regency was in the hands of a woman. He was known as "el doliente" [the afflicted one], she suffered from a chronic illness, and they both preferred sedentary intellectual pursuits over hunting and jousting. The couple eventually had three children, María, Catalina, and a son who ruled as Juan II. Throughout his reign, Enrique depended on his wife, whom one chronicler noted governed "as much like a man as like a woman." Almost immediately she faced challenges by Pedro Tenorio, Archbishop of Toledo, and Juan García Manrique, Archbishop of Santiago.[5] When a *cortes* was convened in Burgos 1391 to resolve those disputes, Enrique's brother, Fernando and his wife-to-be, Leonor of Albuquerque, joined the young king and his wife.[6]

The two couples could not have been more different. Fernando and Leonor were robust and active extroverts, the opposite of the bookish Enrique and Catalina. Fernando was being groomed to inherit and govern his mother's estates, and was already considered a powerful political figure. Leonor was not only intelligent and beautiful but also rich, shrewd, and ambitious. Known

---

de autores españoles, vol. 68 (1877; reprint, Madrid: Ediciones Atlas, 1953), pp. 277–695 (hereafter cited as "Crónica Juan"); Pedro Carillo de Huete, *Crónica del halconero de Juan II*, ed. Juan de Mata Carriazo (Madrid: Espasa-Calpe, 1946); *Crónica de Alvaro de Luna*, ed. Juan de Mata Carriazo (Madrid: Espasa-Calpe, 1940). See also Fernán Pérez de Guzmán, *Pen Portraits of Illustrious Castilians* (*Generaciones y Semblanzas*), ed. and trans. Marie Gillette and Loretta Zehngut (Washington, DC: Catholic University Press, 2003).

4 Ana Echevarria, *Catalina de Lancaster: Reina regente de Castilla, 1372–1418* (Hondarribia: Neara, 2002); Ana Echevarria, "Catalina of Lancaster and the Castilian Monarchy," in Roger Collins and Anthony Goodman (eds), *Medieval Spain: Culture, Conflict, and Coexistence* (Basingstoke: Palgrave Macmillan, 2002), pp. 79–122.

5 Pérez de Guzmán, p. 12.

6 Echevarria, *Catalina*, pp. 61, 78–9, 119–40.

as "la rica hembra" [the rich woman], she possessed estates so vast that it was said she could walk from Aragon to Galicia and never step foot off her lands. Wealth, beauty, and charisma notwithstanding, much of her influence surely stemmed from the fact that she was aunt to both brothers and six years older than Fernando. Her presence at the *cortes* of Burgos in 1391 signals that she already had sufficient clout to be included in a high-level meeting although she and Fernando were not yet married.[7] They married in 1393, the same year that Enrique assumed his majority, and their combined landed wealth crisscrossed the peninsula and created a potent foundation of political influence.[8]

By 1404, Fernando's power began to eclipse that of his brother the king, whose health was failing. Just before his death in 1406, Enrique designated his 2-year-old son Juan as successor, insisting that Fernando sign a pledge of fidelity to him and appointing Fernando and Catalina as co-regents.[9] Squabbling noble factions tipped the balance of power in Fernando's favor, and in 1408 he sought to limit Catalina's authority. She fought back and they compromised: Catalina handled domestic affairs, Fernando took on diplomacy and military matters. By then, Fernando and Leonor had five sons and two daughters whom they used to build strategic regional alliances. In 1409, Fernando named his sons Enrique, then 9 years old, and Sancho, 8, as masters of the powerful Castilian military Orders of Santiago and Alcántara. With these titles came substantial wealth from landed estates, and Queen Catalina correctly regarded these moves as a threat to her son's authority in Castile. In 1410, Fernando demonstrated his military prowess with the capture of the Muslim fortress of Antequera.[10]

That same year, the political landscape changed dramatically when King Martí (1395–1410) of the Crown of Aragon died without a male heir. Fernando, with Catalina's support, claimed a right to the throne through his mother, Martí's sister, and in 1412 Aragonese magnates meeting at Caspe recognized him as Fernando I of the Crown of Aragon. As his political partner, Queen Leonor now exercised her talents freely.[11] When his reign was cut short by death in 1416, his eldest son, Alfonso V (1416–58), succeeded to the throne. After burying her

---

[7] Alan Ryder, *Alfonso the Magnanimous, King of Aragon, Naples, and Sicily, 1396–1458* (Oxford: Clarendon Press, 1990), p. 3; Echevarria, *Catalina*, pp. 60–61.

[8] Echevarria, *Catalina*, p. 58; Ryder, pp. 53–6, 63–4, 158–61.

[9] Ana Echevarria, "The Queen and the Master: Catalina of Lancaster and the Military Orders," in Earenfight, *Queenship*, pp. 97–9.

[10] Echevarria, *Catalina*, pp. 141–67; Echevarria, "Queen and Master," pp. 101–3; Ryder, pp. 12–14, 43. Fernando and Leonor's son Sancho died in 1416.

[11] Ryder, pp. 14–16; Suárez Fernández et al., *Los Trastámaras*, pp. 81–6; Hillgarth, vol. 2, pp. 215–38.

husband and settling her affairs in the Crown of Aragon, Leonor withdrew to Medina del Campo but hardly retired. She was deeply involved in the affairs of both Castile and the Crown of Aragon, often working through her younger sons, Juan, Enrique and Pedro, the so-called *infantes* of Aragon.[12]

Fernando's move to Aragon and subsequent death left Catalina as sole regent in Castile. Nobles who were comfortable with the idea of a joint regency grew anxious at the prospect of her governing alone and began to oppose her. She was fiercely protective of her young son Juan fearing, with good reason, that were it not for her he would fall under the sway of noble factions.[13] But her zeal to protect the boy made him dependent on her, leading his critics to doubt his fitness to rule. His contemporary Fernán Pérez de Guzmán described Juan as "gentle and calm," who, like his father, preferred literature, art, and ornamentation. His father may have been frail and bookish, but Juan seemed worse. In Pérez de Guzmán's estimation, he was "sorely deficient in other graces that are truly virtues and that are necessary to all men and especially to kings," lacked "the intelligence to rule and bring order to his people," and "never for a single hour" worked "at the art of governing." The Castilian nobility turned on Catalina's advisers, particularly the controversial Alvaro de Luna, the illegitimate son of a minor noble who was approximately 20 when he came to court to serve 4-year-old Juan. Pérez de Guzmán questioned Juan's masculinity when he called his close friendship with de Luna a "very special love," wondering if it was the result of "magic and evil spells." Pérez de Guzmán's critique of Catalina was harsher, misogynistic in tone and substance. He almost sounded relieved when Queen Catalina died in June 1418 and commented that as Juan came into his personal rule "it seemed that he was born again," no longer a submissive weakling under the thumb of his mother who ruled "like a man."[14]

Juan's personal rule, however, remained troubled by his disinterest in governance, his reliance on de Luna and swiftly moving events in the Crown of Aragon. Fernando and Leonor had arranged highly advantageous marriages for their children. Their eldest son, Alfonso, had married María of Castile, King

---

[12] Jerónimo Zurita y Castro, *Anales de la Corona de Aragón*, ed. Ángel Canellas López (9 vols, Zaragoza: Institución Fernando el Católico, Consejo Superior de Investigaciones Científicas 1967–1985), vol. 5, p. 470; Echevarria, *Catalina*, pp. 179, 191–204; Ryder, pp. 53, 55, 57, 63–4.

[13] Didier T. Jaen, *John II of Castile and the Grand Master: Alvaro de Luna* (Madrid: Editorial Castalia, 1978).

[14] Pérez de Guzmán, pp. 51–74; Benito Ruano, pp. 101–6; Echevarria, "Queen and Master," pp. 91–105; and Jaime Vicens Vives, *Juan II de Aragón, 1398–1479: Monarquía y revolución en la España del siglo XV*, rev. ed. Paul H. Freedman and Joseph M. Muñoz i Lloret (Pamplona: Urgoiti Editores, 2003).

Juan's sister, in 1415 while their daughter María of Aragon was betrothed to King Juan himself in 1418. In 1419 their second son, Juan, was betrothed to Blanca, the heiress of Navarre.[15] While no marriage was yet arranged for their third son, Enrique, in 1418 Leonor gave him some of his grandfather's estates in Castile, notably the county of Albuquerque. This endowment, coupled with his mastership of Santiago, made Enrique one of the most powerful men in Castile, but also one seeking a royal marriage.[16]

The *Golpe de Tordesillas*

Enrique's ambitious and audacious seizure of power at Tordesillas was precipitated by the departure of two of his brothers. On May 10, 1420, King Alfonso V set sail for Italy in pursuit of the kingdom of Naples, leaving his wife María of Castile to govern the Crown of Aragon as lieutenant general. Assisted by a royal council separate from the king's, María had full royal authority to govern in his absence.[17] In June, *infante* Juan went to Navarre for his wedding.[18] Enrique took advantage of his brothers' absences and between 7 and July 12 went to the town of Tordesillas where King Juan was presiding over the Castilian *cortes*. With the support of key Castilian allies including the constable of Castile, Ruy López Dávalos, and the bishop of Toledo, Enrique made his move. At dawn on Sunday, July 14, supported by 300 men-at-arms, Enrique entered the king's rooms and put Juan under armed guard. He also seized Juan's sister, the *infanta* Catalina, and his own sister, María of Aragon, Juan's betrothed, sending all three to the monastery of Santa Clara; a few days later they were moved to more secure lodgings in Segovia. As Enrique proceeded to govern the kingdom of Castile in his cousin's place, he attempted to persuade Catalina to marry him.[19]

Enrique may have thought that lineage, wealth, and the support of a powerful cadre of Castilian nobles gave him a clear path to power in Castile, but he miscalculated in terms of his family. His brother Alfonso and their mother,

---

[15] Zurita, vol. 5, p. 512; "Crónica Juan," pp. 374, 376.

[16] Echevarria, *Catalina*, pp. 180, 194; Suárez Fernández, et al., *Los Trastámaras*, pp. 74–6.

[17] She was lieutenant twice, from 1420 to 1423 and 1432 to 1453. Theresa Earenfight, *The King's Other Body: María of Castile and the Crown of Aragon* (Philadelphia, PA: University of Pennsylvania Press, 2010), pp. 1–3, 41–66.

[18] The wedding was June 10, 1420. "Crónica Juan," pp. 382–3; Ryder, p. 81.

[19] "Crónica Juan," p. 382; *Crónica de don Álvaro de Luna*, pp. 35–9; Jaen, 35–54; Suárez Fernández et al., *Los Trastámaras*, pp. 74–7.

troubled by his actions, did not rush to his side. In addition, he presumably did not foresee that María of Castile, the imprisoned King Juan's older sister and Alfonso's wife, would prove a powerful opposing force. Although queen-lieutenant for barely two months, she was well educated and aided by a highly skilled staff of officials that gave her sufficient clout to oppose *infante* Enrique's actions. She did not hesitate to step into the fray.[20] The volatile atmosphere of that summer and fall, and of the next few years, tested her political savvy as she and Leonor worked both together and at cross purposes to protect their families.

Within days, King Juan's power was more *de jure* than de facto. The Castilian government effectively fell into the hands of Enrique who claimed to exercise a form of tutelage over Juan but took care not to usurp the title of king. Enrique's brothers disagreed on how to handle their ambitious and intemperate sibling. Alfonso was furious with Enrique, who tried to placate his brother with 2,000 infantry for a campaign in Italy, but was told curtly that he needed money not men. *Infante* Juan, once his brother Enrique's rival, now became his ally but not a wholehearted one. Juan assembled an army and a cadre of Castilian nobles on July 24 ostensibly to support Enrique, but they attempted to restore peace by checking the Enrique's power and the growing influence of de Luna. As fighting broke out near Ávila, Leonor, at nearby Fontiveros, grew concerned with the violence. In her letters she told Enrique that many magnates of Castile supported him but despaired that any good would come of the matter.[21] She tried to persuade him and King Juan to work out a compromise. María of Castile, however, disagreed forcefully with her mother-in-law. In a letter to Leonor, she registered her "great displeasure from the damage to his [Juan's] realms" and reiterated her fears for the safety of her brother and sister and worries that the hostilities would prevent the payment of her dowry. By late August, after Enrique had won a series of skirmishes against the king's supporters, she applied diplomatic pressure on Enrique and his allies which continued throughout the

---

20 Earenfight, *King's Other Body*, pp. 1–18; Theresa Earenfight, "Absent Kings: Queens as Political Partners in the Medieval Crown of Aragon," in Earenfight, *Queenship*, pp. 33–51.

21 "Crónica Juan," p. 388. It is not clear whether the chronicler had access to the original letters, but the editor enclosed this material in quotation marks, suggesting that he did quote directly from the letters. Leonor is a frustrating person to study because the sources are scattered, have not been studied, or have not survived. The best edition of her letters ends in 1416. See Carlos López Rodríguez (ed.), *Epistolari de Ferran I d'Antequera amb els infants d'Aragó i le reina Elionor (1413–1416)* (València: Universitat de València, 2004). Some of her correspondence as dowager queen is preserved in the Arxiu de la Corona d'Aragó, but many letters presumably originated from her own court, not that of the Crown of Aragon, and her sentiments can be inferred by the phrasing of the letters written in response.

fall. She sent embassies to her brother, King Juan, the archbishop of Tarazona, and high-ranking nobles with explicit instructions to reiterate her anger over the damage Enrique had done to the kingdom and urging them to work out a solution.[22]

One of María's first letters on August 16, 1420 to Enrique warns him of her concern for Catalina and states clearly her opposition to a marriage between them. Over the next few weeks, she sent letters to Juan II, Leonor, Alvaro de Luna, the archbishop of Toledo, and Enrique's staunch ally Ruy López Dávalos, Constable of Castile, in which she expresses her displeasure and alerts them that she would be watching the "scandalous" events in Castile very carefully.[23] Her letters to Leonor show an increasingly strained relationship between the two women. Both María and Leonor sought a peaceful resolution to the crisis, but each woman put the needs of her own immediate family members ahead of those of royal cousins or in-laws. Leonor protected Enrique, sometimes to the point of putting at risk her own daughter, held under guard by her son. In her letters to Leonor, María speaks of her fears for the physical safety of her brother and, in particular, her sister to whom she was quite close. María tells *infanta* Catalina of her actions in support and of the indignation of high-ranking nobles and prelates.[24] She worries that the hostilities would prevent the final payment of her own dowry, which Alfonso was counting on to support his army in Naples.[25]

Enrique and his allies held the upper hand, however. Juan's position reached a low point in September when Enrique strong-armed the *cortes* of Ávila into officially recognizing his seizure of the throne. He coerced Juan to proclaim publicly that Enrique had acted at Tordesillas as Juan wanted, that he was not a hostage and was in fact free to move around.[26] It is doubtful that anyone, regardless of allegiance, believed Juan wanted to be deposed, or that he and his wife and sister were under anything other than a courteous house arrest, under the watchful guard of Enrique and his allies.

The actions of María of Castile are particularly important in this early stage, when she worked both with and as a counterbalance to Leonor. As queen-lieutenant in the Crown of Aragon, she had to act swiftly to protect her brother and sister from physical harm and the crown from entanglement

---

22 "Crónica Juan," pp. 384–6; Benito Ruano, pp. 21–4, 74–9; Ryder, p. 81.

23 ACA DR: 3108, 98v–101v (8/16/1420 to 9/4/1420). Many of these letters were copies of the material contained in her letter to Enrique and Juan II, what we call a blind copy to multiple recipients.

24 ACA DR: 3108, 103v–104r (9/16/1420).

25 ACA DR: 3108, 104v–109r (8/16/1420 to 9/16/1420.

26 "Crónica Juan," pp. 396–7.

in civil war. Alfonso was concerned that war with his brothers in Castile would have forced him to abandon his campaigns in Italy, and he relied on María to use her network of allies to avoid it. In her letters, María intensified the pressure on Enrique and his allies. She reiterated her concerns of the consequences should Catalina marry Enrique against her wishes and urged them to work out a solution. Leonor feared that an amicable accord could not be reached but did not give up. On September 13, in response to the decision at the *cortes* of Ávila that legitimized Enrique's actions, María sent a delegation directly to King Juan in Castile. She gave detailed instructions on how to proceed, asserting the king's legitimacy and the support he had from her and Alfonso. In her letters, she asked Juan and Luna to negotiate a resolution with Castilian nobles and prelates, pleaded with Leonor to try to convince Enrique to relent, and sent ambassadors with personal letters to Juan, María of Aragon, and Catalina with reassurances that she was doing all she could.[27]

The Wooing and Wedding of a Reluctant Infanta

While María of Castile was waging an epistolary diplomatic war, Enrique not only tried to subdue and govern Castile but also attempted to convince Catalina to marry him. She had been earmarked to marry one of the *infantes*, but she made it clear that she did not want to marry Enrique. She preferred instead to marry someone from outside Castile or Aragon but tactfully did not give reasons. He had plenty of reasons to want to marry her. Perhaps he was motivated by fraternal rivalry because both he and his brother Juan had courted Catalina, or he may have been frustrated because he was left out of the marriage plans. But Enrique surely found Catalina attractive in more ways than physical beauty, intellect, and charm. While he already possessed considerable landed wealth and prestige as the Master of Santiago, he coveted her dowry which included the lucrative marquisate of Villena. But most importantly, a marriage to the *infanta* would allow him to more legitimately hold the kingdom he seized at knifepoint. Enrique was an obstinate man and a persistent pursuer. No matter what his reasons, the more he persisted, the more she resisted him, ignoring the pleas of barons, royal imperatives, and threats from the bishop of Palencia.[28]

---

[27] ACA Curie [C]: 3163, 21r–27r (9/13/1420). Juan married María of Aragon on October 20. "Crónica Juan," pp. 384–5, 389–94.

[28] "Crónica Juan," p. 382; Benito Ruano, pp. 21–4, 74–81; José Manuel Nieto Soria, "La monarquía como conflicto de legitimades," in José Manuel Nieto Soria (ed.),

A virtual prisoner of her cousin and suitor, *infanta* Catalina was physically isolated from her family and did not know that her sister María was working on her behalf. Enrique won her hand by coercing her nursemaid to persuade her to save her brother's realms by marrying him. With her brother under guard and Castile on the brink of civil war, Catalina relented. In August, after Enrique had taken her alone up to the ramparts of Alamín on the road between Ávila and Talavera de la Reina, she finally agreed to marry him. King Juan had little choice but to approve reluctantly of the marriage because, as some chroniclers suggest, he was persuaded by de Luna's argument that Enrique would be distracted because he "would linger in bed with his wife." De Luna was suggesting that even a man as assertively masculine as Enrique would be easier to defeat when under the influence of a woman's sexual charms. They married November 8 "without any ceremony."[29] María of Castile did not hide her anger and anguish. In a terse emotional response to a letter from her brother informing her of the wedding, María expressed outrage at her sister's marriage, considering it an offense and entirely "against the princess's wishes."[30] But Catalina surprised everyone, adroitly moving from reluctant *infanta* to dutiful wife. For the moment, her consent, acquiescence, and tact nullified any legal objections, and made possible the peaceful resolution that soon followed.

Shortly after the wedding, however, Enrique's scheme began to fall apart. On November 29, while he was at Mass, Juan, de Luna, and a handful of allies, under the pretext of going hunting, escaped from Talavera de la Reina. It was a well-planned maneuver, and its success was abetted by *infante* Juan's cautious stalling tactics in opposition to his unruly brother and by the intervention of María of Aragon and Catalina who, upon hearing that Enrique was about to pursue Juan and de Luna, walked unescorted through a muddy field to plead with Enrique to avoid battle. He ignored them, but he lost a skirmish against the king's forces at the castle of Montalbán where King Juan was safe. Leonor and her advisers, notably the archbishop of Toledo, pressured Enrique to relent. King Juan, aided by de Luna, took advantage of increasing opposition to Enrique among the Castilian towns and nobility to rebuilt his bases of support. On December 10, the king's forces subdued Enrique, Constable Ruy López Dávalos, Garcia Fernández, and Pedro Manrique though they then fled to Ocaña where Enrique held out for 23 days. In early January 1421, Leonor brokered a meeting

La monarquía como conflicto en la corona castellano-leonesa (c.1230–1504) (Madrid: Silex, 2006), pp. 13–17.

29 "Crónica Juan," pp. 388–90; *Crónica de Álvaro de Luna*, p. 41; Benito Ruano, p. 76; Jaen, p. 42.

30 ACA C: 3222, 36v–37r (12/1/1420).

between King Juan and *infante* Juan in a boat on the Tagus River. *Infante* Juan begged the king to forgive Enrique, who then recognized Juan as legitimate king of Castile.[31]

Enrique's failure was the result of a host of political, military, and familial factors. Leonor's obvious disapproval of his action, María of Castile's opposition, Alfonso V's unfavorable reaction, *infante* Juan's tepid support and the increasing opposition of high-ranking nobles, clerics, and townspeople surely led Enrique to conclude that he overreached by wanting both the realm and the bride. He had gambled that with Catalina would come the legitimacy he needed to secure an illegal usurpation, but marriage to an *infanta* was insufficient to overcome the presence of a legitimate, adult, anointed king. Enrique's efforts failed to secure him a kingdom of his own but did get him a dutifully compliant wife and her dowry lands that he hoped would provide additional resources in his opposition to Juan II and de Luna.

Relative calm prevailed from January through April 1421 but tensions flared when Enrique and Catalina attempted to take possession of the marquisate of Villena. This was a risky move. A key provision of the restoration of Juan's authority was the annulment of all royal donations of property made from July to January. The marquisate of Villena, part of Catalina's dowry, was one of those donations. The Villena town council received Catalina as their lady but was reluctant to admit Enrique as lord. In a clear signal that Enrique was losing ground, townspeople were joined by some nobles who thought that King Juan should take possession for Catalina. Juan's council, led by Alvaro de Luna, advised him to annul her dowry, but Juan in the end disagreed and permitted Catalina and Enrique to take to possession of Villena. Enrique retaliated against the nobles who opposed him and the king's orders and gathered an army at Chincilla in Catalina's name. Fearing that things would again spin out of control, Leonor took a lead in the negotiations for peace, while Castilian Queen María and Catalina acted as messengers and go-betweens in the negotiations, which included the pope. Recognizing Juan II's growing power, Enrique relented and by the end of May began to make conciliatory moves toward the king. Seizing the moment, Leonor met with King Juan in secret, asking him to be merciful toward Enrique, if for no other reason than to protect his sister from harm.[32] Leonor's intervention bought Enrique a reprieve that protected his freedom, his wife, and her estates at Villena.

31 "Crónica Juan," pp. 390–98; Carillo de Huete, pp. 1–5; *Crónica de Álvaro de Luna*, pp. 45–50; Jaen, pp. 43, 48–50.

32 "Crónica Juan," pp. 400–408; Suárez Fernández et al., *Los Trastámaras*, pp. 80–82; Hillgarth, vol. 2, pp. 305–6.

A few months later, Enrique, either obstinately hopeful or reflexively belligerent, once again mustered troops. This time he faced not only King Juan's troops but also those of his brother Juan, and he soon lost battles, prestige, and allies. In early June 1422, Catalina wrote to her brother, King Juan, asking him to provide safe passage for her and Enrique to come to court. They arrived on June 13. The chronicler tells us that Enrique, on bended knees and pleading that he was just "un simple caballero" [a simple knight], begged for mercy. Alfonso V, although strongly opposed to Enrique's actions, sent letters from Italy suggesting that he would guarantee his brother's good behavior if Juan would assess a light penalty. But Juan was in no mood to be merciful toward his brother-in-law. He imprisoned him, seized his possessions, and punished his allies.[33] Even though she was not directly involved in Enrique's actions, in strict legal terms Catalina, as his wife, was his accomplice, and this brought her close to treason. Juan revoked the estates of Villena from her dowry and expelled his sister from the kingdom. He accepted the request of María of Castile and Alfonso that she be allowed to live in the Crown of Aragon under their protection. And so, on a mule with only a small retinue, Catalina left the realm of her birth and went to Valencia.

Subduing a Contumacious *Infante*

Alfonso V returned to Spain in December 1423 after three years in Italy, and María of Castile stepped down as his lieutenant. His presence was sufficient to curtail his younger brothers, but Enrique remained a dangerous enemy with potent allies. In 1427–28, he felt strong enough again and provoked his brothers King Alfonso and his brother Juan, who became king of Navarre in 1425, into another fight with Juan of Castile, ostensibly over the control of Enrique's lordships in Castile. It was also a challenge to the power of de Luna's role in Castilian government. Initial hostilities between Navarre and Castile threatened to spill over to the Crown of Aragon, but full-scale war was narrowly averted in 1429 only by direct intervention of María of Castile. With the cardinal of Foix at her side, and perhaps the tacit approval of Alfonso, she pitched her tent between the opposing armies and refused to budge until her brother, her brothers-in-law, and her husband agreed to a peaceful settlement that saved Enrique from imprisonment. Juan II offered a truce as long as the *infantes* ceased interference

---

[33] "Crónica Juan," pp. 406–7, 412–17; *Crónica de Álvaro de Luna*, pp. 54–61; Jaen, pp. 62–3; Benito Ruano, pp. 24–5; Suárez Fernández et al., *Los Trastámaras*, pp. 83–5; Ryder, pp. 103, 115 n.1, 121, 129.

in Castilian affairs. Their mother, Leonor, who had never failed to come to their defense, earned a short imprisonment the following year.[34]

Enrique was nothing if not tenacious. Three years after his mother's death in 1435, he reappeared as an adversary of the king in the Castilian civil war (1438–45). In this conflict, the Queen of Castile, María of Aragon, took her brother Enrique's side, an action that was not just a sign of family solidarity but also a slap in the face of her husband and an indirect blow at de Luna. She and her sister Leonor, wife of King Duarte of Portugal (1433–38), eventually attempted to broker peace. On May 19, 1445, Enrique made one last grab for power, but it ended badly. Juan of Castile and Luna mustered an army and won a decisive victory at the battle of Olmedo. Enrique died of his wounds a few days later.[35]

Juan II of Castile got his kingdom back but paid a tremendous price. His younger sister, Catalina, died in exile in 1439, and Juan owed his present position to his favorite, his mother-in-law, wife, older sister, and brother-in-law. His reign was still fraught with tension. Some Castilian nobles remained powerfully opposed to his rule and de Luna's influence. De Luna would fall hard, dying at an executioner's hand in 1453. Juan's faithful wife, María of Aragon, bore him four children, but by all accounts it was not a happy marriage. Unlike her mother, sister-in-law, and most Spanish queens, she had little influence at all in her husband's political actions and spent most of her married life overshadowed by Alvaro de Luna. María was a dutiful wife in terms of sexual fidelity, but her obedience was not limitless. She clearly drew the line at the role de Luna played in Juan's reign when she opposed Juan's participation in the civil war of 1438–45. Her sister Leonor, on the other hand, was happily married to King Duarte of Portugal; she was a force to reckon with in his reign, and more often than not she was openly critical of their actions.[36]

María of Castile and her mother-in-law Leonor had never been close, but Leonor's support of Enrique made their relationship tense and antagonistic. The marriage of María and Alfonso deteriorated too.[37] After he fell seriously ill in July 1426, they mended their relationship a bit, but they were rarely together after that. In 1432, he left to conquer and govern Naples and never returned. Their marriage, a personal failure, thrived as a political partnership. María of Castile stayed in Spain, governing as queen-lieutenant, and together she and Alfonso ruled the Crown of Aragon until their deaths in 1458. She also remained close

---

34 "Crónica Juan," pp. 474–9; *Crónica de Álvaro de Luna*, pp. 77–83; Jaen, pp. 87–91; Earenfight, *King's Other Body*, p. 67; Ryder, pp. 159–74.

35 Leonor and Duarte married in 1428. Ryder, pp. 221, 268–9; Zurita, vol. 5, pp. 741, 746.

36 Benito Ruano, pp. 36–8, 84–6.

37 ACA C: 2678, 119r (12/1/1424); Ryder, pp. 123–4, 140–41.

to her sister Catalina until the latter's death in 1439. Catalina had continued to defend her husband Enrique though they spent much of their married life apart as fugitives or prisoners and had no children. Nineteen years after their marriage, she died as the result of complications from childbirth.

Kingship, Queenship, and the Interplay of Gender in Monarchy

The *golpe de Tordesillas* generally merits a few paragraphs in most political histories of medieval Spain. Eloy Benito Ruano and José Manuel Nieto Soria both regard *infante* Enrique as a willful and obstinate man who seemed to think that marrying Juan II's sister would legitimize his illegal actions and bring him a crown of his own. They argue that Enrique's ambitions dovetailed with those of the rest of his family and that he was motivated by disdain for Juan's submission to his mother, his uncle and de Luna.[38] Luis Suárez Fernández takes these arguments a step further, emphasizing that Juan's poor governing skills empowered factions of wealthy and embittered Castilian nobles who sought to limit royal power and dared to oppose Juan openly. These conditions fueled Enrique's personal ambition and created a political volatility that continued throughout the reign of Juan and his son, Enrique IV (1454–74).[39]

Infante Enrique wanted a kingdom of his own, like his elder brothers and his cousin, but his *golpe* was more than simply a power grab. The conflicting family interests, particularly Enrique's determined intent to marry the *infanta* Catalina, reveal that the *golpe* of Tordesilla was as much about women as men. Focusing on the men involved fails to consider how much Enrique's success or failure depended on the Trastámara queens and an *infanta*, who were key negotiators and the objects of carefully wrought marital strategies. Situating queens in the *golpe* widens the focus to include crucial elements such as marriage, dowry, and inheritance and demonstrates that monarchy was not sole rule by a man, but a dynamic relationship that involved the entire royal family. This move, in

---

38 Benito Ruano, pp. 21–4; José Nieto Soria, "Propaganda política y poder real en la Castilla Trastámara: Una perspectiva de análisis," *Anuario de Estudios Medievales*, 25/2 (1995): pp. 489–515.

39 Luis Suárez Fernández, *Nobleza y monarquía: Puntos de vista sobre la historia política castellana del siglo XV*, 2nd edn (Valladolid: Universidad de Valladolid, 1975), pp. 74–101; William D. Phillips, *Enrique IV and the Crisis of Fifteenth-Century Castile (1425–1480)* (Cambridge, MA: Medieval Academy of America, 1978).

turn, illuminates attitudes toward women, and especially queens in positions of power, and the ideas of gender that undergird monarchy.[40]

The language of the chronicles eloquently express late-medieval social and cultural attitudes toward masculinity, femininity, and monarchical power. They portray Enrique as arrogant, ambitious, belligerent, and wily and Juan II of Castile as weak, amiable, submissive, and bookish. The chroniclers' message is clear: *infante* Enrique is assertively masculine, King Juan submissively feminine, and masculine is definitely preferred.[41] Juan's reliance on his favorite, Alvaro de Luna, certainly helped cement his reputation. While there is no credible evidence that Juan held de Luna as anything more than a mentor or perhaps a father figure, what mattered to his contemporaries was his docile submission to him. For monarchy to succeed, the king may never appear to be more ruled than ruler. Juan's deference inverted the cultural norm, making him appear weak and feminine, more as a queen than a strong and masculine king. Worse, de Luna was a man of low rank and illegitimate birth. Juan's dependency on de Luna doubly diminished his royal masculinity, making him appear more feminine than if he simply had been under the thumb of noble advisers. The message is clear: submission and deference define femininity while intellect and leadership define masculinity.

Equally damaging in the eyes of his contemporaries, however, was Juan II's reliance on women. Queens are instrumental to a king's success, and a good Spanish queen was the king's partner, expected to rule alongside him. Queens Catalina, Leonor, and María of Castile possessed formidable resources of power, but they were careful to stay within the proscribed boundaries of their official authority, never appearing to be anything other than a good wife, mother, and sister. There is nothing exceptional in their actions, but no matter what Juan did, he suffered by comparison. He seemed less manly in both appearance and rulership than his mother, who as queen-regent took council with male advisers and followed traditional norms of queenship. Pérez de Guzmán lamented that "when King Fernando of Aragon died [in 1416], peace and harmony also died in Castilla." Because the kingdom was then ruled by Catalina as sole regent, Pérez de Guzmán was implying that no good could come of rule by a woman,

---

[40] Theresa Earenfight, "Without the Persona of the Prince: Kings, Queens and the Idea of Monarchy in Late Medieval Europe," *Gender and History*, 19/1 (2007): pp. 1–21; Elizabeth A. Lehfeldt, "Ideal Men: Masculinity and Decline in Seventeenth-Century Spain," *Renaissance Quarterly*, 61/2 (2008): pp. 463–94.

[41] Antonio Feros, *Kingship and Favoritism in the Spain of Philip III, 1598–1621* (Cambridge: Cambridge University Press, 2000); J.W. Elliott and L.W.B. Brockliss (eds), *The World of the Favourite* (New Haven, CT: Yale University Press, 1999).

considered by nature to be disorderly and unruly. But Catalina governed well as sole regent. It was only after her death in 1418 that violence ensued and only then because young Juan failed to provide a strong masculine presence.[42] A king dominated by a queen mother in his youth was bad enough, but Juan as an adult was held hostage by his cousin and dominated by his favorite. While his aunt Leonor alternately opposed and supported her son Enrique's usurpation, his own sister María worked assiduously to save him from deposition or death. Leonor and María were careful to govern beside, never from above, but their actions, swift and effective, made it clear to all just how weak and easily governed Juan was.

The women in Juan's life, no matter how strong, were not criticized openly as threats to his masculinity. Except for harsh comments on Catalina's manliness, there was no public outcry against either Leonor or María of Castile. Queens Catalina, Leonor, and María of Aragon were models of motherhood that supported the king as father. Although María of Castile and her sister, *infanta* Catalina, did not have children, in neither case were they faulted for this.[43] Where all these women performed best, however, was in the political realm. In this, they conformed to the accepted norms of queenship for both Castile, where the regency was considered a natural offshoot of a mother's duty as guardian and tutor of her children, and the Crown of Aragon, where the office of the queen-lieutenant, established in the thirteenth century, was taken for granted as the queen's prerogative.[44] They understood their place in the largely, but not entirely, masculine institution of monarchy, but by doing what good medieval Spanish queens were supposed to do, they upset the gender balance.

Enrique III and Juan II were perceived by their contemporaries to be passive when they should have been active, feminine when they should have been masculine. Fernando I, Alfonso V, and Juan of Navarre, on the other hand, were always assertive, never submissive and thus models of the masculinity deemed necessary for a good king. Juan II upset the masculine-feminine balance of the familial and political dynamics of monarchy. His masculine reputation was saved by the fact that his marriages to María of Aragon and later to Isabel of Portugal were conventionally successful and without strife. María of Aragon was deferential and shadowy, almost entirely supplanted in her expected role of intimate and trusted adviser by de Luna. Although not a cuckoo in the

[42] Pérez de Guzmán, pp. 12, 53–7.

[43] María of Castile suffered from a variety of medical ailments, which made her contemporaries more forgiving of her and far more critical of Alfonso who was criticized for failing in his duty to live with his wife and produce children.

[44] Earenfight, "Absent Kings," pp. 33–9, 43–4; Earenfight, *King's Other Body*, pp. 1–18.

marital bed, he clearly shoved her away from the king's side in governance. No one questioned the paternity of Juan's four children, leaving intact his heterosexual virility and potency. This suggests that the problem was not Juan's physical body, it was his kingly body—infantilized, submissive, ruled instead of ruling, dependent on both low-born men and royal women, and therefore more feminine than masculine. This made him a socially acceptable target for his sexually and militarily assertive masculine cousin and fueled the anxieties of Castilian nobles who grew more alarmed by Juan's dependency on de Luna than on the women in his life.

The problem then is less about the queens and more about the kings. Anxiety concerning masculinity often occurs in a society in transition or decline.[45] Juan II inherited political volatility from the disordered fourteenth century and *infante* Enrique's actions were produced by and resulted from anxieties both political and personal. But his reaction to this disorder—the violent seizure of the king, his aggressive pursuit of Catalina, his contumacious bellicose actions after 1423—eloquently expressed his belief that a more masculine king was necessary and that he was just the man for the job. The unstable relations of power in Juan's reign persisted in that of his son, Enrique IV, who faced scathing criticisms throughout his reign clearly revealing fears that unstable gender roles disturbed the social and political order. Like his father, Enrique relied on favorites, was denigrated as a weakling, and was under near-constant threat from noble factions. Unlike his father, he was called a bad husband, a cuckold, and a homosexual, raising questions about the paternity of Juana, his eldest daughter, which led to a war of succession ultimately won by his younger daughter, Isabel, whose paternity was certain.[46] Critics feared that "the office of the king" was lacking, by which they meant an assertive heterosexually masculine king who ruled, rather than submitted.[47]

Once again, the realm was saved by a woman. The "quasi-miraculous" reign of Isabel and her husband Fernando II of Aragon (1474–1516) restored Castile from anarchy to order.[48] Fernando del Pulgar credits this "marvelous thing"

[45] Lehfeldt, "Ideal Men," p. 465. See also Barbara Weissberger, *Isabel Rules: Constructing Queenship, Wielding Power* (Minneapolis, MN: University of Minnesota Press, 2004), pp. 69–95.

[46] On the sexual dynamics of Enrique's troubled marriages, see Weissberger, *Isabel Rules*, pp. 71–9.

[47] Fernando del Pulgar, *Letras: Glosa a las coplas de Mingo Revulgo*, ed. J. Domínguez Bordona (Madrid: Espasa-Calpe, 1929), p. 133.

[48] See Theresa Earenfight, "Two Bodies, One Spirit: Isabel and Fernando's Construction of Monarchical Partnership," in Barbara Weissberger (ed.), *Queen Isabel I of Castile: Power, Patronage, Persona* (Woodbridge: Boydell, 2008): pp. 3–18; cf. Elizabeth A. Lehfeldt, "The

with Isabel's diligence and good government, but the evidence suggests that the success of Isabel and Fernando is more than just a question of her "masculine" talent for administration and diplomacy.[49] Isabel's success, like that of Leonor of Albuquerque and María of Castile, was due to her understanding of the gender norms and codes of her age. She had a talent for conveying her authority so that it did not challenge Fernando's masculinity, but rather it strengthened it. Like Leonor of Albuquerque, she was attentive to conventionally feminine traits. A devoted mother to five children and faithful wife who sewed her husband's shirts and tended his wounds, Isabel astutely mingled these qualities with masculine traits of governance, including participation in the conquest of Granada. She boldly, and famously, carried an unsheathed sword to her coronation. That action was controversial but not fatal, and throughout her reign she was careful that her femininity counterbalanced and remained sensitive to Fernando's unambiguous masculinity. She ruled Castile in her own right but astutely ceded to him control over military affairs and foreign diplomacy. She accepted his extramarital affairs like a faithful wife but also made it clear that she was hurt by them. He was the sexually assertive provider, procreator, and protector, not the least feminine and certainly not submissive to his wife even as he deferred to her superior authority in Castile.[50] The lesson they learned and used to good effect was that monarchy is an institution that functions best when masculine and feminine forces are carefully balanced.

Queen at War: Shared Sovereignty and Gender in Representations of the Granada Campaign," in Weissberger, *Queen Isabel*, pp. 108–19. For context, see Hillgarth, vol. 2, p. 342.

[49] Fernando del Pulgar, p. 224; Earenfight, "Two Bodies," pp. 3–18.

[50] Lehfeldt, "Ruling Sexuality," pp. 33–4; Weissberger, *Isabel Rules*, pp. 28–68; Earenfight, "Two Bodies," p. 18.

Chapter 11

Don Alvaro de Luna and the Indictment against Royal Favoritism in Late Medieval Castile

L.J. Andrew Villalon

One day in the early summer of 1453, an armed escort entered the plaza at Valladolid to the sound of wailing trumpets and a herald, loudly proclaiming a royal death sentence.[1] At some distance rode the condemned man shrouded in a black cape astride a mule decked in mourning, a lone Franciscan friar walking at his side.[2] After a day's stay of execution to prepare himself and arrange his

1 This chapter grew out of a paper delivered in 1997 at the Congress on Medieval Studies held at Western Michigan University. I owe particular thanks to Professor Emerita Lynne Echegaray who was kind enough to read several incarnations of this article and make quite a few suggestions for its improvement, most of which I have heeded. Unless otherwise noted, all translations are my own.

2 The official chronicle of Juan II was composed by several authors, the only one whose identity we know for certain being Alvar García de Santa María, a member of the kingdom's most famous *converso* family. See "Crónica del serenísimo príncipe don Juan, segundo rey deste nombre en Castilla y en León," in Cayetano Rosell (ed.), *Crónicas de los reyes de Castilla*, vol. 2, Biblioteca de autores españoles, vol. 68 (1877; reprint, Madrid: Ediciones Atlas, 1953), pp. 277–695 (hereafter cited as "Crónica Juan"). Other significant accounts of the reign include one written by the king's falconer, Pedro Carrillo de Huete, and its subsequent reworking attributed to a major political figure, Bishop Lope Barrientos. See Pedro Carillo de Huete, *Crónica del halconero de Juan II*, ed. Juan de Mata Carriazo (Madrid: Espasa-Calpe, 1946); Lope Barrientos, *Refundición de la crónica del halconero*, ed. Juan de Mata Carriazo (Madrid: Espasa-Calpe, 1947). The most positive account of de Luna is the so-called *Crónica de don Alvaro de Luna*, officially anonymous but widely believed to have been written by his loyal retainer, Gonzalo Chacon, who would later become an important official in the reign of the Catholic Monarchs. See *Crónica de Alvaro de Luna*, ed. Juan de Mata Carriazo (Madrid: Espasa-Calpe, 1940), especially pp. 428–35 (hereafter cited as *Crónica Alvaro*). By contrast, the most unfavorable view of the constable can be found in the work of Alonso de Palencia, later the official chronicler to Juan's son, Enrique IV (1454–74). See Alonso de Palencia, *Crónica de Enrique IV* (3 vols, Madrid: Ediciones Atlas, 1973–75), vol. 1, pp. 42–9.

worldly affairs, Alvaro de Luna had spent much of the night in prayer. Early that morning, having confessed and heard Mass, he took a light breakfast, then mounted his mule to ride the last several hundred yards to the carpet-strewn scaffold covered by an awning.

Upon arriving, he dismounted without hesitation and after exchanging a few words with the guards, climbed the steps. When his executioner expressed regret, Don Alvaro replied that he must do his duty, requesting only that it be quick and clean. Having handed his cape and ring to a loyal page, he agreed that his hands must be bound to prevent any instinctive movement to protect his throat, again asking only that the executioner use a silken cord he had brought with him rather than resort to a common rope. The condemned sank to his knees; the executioner swung the axe, then raised the head for all to see. By one account, a loud cry of mourning went up from the crowd.

After three days of public exposure, the corpse was buried in the church of San Andres outside the city walls, in a cemetery ordinarily reserved for "evildoers." The head, displayed on a pole, remained in place for nine days, after which it was reunited with the body. Two months later, both parts were removed to the Franciscan monastery, where the deceased had asked to be interred. Subsequently, Don Alvaro experienced one more move, to the cathedral of Toledo where a sumptuous tomb had been erected.[3]

Thus ended the life of one of history's most famous royal favorites, who rose to become constable of Castile (the kingdom's leading military official), duke of Trujillo, and grand master of the crusading Order of Santiago, a man who guided the destinies of Castile for some three decades. Contemporaries saw in his spectacular rise and fall an example of how fortune's wheel controlled human affairs, first raising men to great heights, then tumbling them into the abyss.[4]

---

3 "Crónica Juan," p. 683.

4 At the end of Juan II's official chronicle, his last chronicler embarks on a rhetorical flight addressed to Boccaccio (d. 1377), whose widely read treatise *De Casibus Virorum Illustrium* dealt with figures whose lives illustrated the workings of fortune. According to the chronicler, the great Renaissance author would undoubtedly have added de Luna to his list of men whom *fortuna* first raised up, then sent plummeting to their destruction. "Crónica Juan," p. 691. An alternate interpretation of de Luna's fall, more typically Christian, was drafted shortly after his death by Castile's great warrior-poet Iñigo Lopez de Mendoza, first marqués of Santillana, who had actually helped engineer the event. In two poems, the *Coplas de don Alvaro de Luna* and the *Doctrinal de privados*, Mendoza argued that his old enemy, whom he compared to Lucifer, had committed crimes and vices for which he deservedly ended on the block. See Michèle S. de Cruz-Sáenz, "The Marqués de Santillana's *Coplas* on Don Alvaro de Luna and the *Doctrinal de privados*," *Hispanic Review*, 49 (1981): pp. 219–24.

Over the centuries, not a few Spanish playwrights have treated his fall as the stuff of high tragedy.

By exploring the circumstances that brought Alvaro de Luna to power, the periodic outbursts of aristocratic violence arising from his presence at the side of Juan II (1406–54), and the spectacular nature of his collapse, this chapter will attempt to shed light on the role of royal favorites in late medieval Spain and the dangers faced by any medieval monarch who relied too heavily upon such a figure in conducting the government of his or her kingdom. The chapter will also examine two documents, drafted 13 years apart that taken together constitute a detailed indictment against this most famous of medieval royal favorites and, by extension, against royal favoritism in general.[5]

The term "royal favorite" (derived from *favori*, a sixteenth-century French designation for such individuals) connotes a person, male or female, who enjoys an extremely close relationship with the monarch and the emoluments that habitually accompany this status, usually including wealth, rank, and influence, and often considerable political power.[6] The relationship between monarch and favorite may, but need not be, sexual.[7] And while it usually involves at least a close friendship between the two, even this may in some instances be lacking. (Consider, for example, the case of Louis XIII of France [1610–43] and Cardinal Richelieu.) This figure who through royal favor occupies a preeminent position in the governance of a kingdom has come to be widely known among scholars as a "minister-favorite" or, to use the Spanish equivalent, a *privado*.[8]

---

5 Both documents are published verbatim in Juan II's chronicle. For an interesting discussion of how some late medieval chroniclers loaded their works with public documents see Chris Given-Wilson's *Chronicles: The Writing of History in Medieval England* (London: Palgrave Macmillan, 2004), especially pp. 14–20.

6 For the derivation of the term, see J.H. Elliott's introduction to *The World of the Favorite*, ed. J.H. Elliott and L.W.B. Brockliss (New Haven, CT: Yale University Press, 1999), p. 1.

7 While the term "royal favorite," especially when applied to a woman, is often used in reference to a monarch's lover, it can equally refer to a person whose close, but not necessarily sexual, connection to a king or queen allowed that individual to help direct affairs of state. A Google websearch for the term "royal favorite" (conducted on July 4, 2012) produced numerous hits referring to royal lovers, mistresses, and concubines.

8 The term "minister-favorite" appears to have been coined by A. Lloyd Moote, "Richelieu as Chief Minister: A Comparative Study of the Favourite in Early Seventeenth-Century Politics," in L.W.B. Brockliss (ed.), *Richelieu and His Age* (Oxford: Clarendon Press, 1992). I.A.A. Thompson, "The Institutional Background in the Rise of the Minister-Favorite," in *World of the Favorite*, p. 14, prefers use of the alternate Spanish word, *valido*, in reference to early modern favorites. See also L.W.B. Brockliss, "Concluding Remarks: The Anatomy of the Minister-Favourite," in *World of the Favorite*, p. 280.

Although biographies treating such men, especially those of the early modern period, are fairly numerous, few works undertake a meaningful comparative study of the sort called for by French historian Jean Bérenger in his seminal *Annales* article of 1974.[9] Bérenger noted the simultaneous triumph of minister-favorites in several early seventeenth-century monarchies and argued that this was not coincidental but almost certainly reflected some change taking place during the period. To further explore the issues raised by Bérenger, J.H. Elliott and Laurence Brockliss organized an international colloquium at Oxford in 1996, from which emerged a collection of essays, *The World of the Favorite*, that has become the most important comparative treatment on the subject. While this collection centers on the early modern period, in particular the seventeenth century, the most frequently mentioned medieval figure is Alvaro de Luna.[10] In fact, James Boyden's contribution to the volume compares de Luna and his spectacular end to a sixteenth-century Spanish counterpart, the Prince of Eboli, and his relatively "soft-landing."[11]

The Rise of Alvaro de Luna

The de Luna family's Castilian branch migrated into the kingdom from neighboring Aragon during the civil wars that overthrew Pedro "the Cruel" (1350–66/1367–69) and replaced him with his illegitimate half-brother, Enrique II (1366–67/1369–79). Upon seizing the throne, Enrique granted properties in Castile to several Aragonese nobles who had loyally supported him, including Alvaro de Luna's grandfather, Juan Martínez de Luna.[12] Around 1388, Don Juan's younger son, Alvaro, fathered an illegitimate child, originally named Pedro. The boy's name was changed to Alvaro at age 7 when he was

---

[9] Jean Bérenger, "Pour une enquete européenne: Le problem du ministériat au XVIIe siècle," *Annales*, 29 (1974): pp. 166–92.

[10] Elliott's introduction to *World of the Favorite* alludes to de Luna five times, more than he mentions any of the great seventeenth-century favorites, including Richelieu, Lerma, and Olivares.

[11] James M. Boyden, "'Fortune has Stripped You of Your Splendour': Favorites and their Fates in Fifteenth and Sixteenth-Century Spain," in *World of the Favorite*, pp. 26–37.

[12] *Crónica Alvaro*, pp. 10–11. Juan Martínez is repeatedly mentioned in Pedro Lopez de Ayala, "Crónica del rey don Pedro," in Cayetano Rosell (ed.), *Crónicas de los reyes de Castilla*, vol. 1, Biblioteca de autores españoles, vol. 66 (1875; reprint, Madrid: Ediciones Atlas, 1953), pp. 393–614. For a more recent edition of the chronicle, see Pedro Lopez de Ayala, *Crónica del rey don Pedro*, ed. Constance L. Wilkins and Heanon M. Wilkins (Madison, WI: Hispanic Seminary of Medieval Studies, 1985.).

recognized on his father's deathbed.[13] After being raised by two uncles, one of whom was Archbishop Pedro de Luna of Toledo,[14] young Alvaro was introduced into the Castilian court as a royal page around 1408.

His family was not disappointed in its hope that the young man (approximately 20 at the time) would ingratiate himself in his new surroundings: "in very little time he won the hearts and esteem of all those who counted most."[15] Apparently 4-year-old Juan II, like those serving him, fell under the spell of the newcomer and the pair became inseparable. "[King Juan] took delight in the young man's friendship as well as his service and always kept him nearby."[16] Attempts by the king's guardians to cool this budding friendship proved unavailing, and in 1414 the queen mother, who had charge of her son, agreed to de Luna's first major promotion to the office of royal *maestresala*.[17] Within a few years it would become evident that under his courtly exterior there lurked the soul of a consummate politician.

De Luna's appearance at court in 1408 came at a turbulent moment in Castilian history. Less than two years earlier, in December 1406, the *cortes* of Castile had gathered in Toledo to discuss Enrique III's (1390–1406) plans for invading Muslim Granada. The king, however, "fell so ill that he was unable to take part in the proceedings."[18] While his younger brother Fernando presided over the *cortes*, Enrique's condition continued to deteriorate and on Christmas Day he died, leaving 22-month old Juan as heir to the kingdom.

---

13 Although de Luna's own chronicler does not mention his illegitimacy, from other sources, in particular the highly negative chronicle of Palencia, pp. 42–3, we learn about this defect and the name change.

14 The archbishop appears to have received his appointment from his own uncle, the Avignon pope Benedict XIII, a member of the Aragonese branch of the family. For clarification of the family's genealogy, see *Crónica Alvaro*, pp. 11–12.

15 *Crónica Alvaro*, p. 14.

16 Barrientos, p. 36.

17 *Crónica Alvaro*, pp. 17–18.

18 A description of the 1406 cortes appears in a short prelude to the chronicle of Juan II. The prelude's heading or title runs "Porque en tanto que duró la enfermedad del Christianísimo rey don Enrique, tercero deste nombre, hasta su fallescimiento, pasaron algunas cosas dignas de memoria, é tales, de que saludables consejos se pueden tomar, determiné de las escribir ante de principiar la crónica del serenísimo rey don Juan segundo deste nombre, hijo suyo," in Cayetano Rosell (ed.), *Crónicas de los reyes de Castilla*, vol. 2, Biblioteca de autores españoles, vol. 68 (1877; reprint, Madrid: Ediciones Atlas, 1953), pp. 259–64. The line "I determined to write about this before beginning the chronicle of the most serene King Don Juan" strongly suggests it was written by Juan's first chronicler, Alvar García de Santa María.

As is often the case, succession of a minor brought in its wake a chaotic state of affairs. In his will, the king had not only established as joint regents his wife, Catherine of Lancaster, and his brother, Fernando, he had also named several trusted officials to look after his son and see to the boy's education. When they arrived at Segovia where the royal family was residing, they found that the dowager queen had ordered the city gates closed against them and adamantly refused to surrender her son into the care of anyone else. Only a hasty compromise which permitted Catherine to retain control over the king's person while compensating the officials for their grudging renunciation of that function prevented a crisis from arising on the eve of coronation.[19]

This clash proved to be a mere prelude to more serious problems. It soon became painfully apparent that the two strong-willed regents did not get along. Despite what appear to have been Fernando's best efforts to arrive at some arrangement with his sister-in-law,[20] matters eventually reached such a pass that, in the words of one chronicler, "nothing was accomplished since decisions reached one day were reversed on the following day."[21] A political crisis was barely averted when the pair managed to agree to pursue the war against Granada proposed by the late monarch, and Fernando assumed control of the military effort. The prince's departure south to organize the campaign triggered another clause from the king's will which called for an administrative division of the realm in the event of the regents' experiencing any prolonged geographical separation. The dividing line was to be the Tagus River which flowed through central Castile: Catherine would govern all Castilian territory north of the river; Fernando would hold sway to the south.[22] Since the queen mother retained control of her son and Fernando remained absent on campaign for long periods, the Castilian situation stabilized for several years, permitting the regency to function however uneasily. In 1410, Fernando captured the fortress of Antequera and became known thereafter as Fernando de Antequera.[23]

Events in the neighboring kingdom of Aragon soon upset this fragile political balance. In 1410, the Aragonese monarch, Martí (1396–1410), died without issue. Following his demise, that kingdom entered a troubled period of interregnum, during which several men claimed the throne. In 1412, with

19 Ibid., pp. 263–4.

20 "Crónica Juan," p. 278.

21 Ibid., p. 283.

22 "Porque en tanto que duró la enfermedad del Christianísimo rey don Enrique," p. 267.

23 Joseph F. O'Callaghan, *A History of Medieval Spain* (Ithaca, NY: Cornell University Press, 197), p. 542.

the very real possibility of civil war looming on the horizon, nine Aragonese magnates met at Caspe to resolve the dynastic crisis. After some deliberation, these arbitrators declared Fernando de Antequera the rightful successor.[24] Later that year, he crossed the frontier between the two kingdoms for the last time and took up permanent residence in his new realm. In 1416, just as he was beginning to settle into the kingship, Fernando died at the age of 35.[25]

He left behind four sons: Alfonso, who succeeded to the crown of Aragon; Juan, who became king of Navarre through marriage in 1420 and followed his brother on the Aragonese throne 38 years later; Enrique, who was appointed grand master of the Order of Santiago; and Pedro [26] These four royal offspring, collectively referred to as the *infantes* of Aragon, were also richly endowed with lands in Castile and continued to play an important role in that kingdom's history for decades to come. Until the mid-1440s, one or another of them would stand at the center of opposition to Alvaro de Luna.

Before departing for Aragon, Fernando had attempted to establish a new regency council, including four of the realm's leading nobles, which was to share power with the queen mother.[27] This arrangement, however, began to break down almost immediately as the other members brought intense pressure on Catherine to end her exclusive control over the king's person. (For the preceding six years, she and her son had lived in near seclusion, mostly in Valladolid.)[28] Although finally forced to surrender the young monarch into the keeping of others, the dowager did everything within her power to retain influence over him. Apparently more concerned with insuring her own position than maintaining harmony among the regents, she soon began to plot with individual members of the council and other great nobles. For their part, most of these magnates acted no less selfishly; having fallen out among themselves, they welcomed the opportunity to enlist her aid in the ensuing power struggle. By the time Catherine of Lancaster died in 1418, the court of her son had once more become a battle ground of bickering factions.

The next year, Juan II reached his fourteenth birthday and declared an end to his minority; his assumption of authority, however, did little or nothing to put an end to the power struggle which divided his leading nobles. Particularly

---

24 "Crónica Juan," pp. 327–8, 333–4, 342–5.

25 Ibid., pp. 346, 370–71. Jerónimo Zurita y Castro, *Anales de la Corona de Aragón*, ed. Ángel Canellas López (8 vols, Zaragoza: Institución Fernando el Católico, 1967–1977), vol. 5, pp. 287–9, 370.

26 A fifth son, Sancho, predeceased his father. Barrientos, p. 23.

27 Ibid., p. 22.

28 Ibid., pp. 24–5.

troublesome was the continuing presence in Castile of two of the *infante*s of Aragon, Juan and Enrique, each of whom became the leader of a rival faction. In addition, many Castilian nobles did not want either man to control the king.[29] In the face of this factionalism, several compromise plans for governing the realm collapsed, and as the struggle for influence over Juan II escalated, "great suspicion and enmity grew up between the two brothers."[30]

For a time, a power-sharing agreement preserved the uneasy peace, but in the summer of 1420 matters came to a head as Enrique, sensing that he was losing the contest, decided on a bold stroke. When the elder *infante*, Juan, and many of his leading supporters journeyed to Navarre for his wedding to Princess Blanche, heiress to that kingdom's throne, Enrique executed a coup d'état. One morning at dawn, in the city of Tordesillas, he and his followers burst into the royal residence, seized control of the king and expelled those of his ministers whose loyalties lay with the other *infante*.[31] Thereafter, for the better part of six months, he held the king under what amounted to house arrest and governed in his name.

Aggrandizement of de Luna and Political Realignment in Castile

It was during this crisis that Alvaro de Luna came of age politically. When Enrique seized the king and arrested or banished his brother's supporters, de Luna was spared despite his close association with Juan Hurtado de Mendoza, a member of the elder *infante*'s inner circle.[32] Thinking it best to placate the frightened and angry young monarch, Enrique permitted his favorite to remain at court, a move he felt safe in making since de Luna was still young and politically inexperienced. Rather than expel him, Enrique tried to buy his support by appointing him to the royal council and paying him a hefty salary.[33]

For his part, while dissembling his intentions well enough to remain in Enrique's good graces, de Luna began scheming to affect the king's release.[34] Late in November 1420, his efforts bore fruit. On one of the brief hunting trips Juan

[29] "Crónica Juan," pp. 379–80; Barrientos, pp. 30–34.

[30] "Crónica Juan," p. 380.

[31] There is disagreement among the chroniclers as to whether this event occurred in June or July, 1420. Cf. "Crónica Juan," pp. 380–82; *Crónica Alvaro*, pp. 35–8; Barrientos, pp. 34–5.

[32] "Crónica Juan," pp. 379–80.

[33] Ibid., p. 381; *Crónica Alvaro*, pp. 37–8.

[34] "Crónica Juan," pp. 389–90; *Crónica Alvaro*, 39–42; Barrientos, 37–8.

was permitted, he and a few of his most trusted followers managed to elude the *infante*'s guards and make a dash to sanctuary in the castle of Montalbán.[35] Although Enrique immediately set off in pursuit, he arrived too late to recapture the royal fugitive. His siege of the castle at first proved effective but ultimately collapsed in the face of superior military forces loyal to the other *infante*, now generally referred to in the chronicles as Juan of Navarre. Having regained his freedom, the king quickly moved against those who had held him captive. Enrique's supporters were stripped of their recent grants and, if unlucky enough to fall into the king's hands, promptly imprisoned.[36]

The king, like most of his chroniclers, credited de Luna for his escape. Afterwards, the favorite's rise was nothing short of meteoric. By the mid-1420s, he was rapidly supplanting all others in the councils of the realm and was well on his way to achieving a hegemony over Castilian politics which he would continue to exercise with only brief interruptions for nearly three decades. In 1421, the monarch conferred upon Don Alvaro the town of San Esteban de Gormaz with the title of count.[37] In the move against Enrique's followers, de Luna profited extensively from confiscations, obtaining from Ruy López Davalos not only the office of constable of Castile but also much of that unfortunate nobleman's estate.[38] These were only the first of many honors and properties showered upon him over the next few decades.

The *privado*'s rising fortunes drove the Aragonese *infantes* to makes peace among themselves and precipitated a major realignment of Castilian politics. By 1425, new lines were clearly drawn. Juan of Navarre joined his eldest brother, King Alfonso V of Aragon (1416–58), in interceding for the freedom of their younger sibling, Enrique, who had been imprisoned in Castile since the failure of his coup.[39] From this point onward, they became perennial opponents of de Luna in the struggle over who would control Castile.

Most of the time it was an unequal contest. Due to his enormous and enduring influence over the king for the better part of 30 years, de Luna effectively ruled the kingdom. Meanwhile, the *infantes* and some of their high-profile supporters spent much of their time outside the realm, either in Navarre or Aragon. Given

---

35 "Crónica Juan," p. 390; *Crónica Alvaro*, pp. 41–3.

36 A notable example of royal retribution can be seen in the case of Garcí Fernández Manrique, Enrique's chief steward, who lost not only lost his newly acquired title to the county of Castañeda, but spent the next six years in close confinement behind the walls of Avila. "Crónica Juan," pp. 415, 449.

37 Ibid., p. 401; *Crónica Alvaro*, pp. 46–9.

38 "Crónica Juan," pp. 424–5; *Crónica Alvaro*, p. 51.

39 "Crónica Juan," pp. 431–4; *Crónica Alvaro*, pp. 54–7.

their secure political base within those two neighboring kingdoms, de Luna's enemies could never be entirely neutralized. They waited in the wings, ready to step forward and provide leadership whenever fear and resentment of the constable might spill over into open rebellion.

Critical to any violent outbreak were the realm's powerful old families, many of which tended to regard someone like the de Luna as a mere arriviste—a "new man" raised above them by the unhealthy excess of royal favor. These entrenched representatives of the established order complained that not only was he a foreigner but, worse yet, one of illegitimate birth. They bitterly resented the complete domination he exercised over the king—even more than they would have resented a similar domination exercised by one of their own number. They also feared his ever-increasing wealth and power. As a result, a not insignificant number of them were on the lookout for a favorable opportunity to bring de Luna down. On three occasions—1427, 1429, and 1438–55—opposition to the favorite spilled over into open rebellion against his dominance. Each time sizeable segments of the Castilian aristocracy joined the *infantes* of Aragon in an attempt to expel him from the body politic; despite some initial success, each attempt fell short of the mark.

Political Crises of 1427 and 1429

In 1427, the *infantes* maneuvered Juan II into appointing a commission to hear complaints against the constable and then to approve, however unwillingly, the commission's recommendation that he be banished from court for 18 months. Typically, at the very moment of success, their alliance began to collapse. Hostility to the favorite had been the cement which held them together; with his removal from the scene, the opposition once again fell to feuding, making possible de Luna's triumphal return long before the 18 months had elapsed. All that had been accomplished was to strengthen the ties between the king and his favorite.[40]

Reestablishment of de Luna's preeminent position at court soon precipitated a second crisis far more serious than the one which had led up to his temporary banishment. In the summer of 1429, King Alfonso of Aragon and his brother, now King Juan of Navarre, entered Castile at the head of a large army.[41] According

[40] "Crónica Juan," pp. 442–3, 446; *Crónica Alvaro*, pp. 62–4.

[41] "Crónica Juan," pp. 451–9; *Crónica Alvaro*, pp. 71–83; Huete, pp. 37–9; Barrientos, pp. 70–79.

to one chronicler, "while acting on the pretence of wishing to meet with the king, they really came in order to meddle in the affairs of the kingdom."[42] Once again, the thinly disguised goal was to find some means of separating Juan II from his constable.

Since the last such attempt, the attachment between the two had grown even stronger; as a result, Juan now proved completely unwilling to endorse any new "compromise" at his constable's expense. He determined to resist the entry of his royal cousins by force, dispatching an advance guard under de Luna to intercept them near the frontier while he himself remained temporarily in the city of Palencia, awaiting the remainder of his army. To all of the great nobles answering his summons, King Juan administered a loyalty oath—a precaution dictated by the fact that not a few of them sympathized with the ultimate goal of the invasion.[43]

Especially suspect was the loyalty of the invaders' younger brother, Prince Enrique. Since the collapse of the last effort to expel de Luna, that mercurial nobleman had sworn "to prevent any entry into the realm undertaken by the king of Navarre and to resist it in any way he could."[44] Nevertheless, on the eve of the *infantes*' incursion, Enrique crossed the Aragonese border in order to meet with his elder brothers. Although he did not openly declare his intentions, there is evidence that he promised to join them with the forces at his disposal once they had actually entered Castile.[45] When the king's call to arms reached him, Enrique failed to answer it. He also avoided taking the new loyalty oath in person, although he did swear through an intermediary.[46] Finally, shortly after his brothers crossed the frontier, he rode out to meet them.[47]

When the Castilian army arrived at the border, Constable de Luna, despite being considerably outnumbered, showed no inclination to back off and await reinforcements. Conflict seemed inevitable until, at the last moment, the queen of Aragon suggested a compromise: in return for the immediate withdrawal of Aragonese troops from Castile, the constable undertook to convince Juan II that the Castilian properties of the two *infantes* should not be confiscated and that preparations for war against Aragon and Navarre should be halted. Both sides agreed, and a battle was narrowly averted.[48]

---

42 *Crónica Alvaro*, p. 72.

43 The oath is printed in "Crónica Juan," p. 454.

44 *Crónica Alvaro*, p. 73.

45 Ibid., pp. 71–2, 76.

46 "Crónica Juan," pp. 454–5; *Crónica Alvaro*, p. 74.

47 "Crónica Juan," p. 458; *Crónica Alvaro*, p. 76; Huete, p. 37; Barrientos, p. 76.

48 "Crónica Juan," p. 458; *Crónica Alvaro*, pp. 77–83; Huete, p. 38; Barrientos, pp. 76–7

The constable was unable or unwilling to convince the king to accept the compromise; perhaps he made little or no effort to do so.[49] In any case, Juan remained determined to punish his cousins.[50] Consequently, a Castilian army commanded in person by the monarch invaded Aragon. When the Aragonese declined an invitation to meet in the field, this force spent the rest of the summer of 1429 doing as much damage as possible to the neighboring kingdom.[51] This second episode ended with the *infantes* once again in exile and de Luna so thoroughly in control of the king that no new threat to his position would arise for nearly a decade.

The Castilian Aristocracy's Final Attempt to Topple de Luna (1438–45)

The third rebellion against the favorite became the most serious domestic crisis Castile had faced since the Trastámara civil wars a century earlier. Beginning in August 1438, it endured for over seven years and came within an inch of success.[52] The spark was provided by the escape of a nobleman named Pedro Manrique[53] whom the crown had imprisoned.[54] While the chronicles fail to explain the motive for his imprisonment, the aftermath leaves little doubt that he blamed the constable for his misfortunes. Having escaped his jailors, he fled to nearby territory controlled by his close friend and relative, Fadrique Enríquez, Lord Admiral of Castile. Despite pressure from the crown, the admiral staunchly refused to surrender the fugitive. Instead, the two men now called on other relatives and friends to help prevent any attempt to retake him.[55]

From the start, the demand of the rebellious nobles that Constable de Luna be removed from power guaranteed them widespread support. One

---

49 Only one source, de Luna's own chronicle, indicates that he made any real attempt to convince the king that he should acknowledge the agreement. *Crónica Alvaro*, p. 87.

50 The king did offer to make peace with Aragon but only on the condition that King Alfonso not interfere in favor of his brothers when the crown confiscated their Castilian holdings. "Crónica Juan," pp. 462–3.

51 "Crónica Juan," pp. 464–5; Barrientos, pp. 79–80.

52 This period is extensively covered in several of the royal chronicles. Although the most complete account of these events is found in "Crónica Juan," pp. 548–652, almost as important a source is the *Crónica del halconero*, pp. 256–469. By contrast, de Luna's own chronicle contains the poorest coverage of these years, devoting only a few pages to the events from 1437 to 1445.

53 "Crónica Juan," pp. 534–5; Barrientos, pp. 6–19.

54 "Crónica Juan," p. 493.

55 "Crónica Juan," p. 548; Barrientos, p. 222.

after another, disgruntled Castilian aristocrats rallied to their side and before year's end most of the high nobility of the north had entered a new coalition dedicated to the constable's overthrow. A letter written to the king in February 1439, illustrates the deep-seated hostility to de Luna which united and motivated these fiercely independent magnates.

> My Lord, it is notorious ... and manifest to all your subjects that the constable has taken possession of your court and of your very person ... May it please Your Majesty to command the constable to withdraw to ... his own estates taking with him his relatives and supporters in order that Your Majesty may remain completely at liberty.[56]

As revolt spread through the Castilian aristocracy, the *infantes* of Aragon saw in the latest crisis a long-awaited opportunity to regain lands confiscated from them a decade earlier. Consequently, in 1439 King Juan of Navarre and his brother Enrique reentered Castile.[57] Although the younger *infante* almost immediately threw in his lot with the nobles who promised to restore his estates, the king of Navarre was not so quick to commit himself.[58] At first, he posed as a possible mediator between the conflicting parties.[59] By year's end, however, not only had he joined the anti-de Luna coalition, for all intents and purposes he had become its leader.[60] The faction gathered new strength in 1440 when it was joined by the *infantes*' sister, María de Aragon, wife of Juan II,[61] and their son, Enrique, the heir to the throne.[62]

After attempts to crush the rebellion had failed, the king tried to placate the opposition by banishing his constable (with the latter's acquiescence) for a period of six months; this time, however, the nobles were not satisfied

---

56 "Crónica Juan," pp. 549–50; Barrientos, pp. 224–7.

57 Both men had been living in Navarre and Aragon since the unsuccessful invasion of 1429. Their eldest brother, King Alfonso, was conducting the campaign that would eventually win him the crown of Naples and their youngest brother, Pedro, had died in the course of that campaign. Huete, p. 255; Barrientos, p. 222.

58 "Crónica Juan," pp. 552–5; Huete, pp. 279–81.

59 "Crónica Juan," p. 558.

60 Ibid., pp. 433–4, 440–2; Huete, pp. 287–92.

61 The queen's adherence to the coalition opposing de Luna may have resulted from her loss of Montalbán to the constable. On the eve of the crisis, the king had pressured her to surrender to his favorite this property she had inherited. While the author of de Luna's chronicle claims that she had done so willing, other chroniclers dispute this. "Crónica Juan," p. 562; *Crónica Alvaro*, pp. 151–2; Barrientos, p. 214.

62 "Crónica Juan," pp. 433–4, 440–42; Huete, pp. 340–43, 356.

with half measures.[63] Calling up their retainers, they quickly raised a military force numbering in the thousands. They seized major royal cities, including Valladolid, Toledo, Burgos, and Segovia.[64] They hurled letters of defiance (*cartas de desafio*) at the favorite and his remaining supporters while clamoring to make the banishment permanent.[65] Eventually, they forced the monarch to summon a *cortes* from which most of the constable's adherents and close associates were excluded and issued on their own authority an ultimatum condemning him as "a capital enemy, a spendthrift, and a devastator of the realm" who would henceforward stand outside the protection of the law.[66]

When the king determined to resist these radical developments, the coalition seized his person in an attack on Medina del Campo,[67] after which he remained a prisoner in his own court. In September 1441, the coalition forced Juan II to appoint a new commission of four charged with dictating a settlement. Since three of them—Queen María, Prince Enrique, and the admiral—were opposed to the constable, it is not surprising that the sentence they handed down stripped him of power, banished him to his estates for six years, and strictly forbade his having any communication with the monarch.[68] The next several years found the realm governed by what amounted to a regency council headed by the elder *infante*, Juan of Navarre. To all appearances, by the end of 1441 the aristocratic coalition had toppled de Luna from power.

Thereafter, however, its members demonstrated an aristocracy's exquisite ability to seize defeat from the jaws of victory. Removal of the hated favorite removed the cement which had bound together its members and, as early as the autumn of 1441, cracks were beginning to appear in what had been a united front. Despite repeated protestations that they would stand together forever to rid the realm of the constable's pernicious presence, the moment they seemingly achieved that end they began to fall out among themselves. Especially ominous for the coalition was a widening gap between King Juan of Navarre and Crown Prince Enrique of Castile.

In 1440, 16-year-old Enrique had joined his mother, his Aragonese uncles, and the majority of the Castilian nobles in their concerted opposition to

---

63 "Crónica Juan," pp. 556–7.

64 "Crónica Juan," pp. 563, 570–71; Huete, pp. 319–20, 334–6.

65 "Crónica Juan," pp. 552–88.

66 Ibid., 570.

67 Ibid., pp. 586–7; Huete, pp. 417–21.

68 The lengthy sentence banning de Luna and related documentation is printed in what appears to be its entirety in "Crónica Juan," pp. 587–607. A slightly abbreviated version appears in Huete, pp. 421–32.

Alvaro de Luna.[69] For several years, he pursued policies which led not only to de Luna's expulsion but also to his own father's imprisonment at the hands of the Navarrese monarch. By the end of 1443, however, the prince was apparently prepared to do a complete about face. Betraying his former allies, he joined his old enemy, de Luna, in an alliance dedicated to freeing Juan II and breaking the power of the Aragonese *infantes*.

Not a few contemporaries attributed Enrique's actions to the preponderant influence of one man, the next great royal favorite, Juan Pacheco.[70] Son of a minor aristocrat in the service of Alvaro de Luna, Pacheco had been introduced into the crown prince's household by the constable, in hopes that through the young man, he might come to exercise influence over the heir.[71] The confidence in his protégé's ability to bond with Enrique proved to be fully justified. By 1440, "the prince so loved [Pacheco] that nothing was done except by his command."[72] Where de Luna miscalculated was in respect to his own influence over Pacheco. Believing it was to his advantage, Pacheco convinced the prince to throw his weight behind the growing faction that opposed his former mentor.

Nevertheless, the situation which resulted from de Luna's fall appears to have satisfied neither the prince nor his favorite. Enrique became increasingly restive at the complete domination of Castilian affairs exercised by his Aragonese uncles while Pacheco realized that, not being a member of the king of Navarre's inner circle, he was unlikely to reap further benefit from the alliance. Consequently, the two young men were open to overtures from Lope Barrientos,[73] Bishop of Avila, and a partisan of Constable de Luna. The bishop suggested the possibility of an alliance between the prince, the constable, and their respective followers

---

69 Most of the chroniclers date the birth of Enrique to early January, 1425. Only the account of Bishop Barrientos gives the year as 1424. "Crónica Juan," p. 429; *Crónica Alvaro*, p. 54; Huete, p. 9; Barrientos, p. 47.

70 Although Enrique IV had several men who might appropriately be designated "royal favorites," the most important was Juan Pacheco, a man endowed with most of the negative characteristics of Alvaro de Luna but few if any of the constable's redeeming virtues. For a recent study of this less famous but equally controversial figure, see Nancy Marino, *Don Juan Pacheco: Wealth and Power in Late Medieval Spain* (Phoenix, AZ Arizona State University Press, 2006).

71 Pacheco's father, Alonso Telléz Girón, Lord of Belmonte, became a supporter of the constable during the 1420s. "Crónica Juan," p. 569; *Crónica Alvaro*, p. 67.

72 "Crónica Juan," p. 569.

73 A Dominican friar, Barrientos, not only served as confessor to Juan II and tutor to his son, Enrique, but over the decades held a number of important positions in both church and state. The prelate's significance as a historical figure is enhanced by the fact that he has left an account of the period. For a brief biography, see Mata Carriazo's "Estudio preliminar," in Barrientos, pp. cxxxiii–cxxxviii.

devoted to liberating the king and, with his support, driving the *infantes* from the realm.[74]

Having struck a bargain, Barrientos then used an intermediary to approach the constable who was confined to his remaining estates. Although such an alliance might prove his best chance of salvation, de Luna hesitated. He reminded his old friend that it was he who would suffer utter ruin if the prince failed to follow through. Even if he were to credit assurances that Enrique and Pacheco could be trusted (a hard assertion to credit given Pacheco's past record), the combined forces which they could muster would still be no match for those of the opposition.

Ultimately, despite reservations, the constable realized that he had little choice. In March 1444, he agreed to the alliance, reserving his public adherence until his allies had drummed up additional support. Winning over other nobles would not only alter the balance of power, it would make it exceedingly difficult for the prince to back out.[75] By this time, the prospects of finding such men had considerably improved. There were supporters of the constable who had kept a low profile but would now rally to his cause. There was also a growing number who, like the prince, were becoming increasingly restive at the domineering attitude of the Aragonese *infantes*. Some whose grievances against crown or constable had driven them to join the aristocratic coalition were willing to switch sides if Juan and his favorite proved willing to redress those grievances.

Around the end of June 1444, the new alliance, now considerably expanded, gathered in the city of Avila where they were soon joined by de Luna. Together, they issued a public demand that the opposing faction set King Juan at liberty.[76] In July, news arrived that the king had escaped his captors and was on his way to join them. Meanwhile, members of the opposing faction decided to disband temporarily and await a more favorable opportunity to regain control of Castilian affairs. While Juan of Navarre and his brother Enrique left the realm, others retreated behind their castle walls and watched as their less-well protected lands fell to the crown.[77]

In the spring of 1445, the Aragonese *infantes* decided to confront the alliance which had driven them out of Castile the previous summer. On May 19, they and their supporters met Juan II's army near the town of Olmedo and in the ensuing battle were soundly defeated.[78] During the fighting, both de Luna

---

74 "Crónica Juan," p. 614; Huete, pp. 449–50.

75 "Crónica Juan," p. 615; Huete, pp. 441–2, 446.

76 "Crónica Juan," p. 621.

77 Ibid., pp. 623–5.

78 Ibid., pp. 625–9; Huete, pp. 463–5.

and the younger *infante* were wounded; while the former recovered, the latter died shortly thereafter.[79] Although hostilities dragged on for several years, for all intents and purposes the crisis of the 1440s ended on the field of Olmedo. In its wake, the *infantes* were again driven from Castile while Constable de Luna regained the power over national policy which he would continue to exercise for the better part of another decade. At this time, King Juan acknowledged his favorite's victory at Olmedo by engineering his election to the grand mastership of Santiago, Spain's principal crusading order.[80]

Aristocratic Indictment of a Royal Favorite

In the winter of 1440, as the crisis deepened, much of the anti-de Luna coalition[81] gathered in the walled city of Avila where they drafted and then handed to a royal delegation a document amounting to a criminal indictment.[82] Not as all-encompassing as the list of charges habitually leveled against heretics, the document is nevertheless wide-ranging, summarizing better than any other document from the period the hatred an aristocracy felt toward a royal favorite, especially one whom they regarded as an outsider, not born to their exclusive circle.

The indictment begins by setting forth the proper duties of kingship. A good king is to be a good Christian, love and fear God, and obey divine commandments. Royal laws are to be drafted for the benefit of the realm and its inhabitants and, once promulgated, remain inviolable. Nobody's goods are to be taken away except for legitimate causes. A king must preserve the honor of his crown as well as promote the well-being of his subjects. "All good princes must love and protect the three estates of the realm, honoring every individual according to his person and his estate." A king must always strive to be more

[79] *Crónica Alvaro*, p. 177; Huete, pp. 465–6.

[80] "Crónica Juan," pp. 635–6; *Crónica Alvaro*, pp. 177–80.

[81] Signatories specifically named by the chronicler included many from the upper nobility of northern Castile: Admiral Fadrique Enriquez; Pedro de Velasco, count of Haro; Pedro de Zúniga, count of Ledesma; Rodrigo Alonso Pimentel, count of Benavente; Juan Manrique, count of Castañeda, Pedro de Acuña, count of Valencia, and Iñigo Lopez de Mendoza, the lord of Hita and Buitrago (and future marqués of Santillana). "Crónica Juan," pp. 558–60; Huete, pp. 317–18.

[82] "Crónica Juan," pp. 560–62. An alternate version of the indictment, with slight differences in wording, appears in Huete, pp. 320–33. Both versions contain a good deal of repetition, often restating what amount to the same accusations in slightly different language. All of the following direct quotations come from Juan's chronicle.

loved than feared "because from love proceeds loyalty, while from hatred comes loathing." It was against this backdrop of correct monarchical behavior that the actions of the royal favorite had to be judged.

"Wishing to make himself sovereign over all," Constable de Luna had acted "out of overweening pride and disordered greed." He had usurped royal power and exercised it both unjustly and tyrannically. He had taken into his hands the appointment of officials on all levels of government, withholding offices from anyone who did not unswervingly support him while distributing them among his followers, including even foreigners, "something which is against the laws and customs of Spain and against the honor of your subjects." According to the document, the fact that the constable was himself a foreigner had been a major cause for his transgressions.

De Luna controlled royal revenues and increased taxes. Through control of the royal mint, he had debased the coinage by striking coins of a weight far below the standard. Such practices produced enormous income, much of which he appropriated to enrich himself and reward his followers. Those drafting the indictment charged that some of these funds had found their way into the fifteenth-century equivalent of "off-shore" accounts, held for the constable in the merchant cities of Venice and Genoa.

Given de Luna's control over appointment and dismissal, all royal councilors and officials lived in such terror of earning his disapproval that they consulted him on all matters which came before them in order to conform their opinions to his. Anyone who did otherwise soon found himself expelled from court—or worse. One result of this sycophancy was the absence of that varied counsel so necessary to good government.

According to his accusers, de Luna had as readily interfered in the affairs of Church as in those of the state. He had named churchmen to office, setting aside legitimate canonical elections while forcing the election of his own candidates, in particular his brother Juan de Luna whom he made archbishop of Toledo. In short, he had conferred upon such people "dignities far above their true merits and taken such dignities away from those who deserved them." De Luna had paralyzed meaningful opposition through a policy of divide and rule, binding men to himself by making them co-beneficiaries of his corruption, while exiling, imprisoning, confiscating the property of, or even murdering all those who dared to stand against him.

The indictment also contains more specific allegations. For example, the constable had appropriated the revenues generated by the *cruzada* in his own town of Marchena. He ran a "protection racket" in the city of Cordoba, permitting and profiting from illicit gambling operations despite laws of both

Church and state which forbade such activity. To support the general allegation that "he had procured the death of many," certain specific victims were named. He is accused of being responsible for the death of the king's close relative Duke Fadrique and having the conde de Luna poisoned to inherit his property. He had procured the death of Fernán Alonso de Robres for having been one of four judges sentencing him to exile and that of the *contador*, Sancho Hernández, for refusing to register a royal grant in his favor. And he had personally beaten to death a squire at the very moment when the victim was clutching the king's shoulders in a vain attempt to find protection—an undeniable case of *lèse-majesté*. Most recently, the constable had seized one of the coalition leaders, Pedro Manrique, who was saved from becoming the next victim only by his timely escape.

While these actions undoubtedly damaged the realm as a whole, the indictment's chief focus involves their effect on the Castilian aristocracy. The aristocrats who were primarily responsible for the document's content wrote into it at great length how their enemy had ridden roughshod over their class interests. The *privado* had seized and killed some nobles while exiling others, in most cases confiscating their property or otherwise profiting from their removal. (Although the document does not mention them by name, any contemporary would have recognized this as a reference to the *infantes* of Aragon.) De Luna had also sown dissension among the nobles themselves, "forbidding them to form alliances and confederations" that were a common feature of aristocratic life in fifteenth-century Castile. His complete control over royal offices and revenues had robbed the king of the love and loyalty due from his most powerful subjects, who now looked to please the constable. A reader of this document is left with the distinct impression that the aristocratic class had suffered most intensely from de Luna's reign of terror.

The indictment is an obvious instance of the time-honored plea of all monarchical government: responsibility for the evils residing in the body politic lies not with the monarch but with his evil councilors. Royal culpability, however, could not be entirely overlooked. For decades, Juan II had habitually conceded to his "evil councilor" the power to commit the crimes for which he stood indicted. "Your lordship has given full effect to his abhorrent, tyrannical, and illicit appetites which have been the cause of great damage to your realm." In order to explain royal behavior that so clearly transgressed the duties of monarchy, those drafting the indictment resorted to another time-honored explanation for evil: Juan II had given his favorite enormous scope to commit crimes as a result of having been bewitched! Such an explanation not only transferred moral culpability from the king to the constable, the obvious bewitcher, it also permitted de Luna's accusers to spread their charges into the realm of sorcery.

> Most excellent prince, all who see you permit such grave ... and detestable enormities ... can only believe that the constable has bound your bodily and intellectual powers through magic and diabolical incantations in such a manner that you cannot do otherwise than he wishes; nor can your memory remember, nor your understanding understand, nor your voice speak, except as he wills ... so much so that not even a member of the world's strictest religious order can be found who is so bound to his superior as is your royal person to the will and desire of the constable.

The Favorite's Fall and a Royal Indictment

When it finally came, the constable's spectacular exit from the scene was brought about not by aristocratic opposition of the sort he had faced and overcome for decades, but by losing the backing of the king whom he had served. Acting in part at the urging of leading nobles like the marqués of Santillana and of his new queen, Isabel of Portugal, who resented the favorite's influence over his husband, Juan II finally surrendered Alvaro de Luna to a merciless legal proceeding conducted by his enemies, one that condemned him to death.

Three weeks after the execution, Juan II issued a lengthy royal letter to his subjects, explaining why he had cut off the head of the man who had long been his closest friend and had long directed the destinies of Castile.[83] Although four times the length of the aristocratic indictment of 1440, this letter adds only one or two accusations to the list, for the most part repeating charges which the aristocrats had leveled against the constable 13 years earlier. In fact, despite a considerable increase in verbiage, there are actually several significant omissions from the royal list.

Clearly missing are the specific charges laid out by the nobles: the death of the royal duke Fadrique, the poisoning of the Conde de Luna, the judicial murders of Fernán Alonso de Robres and Sancho Hernandez, the imprisonment of Pedro Manrique, and that spectacular bludgeoning of a squire who attempted to find safety in the king's presence. While it is possible that Juan believed his constable to be innocent of these charges, the tenor of the document suggests a more likely

[83] The document, dated June 20, 1453, is reprinted in what appears to be its entirety in "Crónica Juan," pp. 684–91.

and more cynical explanation for their absence. All such actions would have involved either the king's active participation or, at the very least, his acquiescence and therefore could not, by any stretch of the imagination, be excused on the grounds of royal ignorance. Their inclusion in the royal indictment would have undercut what is in reality a highly self-serving document, one which tried hard to portray its author as a man "kept in the dark" by his "evil counselor," only at the very end coming to realize the extent of the latter's crimes and corruption.

Among the charges that are directed against the favorite, a great many are clearly aimed at exculpating the king. De Luna is accused of controlling all information which reached his royal master. He appointed or approved all those who served near the king's person. Wise counselors and devout clerics were systematically turned away from court to be replaced by de Luna's minions, who spied on everything the king did and reported every conversation he had. Only those nobles who had the constable's permission were allowed to come to court; to assure their acquiescence, he bribed them, forced them to swear fealty to him, even held members of their families as hostages.

In a supreme example of chutzpah, King Juan even attempted to shift some of the blame for the activities of his favorite onto the nobility, suggesting that they, either through avarice or cowardice, had not adequately warned him of what was happening. Naturally, such warnings as the letter of 1440 on which the present royal letter was largely based or the aristocratic uprisings which had repeatedly convulsed the kingdom and which might reasonably have been expected to serve as a wake-up call, were passed over in silence.

On the other hand, while minimizing his own involvement, the king seems to have realized that there were limits to how far he could realistically distance himself from the actions of his constable without totally sacrificing royal credibility. It is not surprising that in shouldering some responsibility for the situation, Juan II decided not to adopt the excuse for inaction put forward by the aristocrats in 1440, to wit, that he had spent the majority of his reign bewitched. On the other hand, the royal alternative to this unflattering explanation is even more delicious. The king explains his decades-long failure to act as a near-divine forbearance, exercised in a *vain attempt to save the constable's soul.*

> For a long time I tolerated these acts with great patience following the example of Our Lord's conduct with sinners whose death and damnation he does not desire, but rather that they may be converted and live. Many times have I remonstrated with the grand master, calling on him to emend and correct his ways, hoping that

> he would indeed do so, but he with hardened heart never wished to obey me or do as I asked ...[84]

Conclusion

I.A.A. Thompson argued that in the early-modern period the royal favorite played several potentially positive roles, one of which was to act as a lightning rod drawing off criticism that would otherwise be directed at the monarch: "The *valido* was the political persona of the 'Christian Prince,' the negative identity of a king who could do no wrong."[85] While this observation may hold true for Europe of the sixteenth and seventeenth centuries, the career of Alvaro de Luna indicates that it is by no means a universal truth. In fifteenth-century Castile, Constable de Luna's presence generated the storms that periodically threatened the stability of the kingdom and, by extension, the security of the monarchy. Opposition to his rule became an issue around which a broad spectrum of the *nobleza* could unite, producing not only constant tension but even periodic uprisings. The detrimental effect of the favorite became especially acute when, as in de Luna's case, he emerged not from the old nobility but instead was a "new man" of lesser origins, a fact that rendered him even more odious in the eyes of the aristocracy. In short, the presence of Alvaro de Luna acted as a constant irritant, tending to undercut royal authority within what was still the most powerful sector of society, the Castilian aristocracy.

Nor is the constable the only example of this phenomenon. In 1454, Juan II's son and successor came to the throne as Enrique IV, a monarch who seems to have become known even in his own lifetime by the unflattering sobriquet *el Impotente*. Many of the troubles that afflicted that king's very troubled reign can be traced directly to the activities of his own royal favorite, Juan Pacheco. Originally put in place by the constable, Pacheco would prove to be every bit as corrupt and grasping as his predecessor and just as talented a political survivor without demonstrating any of de Luna's redeeming qualities.

By contrast, the absence of such a figure from the final reign of the century, that of the Catholic Monarchs, Fernando and Isabel (1474–1516), constitutes one major reason for their highly successful dealings with their upper nobility. If the royal pair can be said to have shown extraordinary favor to any one individual, that man was Pedro González de Mendoza, cardinal-archbishop of

84 Ibid., p. 68.

85 Thompson, p. 19.

Toledo, whose influence led one writer of the period to dub him "*el tercer rey*."[86] Mendoza, however, was a figure struck from a very different mold than either de Luna or Pacheco. By no stretch of the imagination was he a "royal favorite" in the same sense as the other two. Considerably senior to the monarchs, he had played a key role in Castilian politics for some two decades before they came to the throne. What is more, he was no arriviste; he belonged to one of Castile's leading noble families. In short, Mendoza was a man whose age, wisdom, service, and family ties commanded the respect of virtually all members of his class.

The constable's career also illustrates the habitual inability of an aristocracy to bring down a royal favorite who had not lost the favor of his king. On two of the three occasions when the nobles rose up against de Luna, they managed to secure his banishment from court. On one of those occasions, that banishment was declared to be permanent. Paradoxically, however, it was the very victory of such a coalition which ultimately proved its undoing. For once the royal favorite—the focus of opposition and, therefore, the raison d'être for aristocratic unity—was successfully removed, the anarchic tendencies of the class reasserted themselves with a vengeance. Nobles soon reverted to the scramble for individual or family advantage which habitually absorbed their efforts. And this reversion to the normal state of affairs, in turn, afforded the banished favorite a fine opportunity to repair his fortunes and regain his place, often with the aid and approval of some of those who had recently helped oust him from power. As long as the favorite retained royal favor, aristocratic opposition was unlikely to topple him. In the end, Alvaro de Luna, constable of Castile, grand master of the military order of Santiago, a man referred to by his chronicler as "the greatest lord without a crown," fell victim not to his aristocratic enemies but to the king he had long served.

In conclusion, any medieval monarch wishing to maximize his chances for a successful reign would have been well advised to heed that famous fatherly advice tendered many centuries later by the English writer Rudyard Kipling in a poem directed at his son, to wit, "[let] all men count with you, but none too much!"

---

[86] Pedro Martir de Anglera, *Epistolario*, vol. 1, ed. José López de Toro, Documentos Inéditos para la Historia de España, vol. 9 (Madrid: Imprenta Gongora, S.L., 1953), pp. 31–2.

Index

Note: References to figures are listed in *italics*.